INDIA-UZBEKISTAN

Perspectives on Connectivity Between South and Central Asia

INDIA-UZBEKISTAN

Perspectives on Connectivity Between South and Central Asia

Editors

Ramakant Dwivedi

Abdusamat Khaydarov

The India-Central Asia Foundation
New Delhi

The Diplomatic Academy
at the UWED
Tashkent

PENTAGON PRESS LLP

First published in 2025 by
PENTAGON PRESS LLP
206, Peacock Lane, Shahpur Jat
New Delhi-110049, India
Contact: 011-26490600

Typeset in AGaramond, 11.5 Point
Aegean Offset Printers, Greater Noida

ISBN 978-81-980002-6-2 (HB)

www.pentagonpress.in

Contents

Foreword

Today, the rapidly changing world needs an example of successful interregional cooperation. Such a model could be Uzbekistan and India, which celebrated the 32nd anniversary of the establishment of diplomatic relations in March this year and demonstrate remarkable progress in their development. Confirmation of such a successful growth of collaboration is the assessment of the President of Uzbekistan Shavkat Mirziyoyev, who noted that: "The historical bonds of friendship, cultural and spiritual rapprochement that have been formed between our peoples for centuries are now receiving new content." These words sound like a call for new initiatives aimed at deepening cooperation between our countries.

Indian Prime Minister Narendra Modi, has emphasized the importance of joint efforts to achieve common goals: "India and Uzbekistan jointly took the initiative to hold the India-Central Asia dialogue, which began its journey from Samarkand. "Cooperation between India and Uzbekistan and other Central Asian states serves the goals of peace, stability and prosperity in our region". In this regard, it is appropriate to quote once again the words of N. Modi, who noted that "Mutual cooperation between India and Central Asia is necessary for regional security and prosperity. I want to make it clear that Central Asia is central to the Indian vision of an integrated and stable neighborhood."

Such statements by our leaders not only indicate the desire of both countries for mutually beneficial cooperation, but also emphasize the key role of Uzbekistan and India in strengthening the interconnectedness of the regions of Central and South Asia.

A striking case of how bilateral cooperation can contribute to the achievement of common goals of interregional cooperation are joint projects and initiatives in the fields of trade, investment and culture. The development of cooperation in the field of education and science, as well as the implementation of joint innovative projects in the field of high technologies contribute to the expansion and strengthening of close economic and cultural ties.

Of particular note is the significant deepening of cooperation in the field of security and combating cross-border threats. Today, in the face of modern challenges such as terrorism and extremism, Uzbekistan and India demonstrate a strong commitment to ensuring stability and security in the vast macroregion. As President Mirziyoyev emphasized, "Together we will be able to more effectively counter terrorism, extremism, and transnational crime, including in cyberspace."

As key players in the Central and South Asian region, Uzbekistan and India recognize their role and responsibility in maintaining stability in Afghanistan and its development. Afghanistan, as a connecting bridge between Central and South Asia, needs international support to achieve peace and stability after four decades of bloody conflicts. Today, our countries are providing humanitarian assistance to the people of Afghanistan in order to prevent a catastrophe in this long-suffering country.

It is difficult to underestimate the significance of these efforts aimed at preventing a humanitarian catastrophe, stabilizing the situation in Afghanistan and developing economic ties between Central and South Asia. The support and involvement of Afghanistan in regional projects will contribute to ensuring long-term peace and prosperity in this key geopolitical macro-region of the world. This support, in turn, reflects the mutual desire of Uzbekistan and India to build bridges of cooperation between Central and South Asia.

Mutual understanding based on respect for the national interests of the parties demonstrates how common efforts can contribute to achieving impressive results in consolidating peace through the development of mutually beneficial cooperation.

Currently, assessing the multifaceted ties between Uzbekistan and India, we could say that an important result of the development of bilateral cooperation over the past three decades has been not only deepening of bilateral relations, but also the significant contribution of Uzbekistan and India to strengthening the interconnectedness between Central and South Asia. The assessments and initiatives of the leaders of our countries not only reflect current achievements, but also inspire us to strengthen further cooperation at the international level aimed at achieving common goals of sustainable development, peace and prosperity.

First Deputy Chairman of the Senate of
Oliy Majlis of the Republic of Uzbekistan
Rector of UWED

S. Safoev

Preface

General

India and Uzbekistan celebrated the 32nd anniversary of the establishment of diplomatic ties in March this year. For India, the developments in Uzbekistan would continue to be important as Tashkent is part of its extended neighbourhood. The foreign policy of India which was formulated and pursued by Jawaharlal Nehru has high appeal to the peoples of Uzbekistan. Indeed, his visit to Tashkent in June 1955 continues to be cherished. In the twenty-first century, enhanced cooperation between India and Uzbekistan assumes a higher relevance. There are obvious areas of cooperation to mutual benefit. We believe that the potential to gainfully contribute to the shaping of events in Central Asia and contiguous regions is high and deserves to be pursued in a sustained manner. For more than 32 years, the sovereign Uzbekistan has been developing as an independent actor in international relations. Having been recognized by the international community as one of its members, Tashkent is demonstrating important foreign policy initiatives.

Uzbekistan is especially dedicated to fostering regional collaboration between Central Asia and South Asia. An international summit "Central and South Asia: Regional Connectivity Challenges and Opportunities" took place in Tashkent from July 15-16, 2021 as an initiative of the President of Uzbekistan. The summit discussed three common themes - Economy, Security and Culture. It revived historical ties between Central and South Asia. Tashkent is keen to see the conference as a launch pad for Central Asia's deeper engagement with South Asia. A major objective of the summit was the development of solid foundations for closer interaction between Central and South Asian regions, identifying specific projects of a strategic nature.

In the multi-vectored foreign policy of Tashkent, India takes an important place. India was one of the first to recognize Uzbekistan's independence. India's unselfishness and desire to help Tashkent were felt in all of its actions. And this is no accidental occurrence. The roots of India-Uzbekistan connections and friendship lie in centuries long past. People of India and Uzbekistan enjoyed trade and spiritual relations for centuries. Archeological excavations at many sites in Uzbekistan testify to this. Uzbekistan's independence has ushered in a new stage of interactions between New Delhi and Tashkent.

It is against this backdrop that we felt the need for scholarly exchanges on matters of common interest. This joint study has taken the shape of the book after months of planning, discussions and exchanges with the Diplomatic Academy, University of World Economy and Diplomacy, Tashkent.

Coverage of Topics

This volume is a collection of 20 papers written by scholars from India and Uzbekistan, the authors strived to show the process of formation and the development of relations between the two countries and the entire gamut of issues mentioned below.

An Indian perspective of Indo-Uzbek relations is provided in Dr Ramakant Dwivedi's paper. It argues that this relationship is an evolving partnership that seeks to further strengthen their ties on the basis of mutual understanding, mutual respect; fight against terrorism and fundamentalism and to work together for regional peace and progress. He underlines the fact that India has the requisite technology, talented human resources and financial capacity to be a constructive partner of Uzbekistan in its own journey towards prosperity.

Anil Sharma provides in depth analysis of all the aspects related to foreign direct investments in Uzbekistan. He lays out a road map for enhancing economic ties between India and Uzbekistan.

Dr. Anita Sengupta examines Digital Diplomacy, Branding and the multiple facets of Indo Uzbek Relations in the Post Pandemic Era. Digital diplomacy happens in multiple ways and has emerged as the centre piece of its global agenda with a focus on human centric approach to technology. Digitization has impacted the practice of diplomacy in innumerable ways. This is useful not just in influencing larger public opinion on issues of significance but also in showcasing cultures and traditions that are a part of nation branding for most states today.

Dr Rashmini Koparkar provides detailed examination of India-Uzbekistan cultural relations since ancient times till present time.

Prof P L Dash provides critical study of India-Central Asia relations spelling out the areas of intense engagement. He further describes various models focusing on various areas of cooperation and collaboration between India and Central Asia.

Prof Rashmi Doraiswamy describes importance being Al Beruni who was a mathematician, geographer, astronomer, historian, linguist born in Uzbekistan. She further examines various aspects associated with Al Beruni. Al Beruni was one of the many polymaths that the Islamic Golden Age threw up between the 8th to the 12th centuries, in the Central Asian region.

Prof Sanjay Kumar Pandey and Rahul Gupta critically examines status of Regional Cooperation in Central Asia. They describe the possible trajectory of the said cooperation both in historical and current period. They evaluate some recent trends in regional cooperation in Central Asia, especially since 2016 when the push came, first from Uzbekistan and subsequently from Kazakhstan and others, for upgrading the level of cooperation in the region.

Prof Tabasum Firdous and Dr Fozia Jan spell out priorities of India foreign policy with respect to Uzbekistan. Over the past few decades, India's aspirations and actions in its neighbourhood have been in sync with the broader regional and global environment. They underline that Indian foreign policy framework has become more vibrant and robust.

Ramanshi Dwivedi assesses the efficacy of Indo-Uzbek relations in bringing South Asia and Central Asia together. She examines the contribution of Ideologists of Uzbekistan in enhancing Uzbek-Indian Relations. She stresses on linguistic contacts between India and Uzbekistan during the medieval period.

Amb Abdusamat Khaydarov analyzes India's contribution to the development of world civilization. The author focuses on the main spheres to which Indian scientists of antiquity made a significant contribution, which served as one of the foundations for the development of modern human civilization. In particular, the achievements of ancient India are shown in the field of astronomy, medicine, mathematics, philosophy and other sciences are shown. At the same time, the modern achievements of India are reflected since the declaration of independence and the adoption of the Constitution in 1950. Modern foreign policy of India, bilateral Uzbek-Indian relations, problems of interconnectedness of Central and South Asia, as well as the place and role of India in world politics and economy have been examined.

Amb Dilshod Akhatov and Sadriddin Suyarov, analyzes Uzbekistan's foreign policy, especially in the context of its relations with India. Authors analyze the role of the President of Uzbekistan, Shavkat Mirziyoyev, in shaping the country's foreign policy, especially in the context of Uzbekistan's action strategy for 2017-2021 and the development strategy "Uzbekistan 2030".

Amb Ibrahim Mavlanov analyzes the process of formation of India's geopolitical and geo-economic interests in Central Asia and the Shanghai Cooperation Organisation (SCO). Author bases his study on the analysis of specific events in the international arena in recent years, related to the speeches and initiatives of the President of the Republic of Uzbekistan. He analyzes the proposals of Indian Prime Minister Narendra Modi at the meetings of the Council of Heads of State of the SCO member states. The author bases his assessments on the study of official documents of the SCO and materials of consultative meetings of the heads of Central Asian States. He tries to explore and understand the main aspirations of India in the region of Central Asia and the SCO. The article proves that modern developing India has geopolitical and geo-economic interests in the region of Central Asia and the SCO.

Prof Rustam Dzhumaev examines the main directions of political, economic, socio-cultural cooperation between Afghanistan, India and Pakistan. He underlines the problems and prospects in the development of transport and logistics corridors Between central and south Asia. He also pays attention to the problems of combating threats of terrorism and issues of strengthening global and regional security. He critically examines the "Strategy Uzbekistan 2030", as well as the ideas and initiatives of the President of Uzbekistan Sh. M. Mirziyoyev, for international cooperation and peace.

Dr Sherzod Arapov and Abdulaziz Rakhmatullaev analyze the current state of regional cooperation in Central Asia and review the main directions within the framework of the SCO. She examines cultural ties between Uzbekistan and India dating back to the Great Silk Road and its significance for modern cooperation. She analyzes the role of the SCO in fostering economic integration between its member states, including Uzbekistan and India.

Dr Hilola Mustapova explores India's evolving geopolitical and geo-economic interests in Central Asia since the region's independence in 1991. Focusing on political, economic, and cultural aspects, she emphasizes India's efforts to establish relations with Central Asian states, motivated by a shared historical connection and concerns about regional security, terrorism, and religious extremism. Her analysis touches on India's strategies, including participation in initiatives such as the North-South International Transport Corridor (NSITC) and the Turkmenistan-Afghanistan-Pakistan-India (TAPI) gas pipeline project, to promote trade, energy security, and connectivity with Central Asia.

Dr Saodat Ubaydullayeva analyzes the inter-connectedness between Central Asian states and Afghanistan in the context of security and development of the region. She analyzes the relationship between the Central Asian states and Afghanistan in the context of security and development in the region. She highlights the role of Afghanistan in the system of complex inter-connectedness of regional security in Central Asia and its importance for regional cooperation between central and south Asia.

We are happy to offer this volume to scholars, policy makers, diplomats, entrepreneurs, academics and decision makers in both countries as well as those with a similar interest in the foreign policies of the India and Uzbekistan and Central Asian affairs.

We hope that this book would contribute towards a greater and enlightened appreciation of Indo-Uzbek relations.

Acknowledgements

We would like to thank all the authors of papers published in the book. Without their dedication and persistent hard work, this book may not have seen the light of the day. Prof Mamidala Jagadesh Kumar, Chairman, University Grants Commission and Amb K Raghunath, Former Foreign Secretary, Ministry of External Affairs, Government of India and Amb Gitesh of regional cooperation, the course of their development, as well as consider the key problems of intra-regional cooperation. The article focuses on two areas, regional and economic cooperation.

Dr Umidhon Azamkhujaev examines the issue of legal regulation and functioning of international transport corridors within the framework of European Union (EU) and Association of South-East Asian Nations (ASEAN) economic integration in order to identify the necessary legal framework for the successful functioning of the corridors. He also concludes that international transport corridors cannot function effectively in the absence of multilateral treaties aimed at economic integration and cites the North-South International Transport Corridor (NSITC) as an example.

Dr Rustam Mahmudov examine prospects for development of cooperation between Uzbekistan and India in scientific and technical sphere, which can give an additional impetus to the expansion of bilateral trade, economic and investment ties. He analyzes the measures taken by Uzbekistan towards the development of high-tech industry after the start of socio-political reforms in 2016. In addition, he analyzes India's performance in digital technology development, startup ecosystem, IT services, software products, ER&D and specialized education. Prospects for technological cooperation between Uzbekistan and India are examined through the prism of the Fourth Industrial Revolution.

Prof Anri Sharapov analyzes various aspects of India's history, culture and political structure, focusing on the historical context and contemporary realities. He examines: ancient and modern Indian civilization, including the role of ancient India as a center for the development of science, philosophy and spiritual culture. Archaeological findings and ancient history part discusses the archaeological evidence for a highly developed Indian civilization in antiquity, including the Harappan civilization. Diversity of centers of power in India's history and its democratic status are analyzed, including historical peculiarities in comparison with China. International relations theory section analyzes the specificity of Indian IRT and how it differs from Western concepts, focusing on the historical and cultural foundations.

Dr Gulchehra Isamuhamedova analyzes the prospects and problems of expanding trade and economic cooperation between Uzbekistan and India

Sarma, Former Secretary West, Ministry of External Affairs, Government of India for their guidance. It is a pleasure to say a special word of thanks to ICAF team in New Delhi and Diplomatic Academy team in Tashkent, particularly, Prof Sodyk Safoev, *First Deputy Chairman* of the *Senate* of the *Oliy* Majlis of the Republic of Uzbekistan and Rector of the University of World Economy and Diplomacy (UWED). Thanks to Amb Dilshod Akhatov, ambassador of Uzbekistan in Germany (former ambassador of Uzbekistan in India), Prof Ibrahim Mavlanov, Dean of Applied Diplomacy Faculty of the Diplomatic Academy (former ambassador of Uzbekistan in India) for their guidance and support.

Grateful for cooperation and encouragement from Renu and Ramya.

We would like to thank Pentagon Publishers for copy-editing and publishing the book in record time.

Ramakant Dwivedi
New Delhi
October 09, 2024

A Khaydarov
Tashkent
October 09, 2024

About the Contributors

Dr. Ramakant Dwivedi is, currently, Director of the India Central Asia Foundation (ICAF), New Delhi. He has a PhD from the Central Asian Studies Division of the School of International Studies (SIS), Jawaharlal Nehru University (JNU), New Delhi. Dr. Dwivedi was a Visiting Research Fellow at the Al-Beruni Institute of Oriental Studies, Tashkent (1998-2001). He was Associate Fellow at the Institute for Defence Studies and Analyses (IDSA), New Delhi (2003–2007). He had worked as Officer on Special Duty (OSD) and Gp Director of Afghanistan, Central and West Asia Desk with the National Security Advisor Office, Prime Minister Office, Government of India (2007–2024). He has looked after a variety of domains assigned to him during the service.

His major areas of research are national security, foreign policy, ethnic issues and religious extremism in Eurasian region (Russia, Caucasus and Central Asian countries). He holds a Diploma in Russian Language from the University of World Economy and Diplomacy, Tashkent and a Diploma in Uzbek Language from the Tashkent State Institute of Oriental Studies, Uzbekistan. He has widely travelled in the Eurasian region. Dr Dwivedi was awarded Nehru Memorial Scholarship for Doctoral Studies by Jawaharlal Nehru Memorial Fund, Teen Murti House, New Delhi. He has represented India in 14 countries as domain expert and part of official delegation for scholarly presentations.

His published works include 42 research papers in national/international journals, edited books. He edited *India and Central Asia: Advancing the Common Interest* (IDSA & Anamaya Publishers, New Delhi, 2004), *India-Tajikistan Cooperation: Perspectives and Prospects* (Anamaya Publishers, New Delhi, 2007), *India-Kazakhstan Perspectives: Regional and International Interactions* (Al-Farabi Kazakh National University Press, Almaty & Anamaya Publishers, New Delhi, 2007), *India-Turkmenistan Relations* (Anamaya

Publishers, New Delhi, 2007), *Indo-Uzbek Perspectives on the Environment and Sustainable Development* (Anamaya Publishers, New Delhi, 2007), *India-Kyrgyz Relations: Perspectives and Prospects* (Anamaya Publishers, New Delhi, 2008 - Russian edition brought out by Diplomatic Academy, Ministry of Foreign Affairs, Bishkek), *Contemporary Indo-Uzbek Perspectives on Bilateral and Regional Issues* (Anamaya Publishers, New Delhi, 2008) and *Indo–Kyrgyz Relations: Challenges and Opportunities* (Pentagon Press LLP, New Delhi, 2023 - Russian edition brought out by Diplomatic Academy, Ministry of Foreign Affairs, Bishkek.)

Dr Dwivedi is fluent in Dari, Farsi, Russian, English, Hindi and Urdu Languages. He has functional knowledge of Uzbek Language.

Dr. Dwivedi is Founding & Life Member of the India – Central Asia Foundation (ICAF), New Delhi; Life Member, United Services Institution of India (USI), New Delhi, Life Member, India Islamic Cultural Centre (IICC), New Delhi and Associate Member, Institute for Defence Studies and Analyses (IDSA), India International Centre (IIC), Press Club of India (PCI), New Delhi.

e-mail: ramakantdwivedi2012@gmail.com

Anil Sharma is a Chartered Accountant by profession. He is a Member of National Financial Reporting Authority, Ministry of Corporate Affairs, Government of India and an Adjunct Faculty with the Indian Institute of Corporate Affairs. He was an Independent Director with UCO Bank for 2016-19. He is actively associated with various NGOs working in social Sector.
e-mail: anil54@gmail.com

Dr. Anita Sengupta is an area studies specialist engaged with the study of the Eurasian region. Her areas of interest include issues of identity politics, migration, gender, borders, critical geopolitics and logistics. She is a regular commentator on debates on Asian affairs. She has been Fellow, Maulana Abul Kalam Azad Institute of Asian Studies, Kolkata, Senior Fellow, Indian Council of Social Science Research, New Delhi and Director, Calcutta Research Group, Kolkata. She is currently Director, Asia in Global Affairs, Kolkata.
e-mail: anitasengupta@hotmail.com

Dr Rashmini Koparkar is Assistant Professor at the Centre for Russian and Central Asian Studies, School of International Studies, Jawaharlal Nehru

University (JNU), New Delhi. She has formerly worked as Research Fellow at the Indian Council of World Affairs (Aug 2019- Feb 2020) and as Research Associate at the Vivekananda International Foundation (2016-18). She has published a monograph on 'Issues and Dynamics of the Fergana Valley: Regional Implications' with the Vivekananda International Foundation. Her research interests include Politics and Foreign Policies of Central Asian states, India's engagements in Eurasia, and issues of Identity and Nation-Building. Dr Koparkar was awarded PhD in 2016 from the Center for Russian and Central Asian Studies, JNU. Her PhD thesis was titled, 'Nation-Building in Post-Soviet Central Asia: A Case Study of Uzbekistan'. She has completed M.A. and M.Phil in International Relations from JNU. Dr Koparkar is proficient in Russian language. She has participated in various international and national conferences, and has written number of research papers and articles.
e-mail: rashmini.koparkar@gmail.com

Prof P.L. Dash was Director, Centre for Central Eurasian Studies, University of Mumbai, India. He was Professor of International Relations and Indian Council for Cultural Relations (ICCR) India Chair at the University of World Economy and Diplomacy, Tashkent, Uzbekistan. He was Visiting Professor at the Nanyang Technological University, Singapore and CRRID, Chandigarh, India. He has numerous publications to his credit.
e-mail: pldash50@gmail.com

Dr Rashmi Doraiswamy studied Russian language and literature at Jawaharlal Nehru University, New Delhi. Her doctoral thesis was on Mikhail Bakhtin, the Russian philosopher. She is Professor at the Academy of International Studies (AIS), Jamia Millia Islamia, New Delhi. She is author of *The Post-Soviet Condition: ChingizAitmatov in the '90s* (2005) and *Guru Dutt: Through Light and Shade* (2008). She is editor of *Cultural Histories of Central Asia* (2009), *Energy Security: Central Asia, India and the Neighbourhood* (2013), *Perspectives on Multiculturalism: Pre-Soviet, Soviet and Post-Soviet Central Asia* (2013), *Central Asia and South Asia: Economic, Developmental and Socio-Cultural Linkages* (2017), *Central Asia, China and India: Historical, Economic, Political And Cultural Relations* (2017), *The Russian Factor in Central Asian Culture* (2018) and *Perspectives on BRICS* (2019). She is co-editor of *Being and Becoming: The Cinemas of Asia* (Macmillan, 2002), *Globalisation and the*

Third World (Manak, 2009), *Asian Film Journeys: Selections from Cinemaya* (Wisdom Tree, 2010) and *Window into Russia: Culture and Society in the XXI Century* (2010). She has participated in national and international seminars on cultural issues and has served on several statutory and non-statutory film festival and critics juries in and abroad. She has lectured and written extensively on cultural issues. She was the recipient of the National Award for the Best Film Critic in 1994. She was Coordinator of the UGC Central Asian Studies Programme at the Academy since from 2007 to 2016. She has organized and been co-organiser of workshops, international and national conferences, many of which have been on Central Asia, Russia, Eurasia and Soviet Union. She was Honorary Deputy Director of the Academy of Third World Studies, JMI from October 2005 to May 2007. She was Officiating Director of the AIS from August 2015 to July 2020.
e-mail: rashmidee@gmail.com

Prof Sanjay Kumar Pandey is a Professor at the Centre for Russian and Central Asian Studies, School of International Studies, JNU, New Delhi. He served as the Chairperson of the Centre, and the Director of the Russia and Central Asian Area Studies Programme. He teaches courses on Politics and Society, as well as the Foreign Policy of Russia and the Central Asian States. He was L. M. Singhvi Visiting Fellow at the Centre of South Asian Studies, University of Cambridge; Charles Wallace Trust Visiting Fellow, University of Cambridge; and Visiting Fellow at Cambridge Central Asia Forum, Cambridge.
e-mail: skpandeyjnu@gmail.com

Rahul Gupta is a Research Scholar at the Centre for Russian and Central Asian Studies, School of International Studies, Jawaharlal Nehru University. His research interests span Great Power engagement with Central Asia, with a focus on Russian and European Union's engagement with Kazakhstan.
e-mail: grahul900@gmail.com

Prof Tabasum Firdous is the Director, Centre of Central Asian Studies (CCAS), University of Kashmir. Dr. Fozia Jan is a Post-Doctoral Fellow, Indian Council of Social Sciences Research (ICSSR) at the Centre of Central Asian Studies (CCAS), University of Kashmir.
e-mail: icafindia@gmail.com

Ramanshi Dwivedi is a Research Scholar at the University of Delhi. She is engaged in the pursuit of Political Science with Economics as her minor. Her intellectual fervor is directed towards unraveling the subtleties of International Relations, Diplomacy, and Economic developments. She has demonstrated her scholarly prowess by publishing over 5 articles in esteemed annual journals of the University of Delhi, including "Global Dispatch: A Diplomatic Discourse" by Miranda House, University of Delhi, "Siyasat" by Hindu College, University of Delhi, "The Denouncement" by Lady Shri Ram College, University of Delhi, "Tarikh" by St. Stephens College, University of Delhi and "Habitus" by Kamala Nehru College, University of Delhi. She has also contributed various articles to the Hindu College Gazette. Her publications delve into critical topics such as the 'Ukraine Conundrum,' 'Perilous Waters - Navigating Geopolitical Dynamics in the South China Sea,' 'Karmic Realms of Governance: Interpreting Global Political Power Dynamics Through the Prism of Bhagavad Gita', 'Israel-Palestine,' 'Indian Foreign Policy,' 'Economic Growth: The Megacity Effect on Reforms', and 'Strategizing Diplomacy to Emerging Global Challenges: Navigating Geopolitical Turmoil in the 21st Century'.
e-mail: ramanshidwivedi200308@gmail.com

Amb Abdusamat Khaydarov is currently Director of the Diplomatic Academy at the University of World Economy and Diplomacy (UWED), Ministry of Foreign Affairs of the Republic of Uzbekistan.

From 2014 until the end of 2016, he headed the Political Affairs Department of the United Nations Assistance Mission in Afghanistan (UNAMA). Prior to this, from 2007 to 2014, he was the Head of UNAMA's Western and Southern Regional Offices. Before joining UNAMA, Amb Khaydarov was a career diplomat and an expert on Central and South Asia. Following Uzbekistan's independence in 1991, he held several key positions at the Uzbek Foreign Ministry and later served as the chief consultant on interstate relations and foreign economic relations at the Office of the President of the Republic of Uzbekistan.

Amb Khaydarov graduated from MGIMO in 1976 and later from the Diplomatic Academy under the Ministry of Foreign Affairs of the Russian Federation in 1992. Between 1996 and 1999, he was the ambassador of the Republic of Uzbekistan to Iran. Subsequently, from 1999 to 2000, he served as the Deputy Minister of Foreign Affairs of Uzbekistan.

A prolific writer, Amb Khaydarov has written more than 70 articles, monographs, and books on international relations and security issues, with a particular focus on Afghanistan, Iran, Central and South Asia. He is fluent in Dari, Farsi, Russian, and English.

Amb Khaydarov is a member of the Advisory Board of the India-Central Asia Foundation (ICAF) and the Academic Council of the Diplomatic Academy and UWED under the Ministry of Foreign Affairs of the Republic of Uzbekistan.
e-mail: akhat54@gmail.com

Amb Dilshod Akhatov is currently the ambassador Extraordinary and Plenipotentiary of the Republic of Uzbekistan to the Federal Republic of Germany. He served as the Head of the Main Department of bilateral cooperation of the Ministry of Foreign Affairs of the Republic of Uzbekistan in 2018. From May 28, 2018, to 2020, he held the position of Deputy Minister of Foreign Affairs of the Republic of Uzbekistan. Following this, from 2020 to 2023, he was the Ambassador of the Republic of Uzbekistan to the Republic of India. Amb Axatov is fluent in Russian, German, and English.
e-mail: akhatov@uzbekistan.de

Sadriddin Suyarov, has been in Diplomatic service. He graduated from Tashkent State University in 1985. He worked in the leading media of Uzbekistan, such as the National Television and Radio Company, the National Information Agency of Uzbekistan (UzA), 'Dunyo' Information Agency, 'Uzbekistan Today' Information Agency and others.
Email: sadriddinlatif@gmail.com

Amb Ibrahim Mavlanov is currently serving in the Department of International Finance and Investment at the University of World Economy and Diplomacy (UWED) under the MFA of the Republic of Uzbekistan.

Between 1992 and 2005, he held various significant positions, including Head of the Foreign Economic Relations Department of the Ministry of Foreign Affairs, Head of Uzbekistan's diplomatic mission in Latvia, Chief Consultant on Interstate Relations of the Office of the President of the Republic of Uzbekistan, ambassador of Uzbekistan to India and Bangladesh, and First Deputy Minister of Foreign Affairs of Uzbekistan. Prof. Mavlanov has authored

over 20 books and more than 200 scientific articles on international economic relations, world economy, economic diplomacy, foreign policy, and economic and mathematical methods.
e-mail: ibradjab@yahoo.com

Prof Rustam Djumayev is currently the Dean of the Faculty of Applied Diplomacy at the Diplomatic Academy at the UWED. He earned his academic degree of Doctor of Political Sciences in 1997 and Professor in 1998. He was the Deputy of the 1st and 2nd convocations of the Oliy Majlis of the Republic of Uzbekistan from 1995 to 2005. Between 1993 and 2012, he held significant positions in the administration of the President of the Republic of Uzbekistan. Prof. Djumayev has published five monographs, several textbooks and manuals, and over 100 scientific articles.
e-mail: rustamjuma1960@gmail.com

Dr. Sherzod Arapov is the Dean of the Faculty of International Relations at University of World Economy and Diplomacy (UWED). He is a Doctor of Philosophy in Political Science (PhD). Dr. Arapov has authored several dozen scientific articles. He is fluent in English, Russian, German, and French languages.
e-mail: arapov.sh.@uwed.uz

Dr Umidkhon Azamkhujaev is a lecturer in the International Law Faculty at the UWED. From 2015 to 2023, he served as the Director for Control and Personnel Management of the Uzbek Republican Commodity Exchange Joint Stock Company. He holds a PhD and is fluent in Russian and English. U.Azamkhujaev has authored more than 15 publications.
e-mail: umid.uzbek@gmail.com

Dr. Rustam Mahmudov is a senior research scholar at the Laboratory of Anthropology and Conflict Studies at the Institute for Advanced International Studies (IAIS) and an Associate Professor at UWED. Dr. Mahmudov is responsible for preparing analytical materials, articles, and scientific research on various aspects of socio-political anthropology, ethnology, and conflictology related to Central Asia and Afghanistan at IAIS. Prior to joining IAIS, he worked in various positions at the Tashkent State University of Oriental Studies, the Institute for Strategic and Interregional Studies under the President of the Republic of Uzbekistan, the Ministry of Foreign Affairs of the Republic of

Uzbekistan, and the Center for Political Studies. Dr. Mahmudov has authored over 200 articles on regional and world politics and security, economics, energy, and technological geopolitics.
e-mail: rmaxmudov@uwed.uz

Dr Anri Sharapov is currently an Associate Professor at the University of World Economy and Diplomacy of Uzbekistan. Anri Sharapov teaches such courses as: Regional Studies, Geopolitics, Theory of International Relations. Dr Anri Sharapovhas authored over 40 publications, monographs, and books. He is fluent in Russian and English languages.
e-mail: anri_1@rambler.ru

Dr Gulchekhra Isamukhamedova is currently Project Coordinator, International Organization for Migration (IOM), United Nations Agency in Tashkent. She is also a lecturer at the Department of Foreign Economic Activity and Tourism at the Tashkent State University of Oriental Studies. She is the author of more than 30 publications on international economic relations and security issues, including studies on Central Asia, Shanghai Cooperation Organisation (SCO). She is fluent in Russian, English and French languages.
e-mail: gulchewka@yahoo.com

Dr Hilola Mustapova has been a senior lecturer at the Tashkent State University of Oriental Studies since 2004. She has authored five textbooks and over 30 scientific works, and has participated in numerous international and national conferences. Her research focuses on India's foreign policy, its relations with Central Asian countries, and India's geopolitical and geo-economic interests in Central Asia. Mustapova defended her PhD thesis in 2022. She is fluent in Urdu, English, and Russian.
e-mail: mustapovakhilola@gmail.com

Dr. Saodat Ubdaydullayeva is an Associate Professor in the Department of History, Culture, Politics, and Economy of Korea at the Tashkent State University of Oriental Studies since 2021. She holds a Doctorate in Political Science. Dr. Ubdaydullayeva has authored over 50 publications, monographs, and books on the political aspects of attracting foreign investment in Uzbekistan and regional security issues in Central Asia. She is fluent in Russian and English languages.
e-mail: sadulya75@mail.ru

1

India-Uzbekistan Relations: Enhancing the Partnership

Dr Ramakant Dwivedi

The close friendly relations between India and Uzbekistan have their roots deep in history – from Kushan period till present. The eminent Uzbek scholar Al-Beruni visited India in the 11th century and wrote the famous book, *Kitab-Takkik Al-Hind* – one of the most authoritative books on Indian society and culture. India's first Prime Minister, Jawaharlal Nehru had visited Uzbekistan in 1955 and 1961 when it was part of the erstwhile Soviet Union. This paper is going to provide an objective perspective on historical, cultural and economic relations between India and Uzbekistan.

Uzbekistan's independence on September 01, 1991 has led to the expansion and strengthening of bilateral ties between New Delhi and Tashkent in the political, economic and cultural spheres. India and Uzbekistan signed a Protocol on Diplomatic and Consular matter on March 18, 1992. The mechanism of bilateral consultations between the two countries is an overarching framework for enhancing relations. Since 1992, there have been frequent high level visits. Prime Minister Narasimha Rao visited Tashkent in 1993, Prime Minister Dr Manmohan Singh visited Tashkent in 2006, Prime Minister Narendra Modi visited Tashkent in 2015 and 2016. President Karimov paid State visits to India in 1991, 1994, 2000, 2005 and 2011. Present President of Uzbekistan Shavkat Mirziyoyev has visited India in 2018 and 2019. A virtual India – Central a Submit was held in January 2022. President Mirziyoyev attended virtual meeting of the Head of the States of SCO in July 2023. Number of Agreements and Protocols signed during these visits.

How does all this bear on present day India-Uzbekistan relations and cooperation and what we need to do to realize their full potential?

The political dialogue between India and Uzbekistan has been regular and mutually beneficial. High-level exchanges have indeed set the tempo to chart out the scope and direction of cooperation and have also laid the foundation for understanding of each other's interests and core concerns. Both countries subscribe to common principles of inter-state conduct, peaceful settlement of all differences and rejection of extremism of all forms as well as the principle of non-interference in the internal affairs of other countries.

There is an abiding sense of an intrinsic affinity between India and Uzbekistan. It is this affinity which has been the driving force of the multidimensional exchanges between India and Uzbekistan over the centuries – political, cultural, religious and spiritual, as well as commercial and in human movement and contact. Our mutual affinity has made it possible for the extended neighbourhood idea to become a reality.

India-Uzbek cooperation spans many areas such as economic and commercial, cultural, education and technical training in diverse disciplines, information technology, science and technology, agriculture and civil aviation, etc. India and Uzbekistan have signed several agreements so far to promote cooperation in these diverse fields. Military training and education is another important component of bilateral ties between New Delhi and Tashkent. Politico-military cooperation is an important part of bilateral ties. Given the changed geo-political situation in Eurasia, this assumes greater significance.

India and Uzbekistan have been playing a positive role in the reconstruction of Afghanistan. Given their shared concerns over threats from religious fundamentalism, terrorism, extremism and cross-border terrorism, India and Uzbekistan have underlined the need to further strengthen secular and democratic ideas in international relations. The two countries share common values such as secularism, tolerance and strong opposition to the forces of fundamentalism and terrorism.

Energy security is paramount for a developing country like India, which has begun to grow at an accelerated pace. India's energy consumption is likely to grow. Uzbekistan could provide a modicum of energy security to India. In this regard, the issue of the transport corridor assumes significance. If connectivity issue is resolved between South and central Asia, it would be a win win situation for the countries in both the regions.

Uzbek entrepreneurs can make use of the considerable experience of Indian industry in areas such as textiles (both cotton and silk), pharmaceuticals and medical equipment, information technology and processing of agricultural products, to name only a few. Indian businessmen have already shown interest to invest in some of these areas. It is a matter of satisfaction that our bilateral trade figures for the last several years are following an upward trajectory. I believe that there is still is a considerable space for further strengthening our economic relations. Bilateral trade in 2022 is about $ 690 million. 13th meeting of the Inter-governmental Commission on Trade, Economic, Scientific and Technological Cooperation between India and Uzbekistan was held in July this year to discuss ways and means to exploit the economic potential that exists between New Delhi and Tashkent.

Cultural ties constitute an important pillar of our bilateral relationship. There is a very active Indian cultural centre in Tashkent, which, besides working closely with many Uzbek organizations, also conducts regular classes in Indian classical dance "Kathak", Tabla, Yoga, Hindi language and Indian studies. It is rather difficult to separate the past from the present while discussing Indo-Uzbek cultural ties. The past feeds and enriches the present and provides the ambience for the warm relations that exist between the two countries. There are about 5000 Indian nationals living in Uzbekistan (Tashkent, Qarshi, Andijon, Ferghona, Urgench and Bukhara regions).

In the final analysis, one can say that the goodwill existing between two countries need to be translated into substantive economic, commercial and investment linkages. Enhancing the economic engagement may be a priority of both the governments. Religious extremism and international terrorism would remain challenge to Central Asian security and stability. Indo-Uzbek cooperation would be an important part of the international coalition against such forces. Uzbekistan appreciates the active and constructive stand taken by India on various regional and global issues, for example, the reconstruction of Afghanistan and the fight against international terrorism. India and Uzbekistan have maintained active cooperation at the multilateral fora, particularly the United Nations. Tashkent supports India's permanent membership at the United Nations Security Council (UNSC) and resolution of Jammu & Kashmir issue through bilateral talks between New Delhi and Islamabad. India has been a supporter of evolutionary democracy in Uzbekistan. In pursuing policies for successful economic development with equity, every nation would have to effectively base them on its own history, culture and traditional value systems. Imitative policies, which reflect the conditions in other countries, are not likely to be effective.

For Uzbekistan, India could emerge as a major market for its energy resources. Indications are that Uzbek enterprises and entrepreneurs would welcome Indian participation via joint ventures in areas like manufacture of electronic equipment, precision instruments, optical instruments, textiles, ready-made garments and leather goods. Uzbekistan is in a good position to supply items like phosphorous fertilizers, chemicals and metals to India. Information Technology, hydrocarbons, deepening of bilateral cooperation in the area of small and medium scale business and tourism appear to be candidate areas in Indo-Uzbek economic cooperation with high potential for success.

2

Foreign Direct Investment in Uzbekistan: An Analysis

Anil Sharma

Introduction

Uzbekistan is a resource-rich, strategically located in the heart of Central Asia. As on December, 2023, the Gross Domestic Product (GDP) of the country is US $90.8 Billion having 6 per cent growth rate and having GDP per capita at US$ 2468. The literacy rate in Uzbekistan is 97 per cent. There are 93 local universities and 21 branches of foreign universities. About 63 per cent of the population of 36.8million people aged 14 to 59 years. By 2035, the population is forecasted at 44 million people. The level of urbanization is at least 59 per cent.

Uzbekistan has developed decent infrastructure. The total length of roads exceeds 184 thousand km, electricity network 237 thousand km, railways network 4.7 thousand km and gas pipelines 13.7 thousand km. There are 11 international airports. During the year 2023, the total trade (goods) of Uzbekistan was US $ 68.57 Billion consisting of exports (goods) of US $ 24.43 Billion and Import (goods) USD 38.14 Billion. Major Trade Partners of Uzbekistan are: Russia, 17.9 per cent, China, 17.7 per cent, Kazakhstan, 9.3 per cent, Turkey, 8.1 per cent and South Korea, 4.5 per cent. Main exports products were gold, tourism energy and fruits and vegetables. While industrial goods, automobiles, iron and steel were major imports.[1]

In 2019 Uzbekistan entered the top 20 countries in the world that achieved the greatest results in improving the business environment. Uzbekistan introduced a visa-free regime for the entry of tourists from 86 countries of the world. In this regard, Uzbekistan is becoming the most open country for tourists among the CIS countries. Fitch Ratings affirmed Uzbekistan's outlook as 'Stable' in April, 2022. According to the Gallup rating "Global Law and Order" and "Individual Report on Travel Safety", Uzbekistan is on the 5th place in the list of the safest countries in the world for personal safety, law enforcement and travel.

The introduction of free conversion of the national currency, the reduction of trade barriers and customs payments allowed to significantly increasing the volume of trade. Current foreign policy of Uzbekistan is formed taking into account the dynamic changes in the world and the region as well as large-scale reforms within the country. In the past, large-scale reforms have been carried out in the tax system, the rates of a single tax payment, VAT, property tax, social payment have been reduced, a flat taxation scale has been introduced for personal income, and some types of taxes and obligatory payments have been cancelled. VAT rate has been reduced from 20 per cent to 15 per cent.

The government adopted its "Digital Uzbekistan – 2030 Strategy" in October 2020 to intensify work to upgrade communications infrastructure to the 5G standard. Uzbekistan aspires to become an upper middle-income country by 2030 (US$4,000 per capita) while maintaining domestic social equitability through the halving of poverty by 2026.

It has significant reserves of mineral resources, more than 2,000 deposits. Annually production of gold counted as 90 tons. Uzbekistan has the largest consumer market in the region. The Republic of Uzbekistan has tremendous potential for energy development. It is also important that in terms of low cost of energy (cost per kWh of electricity and m^3 of gas). The country is in second place among the CIS. It has the potential to become a strong regional economy.[2]

Developing tourism is among the major priorities of the Government and the number of foreign tourists was rapidly increasing until the pandemic. Uzbekistan's development strategy for 2022-2026 set the target to increase the number of foreign tourists visiting the country to nine million by 2026.

The government intends to increase the number of students attending university (particularly in technical fields) to 50 per cent of all high school graduates by 2030 and plans to build 30 new universities to accommodate them.

Investment Climate in Uzbekistan

Over the last few years, Uzbekistan has made significant strides to attract more international business and investment. The nation's strategic location as the main land corridor with developed infrastructure helps in booming market with high growth. There is no doubt that ongoing reforms will help to provide great opportunity to each of investors. Uzbekistan introduced a procedure for providing residence permits to foreign investors, subject to investment in the Republic of Uzbekistan. In the case of other types of investments (for example, in shares, replenishment of the authorized capital or acquisition of shares in enterprises), the amount of investments made must be at least $ 400,000. Moreover, an "investment visa" has been introduced for investors who have contributed at least $ 200,000.

To actively attract foreign capital, there are 21 free economic zones (7 pharmaceutical, 12 industrial, 1 agricultural and 1 tourism), a business ombudsman institution has been introduced, the Tashkent International Arbitration Centre has been established. Uzbekistan has risen from the 6th to the 5th group in terms of the OECD country credit risk classification. There are more than 50 international companies with FDI in Uzbekistan. In 2014, Uzbekistan joined the CIS Free Trade Zone Agreement. On December 11, 2020, Uzbekistan joined the Eurasian Economic Union (EAEU) as an observer. On April 9, 2021, the European Union accepted Uzbekistan as the ninth beneficiary of a General System of Preferences Plus (GSP+) trade arrangement, which removed tariffs on two thirds (6,200 titles) of the product lines covered by GSP. On November 1, 2021, Uzbekistan was admitted to the United Kingdom's Enhanced Framework Generalized Scheme of Preferences, which allows zero import duty on more than 7,800 products made in Uzbekistan. The country is also working on joining the World Trade Organization (WTO).[3]

Reforms by the Uzbek Government

The Government of Uzbekistan (GOU) has made efforts to improve the investment attractiveness of the country. The GOU has modernized its legislation through the adoption of the Law on Investments and Investment Activities and other acts that streamlined interactions of investors with the state, reduced the tax load, liberalized access to certain commodities, and started the privatization of major state-owned enterprises.

Uzbekistan's Constitution provides for a presidential system with separation of powers and a representative government. The incumbent, President Shavkat Mirziyoyev, after winning his first Presidential election in 2016, he implemented a reform program. The Development Strategy of Uzbekistan for 2022-2026 was adopted in January 2022.[4]

Under Uzbekistan's law on Public-Private Partnerships, there are new opportunities for foreign investors to participate in large projects, with tenders operated by the Public-Private Partnership (PPP) Development Agency under the Ministry of Finance of Uzbekistan. Since 2018, foreign bidders have signed PPP agreements to implement several fossil fuel and renewable energy projects. The Government wants to attract investments in the amount of $14 billion on a PPP basis to the energy, transport, healthcare, education, ecology, utilities, water management and other sectors in 2022-2026.[5]

The National Program (2019-2030) for the development of the chemical industry has identified 31 projects with a total value of $12 billion. The government plans to increase production of higher value-added goods through mineral processing. Projects in the oil and gas industry are intended to attract about$36.5 billion in investment from various sources through 2030. These projects may represent good export opportunities for suppliers of oil and gas extraction, transportation, processing technologies, and oil services.

Privatisation of Public Sector

The state still plays a significant role in Uzbek economy. State owned enterprises (SOEs) dominate the economy particularly in banking, energy, metallurgy and mining, telecom and transport sector. Uzbekistan is aiming to transfer 20 per cent of public services to the private sector and expand the share of the public sector in its GDP to 80 per cent by 2026. The government plans to transition the banking industry from public to private capital, with a target of expanding the share of private sector to 60 per cent by 2026. The income tax rate for banks will be lowered from the current 20 per cent to 15 per cent starting from2023. State-owned banks (SOBs) are in the process of modernizing their client service systems, transitioning to international financial reporting standards, and improving corporate governance to increase their attractiveness to foreign investors.[6]

Notable progress has been made in development of renewable energy capacity. Uzbekistan already attracted FDI to develop nearly 4,000 MW of solar and wind capacity and plans to build another 4,000 MW generation capacity by 2026, which will increase the share of renewable to 25 percent and displace 3 billion cubic meters of natural gas usage annually.

Changes in Business Laws

Over recent years, a number of structural reforms have been implemented in the sphere of foreign trade aimed at strengthening the export potential, improvement of customs administration as well as creation of an effective system of incentives for businesses to engage in foreign trade activities. In order to stimulate exports of domestic products as well as in accordance with the Resolution of the President of the Republic of Uzbekistan dated May 24, 2019, subsidies and compensations are provided to exporting enterprises to cover interest expenses on pre-export credits of commercial banks and transportation by railroad transport when exporting certain products.

The Resolution of the Cabinet of Ministers of the Republic of Uzbekistan dated December 31, 2020 approved the procedure of financial assistance of the Export Promotion Agency under the Ministry of Investment and Foreign Trade to the exporter organizations for compensation of costs associated with the introduction of international standardization and certification systems both in the country and abroad, registration of national products in foreign authorized bodies and participation in international exhibitions and fairs. An accelerated seven days VAT refund process is introduced for exporters. Uzbekistan has signed bilateral agreements with 54 countries on the avoidance of double taxation.

Role of Multilateral Development Institutions

Asian Development Bank (ADB)

ADB is one of Uzbekistan's largest development partners. ADB's support was focused on reforms for the country's transition toward an inclusive and market-driven economy. ADB is assisting in this transition by providing policy advice, capacity building, and projects that support private sector development, reduce economic and social disparities, and promote regional cooperation and integration. In 2022, ADB committed 5 public sector projects and programs for just over $1 billion to Uzbekistan. This included a $500-million loan to help promote food security, provide social protection for vulnerable groups, and support employment in Uzbekistan amid the corona virus disease (COVID-19) pandemic.

Till December, 2022, ADB has committed 240 public sector loans, grants, and technical assistance totalling $11.5 billion to Uzbekistan. Cumulative loan disbursements to Uzbekistan amount to $7.69 billion. These were financed by regular and concessional ordinary capital resources, and other special funds. ADB's current sovereign portfolio in Uzbekistan includes 32 loans, 1 grant, and 1 sovereign guarantee worth $5.06 billion. Total outstanding balances and undisbursed commitments of ADB's non-sovereign transactions in Uzbekistan as of 31 December 2022 was $327.18 million representing 2.6 per cent of ADB's total private sector portfolio.[7]

World Bank (WB) and International Finance Corporation (IFC)

World Bank Group's financial, technical, and analytical support to the country has grown substantially since 2017, bolstering the Government's efforts to implement a comprehensive program of market reforms. The World Bank's country program in Uzbekistan is the second largest in the Europe and Central Asia region after Turkey. As of December 1, 2022, it consists of 24projects, with net commitments totalling around US$4.6 billion. These projects provide support to the Government in critical areas, such as macroeconomic reforms, modernization of agriculture irrigation and drainage systems, health, education, water supply and sanitation, energy, transport, social protection, urban and rural infrastructure, national innovation, and tax administration systems, as well mitigation of the health, economic and social implications of COVID-19.

IFC is also helping it to increase private sector participation in the economy via PPPs, support the privatization process, enhance corporate governance, continue the transformation of the cotton sector, deepen and diversify the financial sector, including with the development of the microfinance sector and capital markets, and develop an enabling environment for PPPs in support of infrastructure development.[8]

European Bank for Reconstruction and Development (EBRD)

EBRD's clearest contribution to systemic change has been within the energy and financial sectors. In energy beyond financing for private sector renewable energy generation, the EBRD has also financed public grid infrastructure, delivered capacity building to state counterparts, and contributed through policy dialogue to the renewable energy competitive auction process. The EBRD's SME credit lines and support to commercialisation and private sector participation in state-dominated sectors have had a clear role in contributing to systemic changes related to enhancing competitiveness. In addition to increasing the role of the private sector, the EBRD's renewable energy support has had a clear role in helping to promote green energy. EBRD support to the private sector has been channelled through two primary mechanisms: financing for private sector businesses and the Advice for Small Businesses (ASB) Programme. Between 2017-22, the EBRD committed to US$ 210 million of financing for private sector businesses, primarily in the agribusiness and pharmaceutical sectors and launched 258 projects under the ASB.[9]

Foreign Direct Investment in Uzbekistan

The government's efforts to facilitate the entry of foreign businesses into Uzbekistan's economy are already paying off. In the World Bank's Doing Business 2020 ranking, Uzbekistan was among the top 20 most improved economies on the ease of doing business score.

Investment Agreements

The USAID Legal Reform Program has assisted the Ministry of Justice in preparing successful models of an investment agreement and bilateral investment treaties. The model investment agreement has already been used to conclude 22 international agreements, valued at over 2 billion U.S. dollars, with investors from Turkey, Germany, Russia, the U.S.A., Canada, the United Arab Emirates, France, China and other countries. Of these investment agreements, six were in the field of information technology, five in mining, and four in energy.[10]

The important investment agreements entered into by Uzbekistan include with Korea, China, Russia and Turkey. Generally, Uzbekistan's investment treaties adopt a broad, non-exhaustive asset-based definition of investment. Generally, Uzbekistan's investment agreements contain the core set of substantive protections the foreign investments and investors may enjoy under the treaty (namely, the most-favoured-nation; national and fair and equitable treatment (either qualified or unqualified); full protection and security and guarantees against expropriation).[11]

Securing Foreign Investments

Uzbekistan has established the export-import insurance company Uzbekinvest to, inter alia, 'provide complex insurance coverage for foreign investment in priority sectors of the Uzbek economy'. Uzbekinvest's insurance coverage is not contingent on the existence of an investment treaty between Uzbekistan and the investor's state. Further, according to article 50 of the Law On Investments and Investment Activity No. 598 dated 25 December 2019, a foreign investor has the right, but is not required, to obtain insurance coverage from any insurance company operating in Uzbekistan and may insure against political and other risks in 'international organisations, foreign agencies, and other insurance companies'. Uzbekistan is a member of the Multilateral Investment Guarantee Agency.[12]

Persistent Weaknesses and Threats

The Russian war in Ukraine has affected the political and economic landscape of the region, and the full long-term impact is yet to be understood. Russia and Ukraine were Uzbekistan's largest and ninth largest trading partners in 2021. Uzbekistan has also been actively attracting Russian investment capital: the largest state industrial and energy companies of Uzbekistan have signed several billion-dollar loan agreements and MOUs with Russian state banks to finance their projects in the last few years. The status of these agreements may be at risk now.

Insufficient IPR protection remains to be a challenge for foreign businesses in Uzbekistan. On April 26, 2022, President Mirziyoyev signed the decree on "Additional Measures for the further development of the field of Intellectual Property". Despite this progress, IPR enforcement in Uzbekistan remains weak. State-owned enterprises dominate Uzbekistan's economy and limit fair competition in some key industries, including but not limited to energy, telecommunications, automotive, aviation, chemical, mining, etc. Documents required for licensing, registration and other permits may be amended without notice, which creates an opportunity for rent-seeking.

India Uzbek Economic Ties

Present Status

India and Uzbekistan have relations that go back in history. India was one of the first countries to recognize the state sovereignty of Uzbekistan after the latter's independence. There has been significant intensification in bilateral ties in recent years. Bilateral relations encompass a wide canvas, including on political and strategic issues, defence and security, trade and investment, energy, agriculture, education and people-to-people ties.

There are about 11000 Indian nationals, from different parts of the country are, living in various regions of Uzbekistan. They are Involved mostly in pharmaceutical and hospitality businesses; some are university and school teachers; and many serve as doctors in local hospitals and many work in the oil and gas sector. Presently about 4000 students are studying medicine in different medical universities of Uzbekistan.

Bilateral Trade

At present, India and Uzbekistan bilateral trade is at about USD 690 million (as per Uzbek statistics). The major items of India's exports are pharmaceutical products, mechanical equipment, vehicle parts, services, optical instruments and equipment. India's import from Uzbekistan consists largely of fruit and vegetable products, services, fertilizers, juice products and extracts, and lubricants.[13] As per official figures released, India's bilateral trade with Uzbekistan during the last three years is as shown below:

Year (Jan–Dec)	*Imports from India (in US$ million)*	*Exports to India (in US$ million)*	*Total trade turnover (in US$ million)*
2021	461.0	29.0	490.0
2022	654.9	35.6	690.5
2023	584.1	105.7	689.7

Indian Investments in Uzbekistan

Numbers of projects are being implemented by India in Uzbekistan on government to Government basis. Agreements on establishment of cooperation between the Andijon region and the state of Gujarat and between the cities of Samarkand and Agra were signed during the visit of Uzbek President in October 2018. A similar understanding between Haryana and Fergana was also inked in August 2022.India had also opened a credit line of $448 million for four development projects in Uzbekistan, including road construction, wastewater treatment and information technology.

Both India and Uzbekistan have set up National Coordination Committees to oversee the implementation of mutually agreed projects and initiatives. The Committees on both sides review projects through grant assistance, LOC and private investment proposals along with other aspects of bilateral cooperation in trade, investment and education fields. In August 2020, in the first meeting of Uzbekistan – Indian Committee for Coordination and Promotion of Practical Implementation of Bilateral Agreements was held via videoconference where issues related to the implementation of joint projects in agriculture, pharmaceuticals, healthcare, education and infrastructure development.[14] As noted, 98 investment and trade agreements were signed for $ 2.3 billion within the framework of bilateral cooperation.

So far private investment is concerned, there are over 280 companies of Indian origin operating in Uzbekistan and joint projects worth over $650 million were being realised. Indian investments by Indian companies include those in the field of pharmaceuticals like Cadila, in development of airports and cargo complex like GMR, in health care like Ambani Speciality Hospital. Amity University and Sharda University have opened campuses in Tashkent and Andijon respectively. Indian institutions like iCreate are actively cooperating with Uzbek counterparts for promoting start-up ecosystem in Uzbekistan and training entrepreneurs in setting up incubators. Indian companies like Dev IT have entered into bilateral cooperation in field research, technologies, start- ups and innovations with budding Uzbek partners. NTPC is also participating in various tenders including solar PV power plants and consultancy assignment for gas projects in Uzbekistan.[15]

More investments in various fields, including pharma and healthcare, textiles and auto components, agriculture and food processing, and mining and jewellery sector are in various stages of discussion. Uzbekistan has invited Indian companies to explore joint-venture opportunities in seven pharmacological free economic zones. Special attention is being given to the implementation of joint projects with Indian companies in Uzbekistan's free economic zones.[16]

Challenges for Indian Investment

Uzbekistan's status as a landlocked country contributes to connectivity challenges. Air connectivity between the two nations is not as robust as desired, hampering swift and efficient exchanges. The extensive influence of China's Belt and Road Initiative in Central Asian countries, including Uzbekistan, poses a challenge. China's growing presence in the region may alter the economic and geopolitical landscape. The geopolitics of Central Asia, including the presence of other major powers in the region, adds complexity to India – Uzbekistan relations and influences regional dynamics.[17]

Way Forward

India-Uzbekistan relations are a key to India's vision of integrated extended neighbourhood. Trade relations are a natural outcome of strengthening of bilateral relations. There is a pressing need for increased convergence between India and Uzbekistan, spanning economic, diplomatic, and strategic spheres. India and Uzbekistan bilateral trade is well below its potential. There is need to explore initiatives to improve connectivity in facilitating trade between the two countries. India needs to take the relation forward in newer areas like information technology, digital payment solutions and investment in start-ups, space cooperation and Gems and Jewellery, Uzbekistan's cotton industry and rich natural resources such as gold and natural gas offer attractive opportunities for investors from India. Diversifying trade beyond traditional sectors and exploring opportunities in emerging industries can lead to a more robust economic partnership.

India and Uzbekistan have signed a Joint Statement in September 2019 to set up a joint feasibility study for entering into negotiations for a Preferential Trade Agreement (PTA). Indian Prime Minister Narendra Modi and Uzbek President Mirziyoyev instructed their officials to fast-track the conclusion of the ongoing study. There is need to finalise the Bilateral Investment Treaty at the earliest. Further steps are needed to accelerate the preparation and signing of the Agreement on Encouragement and Reciprocal Protection of Investments and the Agreement on Preferential Trade.

Indian companies should capitalize on Uzbekistan's trade agreements and explore mutually beneficial investment projects. This can be achieved by setting up joint ventures in Uzbekistan. Rather than looking for bilateral trade, such joint ventures may enjoy advantage due to Uzbekistan's trade agreements/ treaties with other countries.

India and Uzbekistan need to evolve imaginative policy to overcome the issue of geographical inaccessibility. This will foster improved connectivity, facilitating smoother trade and transit across the region. This move can help overcome landlocked challenges and expand economic horizons. Indian investors should explore joint ventures to be set up in Free Export zones in those sectors in which raw material can be procured locally for manufactured goods to be exported to developed countries.

India should help Uzbekistan in its preparation for becoming member of World Trade Organisation. Indian banks may explore setting up their branches in Uzbekistan to cater the financing requirements of Indian investments and joint ventures.

End Notes

1 www.eoi.gov.in/tashkent>Countryfact sheet- Uzbekistan accessed on March 27, 2024.

2 https://www.state.gov/reports/2022-investment-climate-statements/uzbekistan/ 2022 Investment Climate Statements: Uzbekistan, accessed on June 10, 2023

3 httpps://invest.gov.uz >Why Invest in Uzbekistan- Investment Promotion Agency under the Ministry of Investment and Foreign Trade- Republic of Uzbekistan, accessed on January 17, 2024

4 International Trade Administration, US Department of Commerce, accessed on September 29, 2023

5 https://www.trade.gov/country-commercial-guides/uzbekistan-market-opportunities – Uzbekistan – Country Commercial Guide, accessed on June 10, 2023

6 *Ibid*

7 www.adb.org/publications/series/asian-development-outlook Asian Development Bank Member Fact Sheet – Uzbekistan

8 www.worldbank.org/en/country/uzbekistan- Uzbekistan –World Bank Group FY22-26 Country Partnership Framework, February 2022.

9 The EBRD in Uzbekistan (2017-22) EBRD Evaluation Department – October 2023, accessed on January 17, 2024

10 https://www.usaid.gov:uzbekistan - Boosting Foreign Investment in Uzbekistan, accessed on January 17, 2024

11 https://wwwlex.uz/acts/561818 Lexology: Getting the Deal through- Investment Treaty Practice, accessed on October 14, 2023

12 LRU-598-COH-25/12/2019 – Laws of Republic of Uzbekistan- Law on Investments and Investment Activities (Unofficial Translation), accessed on September 29, 2023

13 http://eoi.gov.in/eoisearch/MyPrint BILATERAL- India – Uzbekistan Relations accessed on March 27, 2024

14 https://pib.gov.in/PressReleasePage.aspx?PDIR=1845984-13th Session of India-Uzbekistan Inter Governmental Commission held in India.

15 Uzbekistan Offers attractive conditions to Indian Investors in IT, Textiles, Electronics, Pharmaceutical and Minerals:Envoy-by Dipanjan Roy Chaudhary, ET Bureau, Apr 01, 2024.

16 wtc@wtcmumbai.org- Uzbekistan invites Indian firms to Joint projects in 7 Pharmacological zones, accessed on January 17, 2024

17 https://universalinstitutions.com/category/current affairs/editorial/Indian Express>India Uzbekistan Relations, accessed on January 17, 2024

3

Digital Diplomacy, Branding and the Multiple Facets of Indo-Uzbek Relations in the Post Pandemic Era

Dr Anita Sengupta

Digitization has impacted the practice of diplomacy in innumerable ways. Using a variety of tools that include social media and messaging applications, digitization has today transformed the way global institutions, governments and populations can be influenced. Diplomats now use digital tools to create trans-national networks that often include both the official ministries as well as non- governmental agencies. This has created avenues for interaction with larger populations that was limited by the tools of traditional diplomacy based on state to state interaction. While this creates the possibilities of contention with an unpredictable online public, it also creates the potential of communication through a virtual presence where conflictual relations do not allow a presence on the ground. Digital diplomacy refers mainly to the growing use of social media platforms by a country in order to achieve its foreign policy goals and proactively manage its image and reputation.[1] This is useful not just in influencing larger public opinion on issues of significance but also in showcasing cultures and traditions that are a part of nation branding for most states today. And here digital diplomacy plays an increasingly significant role. While it is true that nations have always sought to promote their economic, diplomatic and military interests, it is only in the last decade that nations have turned to the explicit use of techniques of branding. Since a significant part of branding is through a digital mode, digital diplomacy has assumed a significant part in determining the relations among states.

Digital diplomacy happens in multiple ways and has emerged as the centre piece of its global agenda with a focus on human centric approach to technology. For instance the development of Digital Payment Index (DPI) for adoption of digital payments, data sharing infrastructures and boosting digital economy has become an intrinsic part of India's digital diplomacy. The Digital India campaign has become an integral part of providing digital solution not only for domestic governance but also across states. The fact that affordable and accessible digital technology can be made available on a large scale has enabled India to promote its digital infrastructure and embark on a digital diplomacy that has significantly contributed to her soft power.[2] India's online payments infrastructure, to power real-time money transfers, for instance could well become an alternative for a technology-driven connectivity initiative. It is a cost-efficient alternative to China's multi-trillion-dollar infrastructure investment in ports and pipelines in an escalating battle for regional influence. In this background, plans announced for an entity backed by Nepal's central bank to deploy India's payments model is a significant development for the Himalayan nation which is often caught in the geopolitics of the region. Closing a soft infrastructure gap marks a stark contrast to President Xi Jinping's attempt to plug the hard infrastructure deficit stretching from Pakistan to Sri Lanka. His Belt and Road programme formally started in 2013 began with the idea of constructing transport corridors as a good way to make friends because such projects provide countries with highly desired funding, jobs, taxes and technical expertise. However, in a number of cases it has led to debt traps. On the other hand, India's direct financial gain from sharing its technology will likely be limited to nominal fees. As an image building exercise this digital diplomacy has enormous value in branding India as a neighbour willing to extend support without expectation of much gain. India now uses different ways to engage with audiences overseas through mobile apps, live streaming videos and a very responsive social media presence.

Such practices of 'nation branding' has proliferated in recent years as more and more governments around the world attempt to harness the power of commercial branding techniques to improve their country's image and reputation across a wide range of sectors.[3] Terms such as 'brand image' and 'brand identity' are increasingly being used to describe the perceptions that are held of nations among their 'stakeholders'. This eruption of the vocabulary of branding into the international affairs of nations has not been without scepticism regarding the appropriateness and relevance of such overtly commercial practices. However, almost every government in the world is now engaged in one way or another with nation branding, more visibly through the commissioning of advertisements in international channels and less visibly though initiatives like the consistent portrayal of certain symbols and images as constituting the essence of the state.[4] The subtle but consistent depiction of yoga and meditation as ways of discovering oneself intermingling with the discovery of India itself, in a recent Incredible India video, is a representative example.[5] However, contending images that reflect political positions and are used to discredit positions are also a possibility. The Hamas that controls the Gaza strip circulated a video that depicted the place as a bustling city with shopping malls, beaches and parks. The Israeli diplomats used the same video to argue that the Hamas had been untrue about the fact that a brutal Israeli siege had destroyed the place.[6]

The success of any brand is determined by its ability to convince people of the viability of the brand. In terms of the state, this would be interpreted as the ability of the state to convince international audiences about the viability of its foreign policy. Global economic forces make developing a good brand more important than ever. Similarly branding now has a very important role in the politics of security. Like commercial brands states are now described as 'friendly' (i.e. western oriented) 'credible' (ally) or in contrast 'unreliable' (rogue state). Therefore, countries could also be at the receiving end of a branding process. The clustering of states as the 'axis of evil' is an example. Similarly, an 'unbranded' state may have a difficult time in attracting economic and political attention. Assertive brand asset management may be viewed as central to keeping both competitive economic and political edge. States, regions and cities now adopt proactive branding strategies in the knowledge that as a strong, attractive place brand they can expand their market and political share by creating a strong brand premium. In fact, place branding specialists emphasize that nation branding encourages one to revisit the debate on nationalism and the role and nature of national identity.[7] 'Chinese Dream' the brand slogan initiated by President Xi and first used by him at the National Museum's

'Road to Revival' exhibition was as much an attempt at national revival is a reflection of the aspiration for extension of Chinese soft power through cultural symbols. This change implies more than merely window-dressing. It implies a shift in political paradigms, a shift from the modern world of geopolitics and power to a post- modern world of images and influence being sought after by states today.

This article is an attempt to examine this through an analysis of how digital diplomacy and a positive branding are transforming India's relations with Central Asia in general and Uzbekistan in particular. It begins with an examination of how the nature of diplomacy is now affected by branding through projection of soft power and then goes on to project this in terms of India's relations with Uzbekistan.

Diplomacy, branding and soft power

Interest in the concept and practice of nation branding has proliferated in recent years as more and more governments around the world attempt to harness the power of commercial branding techniques in order to improve their country's image and reputation across a wide range of sectors. History, of course, is replete with vignettes that are evocative of place branding. The French state has undergone regular re-branding exercises. Other examples include the remarkable transformation of the Ottoman Empire to Ataturk's modern Turkey and of the erstwhile USSR to the Russian Federation. After 1945 the collapse of the Great European colonial empires created a wave of nations. Many of these gave themselves new names. Ceylon became Sri Lanka, Gold Coast became Ghana, Southern Rhodesia became Zimbabwe and its capital Salisbury became Harare. The Dutch East Indies became Indonesia. Its capital Batavia became Jakarta and its multiplicity of languages was replaced by Bahasa Indonesian. The former Belgian Congo became Congo, then Zaire, and then Congo again. Entirely new countries like Pakistan and Bangladesh emerged from what had been the British Indian Empire. Bangladesh has had three names in just over half a century, first it was a part of India as East Bengal, then it became East Pakistan and then Bangladesh.[8] While it is true that nations have always sought to promote their economic, diplomatic and military interests, it is only in the last decade that nations have turned to the explicit use of the techniques of branding. A comprehensive nation branding strategy would also encompass initiatives and programmes to stimulate diaspora mobilization, enhance the coordination of the nation's key institutions and organizations and ensure a reasonable degree of consistency in the country's official communications. Simon Anholt, who introduced the term 'nation brand' went on to argue that with the rapid expansion of globalization, 'place branding' becomes important because every place wants to enhance, reverse, adapt or otherwise manage its international reputation since the world has become one market.[9]

Most of the literature on 'nation branding' focuses on one of the three dominant research areas: the country of origin effects for export products; branding tourist destinations and getting foreign investments. However, there is much more to a powerful nation brand image than simply boosting branded exports around the world. It is now essential for countries to understand how they are seen by publics around the world; how their achievements and failures, their assets and liabilities, their people and their products are reflected in their brand image. Reputation management and influencing public opinion in other countries have become important drivers of foreign politics, and public diplomacy now plays an important role in communicating a nation's policies and cultures to international audiences. The 'brand state's' use of its history, geography and ethnic motifs to construct its own distinct image is a benign campaign that often lacks the deep rooted often antagonistic sense of national identity and uniqueness that can accompany nationalism, yet it is no less significant in terms of 'identity politics'. In fact, place branding specialists emphasize that nation branding encourages one to revisit the debate on nationalism and the role and nature of national identity.

For India it was reflected in the *Incredible India* campaign launched in 2002 by the Ministry of Tourism as a nation branding campaign.[10] It was aimed both at extending the business and leisure traveller's stay in India but also promoting domestic tourism and international financial investment. Typically focusing on the travels of international culinary experts, travel bloggers and in the most recent version a 'yogi on the racetrack' through India, the campaign portrays amazing hospitality in the background of staggering peaks, extended vistas, serene lakes, exotic wildlife and luxurious accommodations. Visualising a joyous colourful celebration of life Incredible India facilitates the idea of seamless communication and global accessibility aimed at creating a relationship between tourism destination marketing and nation branding. The campaign, deemed to be responsible for rise in foreign exchange earnings, increase in tourist arrival and a place for India in the top ten country brands in Future Brand's Country Brand Index was, however, aimed at more than just destination branding. It sought to improve India's share in key Asian markets and to position and distinguish India from Asian competitors, Malaysia, Thailand and Singapore, each with its own brand slogan 'Malaysia Truly Asia', 'Amazing Thailand' and 'Uniquely Singapore'. The policy was aimed at reflecting the fact that in an increasingly globalized world, where the state is situated within the global space and its 'image' in the international community becomes in many ways as crucial as the projection of homogeneity within the state.[11]

Given India's historic and cultural connects to its extended neighbourhood both towards the South and Southeast and the Northwest, its branding as an Asian alternative would be conducive towards the building of an alternative logistic framework for Asian development.[12] It has been argued that India today regards the concept of neighbourhood as one of widening concentric circles around historical and cultural commonalities. Here geography imparts a unique position to India, extending her neighbourhood to East Asia, West Asia, Central Asia, South Asia and South East Asia.[13] India has made a determined effort to reconnect with this extended neighbourhood which it has attempted within a new framework that emphasized economic relations and energy diplomacy rather than the traditional notion of third world solidarity through the non-aligned movement.[14] Analysts have noted that another significant change has been in the transformation in Indian policy from the unilateralism of previous eras to a multilateral approach.[15] And here the Indian position has coincided with the Central Asian one. Multilateral solutions have been sought for in a number of areas with regard to conflict resolution in both India and the Central Asian states. In this connection Kazakh initiatives to collectively deal with security issues has been noted as important by India particularly the progress of the Conference on Interaction and Confidence Building Measures in Asia (CICA).[16]

Similarly bilateral relations have also been developed. India and Kyrgyzstan raised their bilateral relationship to 'strategic partnership' and signed a number of agreements including a bilateral investment treaty on the sidelines of the

SCO Heads of Government meeting in Bishkek in June 2019. In the course of bilateral talks during the Summit it was stated that elevating the bilateral relationship to that of strategic partnership would enable long term cooperation in a number of fields with special emphasis on defence cooperation where a decision had been made to set up a joint working group. Among the agreements signed was a Memorandum of Understanding (MoU) for cooperation between the National Security Council Secretariat of India and the Office of the Security Council of the Kyrgyz Republic. Strategic partnerships indicate a new stage of mature relationship that recognizes equality, mutual advantage and each other's nation security interests. In the view of the persistence and promise of strategic partnerships in international affairs this strategic partnership between India and Kyrgyzstan assumes relevance particularly in the context of changed geopolitical realities in the Eurasian region and transformation of India's own security perception. It also assumes relevance in the context of larger regional arrangements of which India and Kyrgyzstan are now a part.[17]

With the increasing recognition of trade and connectivity as the impetus driving relations among states, there has been in recent years an increasing focus on connectivity as the determining focus of Asian relations in the coming decades.[18] Reflective of this was the fact that lack of connectivity and measures to overcome this was the principle focus of discussion during the first India-Central Asia Summit. On January 27, 2022, a virtual India-Central Asia Summit was held with leaders of Kazakhstan, Kyrgyzstan, Uzbekistan, Tajikistan and Turkmenistan, following the leaders' inability to attend the Republic Day celebrations that they had been invited to as Chief Guests due to a resurgence of COVID-19 infections globally. However, this invitation was reflective of India's renewed engagement with an extended neighbourhood, which looked not just eastwards but also towards the northwest. Connectivity, trade and developing a framework for co-operation on the Afghan situation were part of the agenda.[19] There is a proposal to make the Summit a permanent yearly event with a permanent Secretariat for greater engagement at the ministerial level, a change from the foreign minister level at which it currently exists. This follows the Delhi Regional Security Dialogue was hosted in New Delhi in November 2021. The hosting of the Summit elevates the bilateral relations that India has with the states to a formal multilateral level.

Another is a robust Neighbourhood First policy, which the Vaccine *Maitri* reflected recently. This effort to make Indian vaccines available for all during the pandemic first benefitted the immediate neighbourhood with vaccines being sent to Bhutan, Nepal, Bangladesh, Maldives, Myanmar and Seychelles and Central Asia. Vaccines sent as aid went first and overwhelmingly to the neighbourhood. However, it is being argued that this may not be enough to counter either increasing Chinese influence or India's own image within the region. However, the abrupt end to this humanitarian assistance in the face of a vaccine shortage within India meant not just disruption of vaccine rollout in other states but also squandered the goodwill that India had garnered in the initial phase. A step towards restoring this credibility came with increasing availability of vaccines by the last quarter of 2021 and an offer to share vaccine with Southeast Asian states as part of the Quadrilateral Security Dialogue (QUAD) and G-20. The pandemic revealed the strengths and weaknesses states globally as social welfare policies, rules of economic governance and commitment towards multilateralism came into question. A protectionist tendency had already become visible when the pandemic began with the post-World war consensus under review. As borders were closed and nationalist tendencies gained ground there was also a re-thinking of alliances. And it is here that there could emerge the possibility of projection of India as an alternative.

Diplomacy and the Multiple Facets of Indo-Uzbek Relations in the Post-pandemic Era

Among the many facets of relations between India and Uzbekistan, the development of information technology and the sharing of digital technologies now assume an important position. On 11 December 2020, India and Uzbekistan held a virtual bilateral summit where Prime Minister Narendra Modi and Uzbek President Shavkat Mirziyoyev deliberated on a range of issues important to both the nations including the early conclusion of the bilateral investment treaty, the COVID-19 pandemic, and combatting the threat of terrorism by "destroying" terrorist safe-havens, networks and funding channels. A US $448 million Line of Credit for the development of infrastructure, information technology and sewerage treatment in Uzbekistan has been extended by India. Significant among the agreements were those on cyber security, digital technologies and renewable energy. Among the issues discussed were the situation in Afghanistan and its significance for stability, trade enhancement and security of the entire region.

Indian initiatives in the region, however, cannot be visualized in isolation. Here an understanding of developments within the region and the geopolitical positioning of other states assumes importance. The viability of a proposal for a strategic partnership that was proposed by E.M. Primov and could have assumed relevance for the Central Asian region, i.e. the Russia-China-India triangle called 'Primakov's triangle' in Russian journalism.[20] While it is true that this initiative has been a non-starter in a number of ways, it is also true that one of the issues that it was meant to address was that of stability and development in the areas bordering the three states, i.e. the Central Asian region and Afghanistan. This means that the reason why the 'Eurasian triangle' failed to take off remains significant and this brings into focus the importance of taking a closer look at the region as the determining factor in the evolution of future relations between the states, whether it be between Russia and China or China and India or Russia and the US.[21] In any case, it is important to emphasize that simply focusing on the Sino-Indian interaction as the impediment to a more active Indian role in the region presents a truncated story that fails to take note of the varied and multidimensional interests of other powers and of course of the five states themselves.[22] Here two recent developments are significant. India and Eurasian countries have begun negotiations on a Comprehensive Economic Cooperation Agreement which is roughly the same as a foreign trade agreement. 90 per cent of the rail link of the International North South Corridor is complete. Once it is operational container transportation will be 30 per cent faster.

There have been attempts to promote policies in a multi-dimensional manner. For more than half a century prior to 1991 India's contacts with Central Asia were mediated through Russia. Though India had privileged access to the region it is a fact that India was slow to capitalize on its relations with Central Asia. Part of the reason could have been the fact that India recognized Russia's special interest in the post-Soviet space and endeavoured to work through Russia. The pace of relations accelerated post-1998 as a part of a more pro-active stance followed by India in its policies in general. By then the pace of economic reforms in the country had accelerated and the parameters of India's policy also broadened.[23] The expanding concentric circles of foreign policy now included not just South and South East Asia but also Central Asia and Afghanistan. It accelerated further after 2005 when interest was shown in the region symbolized by the participation of the Prime Minister in the SCO meeting in St Petersburg in 2009. The Kazakh President was the Guest of Honour at the Republic Day celebrations in 2009. A series of important economic initiatives were undertaken, which included the purchase of uranium from Kazakhstan. The Indian President was a guest at the Tajik National Day celebrations in 2009. During the course of this visit the President attended an Indo-Tajik Business Forum and visited the shrine of Mir Said Ali Hamdani, the Sufi saint who spread Islam in the Kashmir Valley. Along with cultural diplomacy, economic diplomacy is increasingly becoming important and there is today cooperation in the field of defence, intelligence sharing, training and assistance and ITEC programmes.[24] Indian engineers completed a transmission line to carry Uzbek electricity deep into Afghanistan and possibly beyond and a forward policy in Afghanistan as well.[25] It is important to keep in mind the fact that India ranked as the third major donor to Afghanistan supporting projects in education, infrastructure, health and other fields.

In fact, connectivity played a large part in the Indian decision to apply for membership to the SCO with the general agreement that for India joining the SCO was about "raising its stakes in Central Asia", of greater connectivity to a wider resource rich region and an opportunity to work on common issues of concern.[26] This in conjunction with Iran's membership would ensure that India would be able to move towards developing a platform for trade and transit through Bandar Abbas and Chabahar eventually linking with the North South Corridor. There also remained the possibility of the SCO acting as guarantor for projects like TAPI and the IPI which have been in the pipeline for a number of years. This would also provide a useful interface for interaction with Afghanistan and its neighbourhood. However, there is also the counter argument that SCO engagement need not be over emphasized as bilateral engagement with the Central Asian states work just as well as illustrated by the uranium supply deal with Kazakhstan during Prime Minister Modi's visit. The Indian alternative through 'Connect Central Asia' that was projected as the policy initiative on the west that would complement its Look/Act East Policy with emphasis on the four "Cs" commerce, connectivity, consular and culture. It is significant that the policy was unveiled at the first India-Central Asia Dialogue, a Track II Initiative at Bishkek in 2012. In addition, the creation of direct air corridors between the two countries and the entire region for both passenger and cargo flights had already been emphasized by India's external affairs minister Subramanian Jayshankar when he hosted the India Central Asia Business Council in February 2020.

The credit to these rejuvenated ties between the two historically connected countries as well as the whole of Central Asia goes to the constructive and coherent approach of New Delhi towards the Heart of Asia after the demise of the former Soviet Union. In 2015, PM Narendra Modi visited Uzbekistan and brought to the forefront the "region's strategic importance for India" and adopted a coherent strategy to upscale its relationship with Central Asia and bolster their ancient socio-economic and traditional ties. Terrorism being a common threat, both countries signed an agreement establishing a joint working group on counter terrorism and agreed to expand cooperation in the fields of defence and cyber-security. Former Uzbek President Islam Karimov made strengthening relations with New Delhi Tashkent's top foreign policy goal. For strengthening the bilateral relations, Uzbek president Mirziyoyev visited India in 2018 as well as in 2019 and signed a number of MOUs on trade, tourism, import of Uranium from Uzbekistan, technology and innovations. Even in 2020, when the world is facing grave economic crisis, the virtual India-Central Asia Dialogue including Afghanistan, was held on 28 October 2020. India gifted HCQ and Paracetamol tablets sought by Uzbekistan, along with lifting ban on export of essential medicines to fight COVID-19. India also conducted e-ITEC programmes for capacity building of Medical professionals from Uzbekistan. 660,000 doses of Covishield vaccine were delivered from Serum Institute of India to Uzbekistan under the COVAX initiative on 17 March 2021. In India's fight against the second wave of COVID-19, Uzbekistan provided 100 Oxygen concentrators and 2000 injections of Remdesivir.[27]

New Delhi announced its one-billion-dollar line of credit to five Central Asian Republics to widen the connectivity, energy partnerships and reinvigorate trade and commerce.In addition, a Line of Credit Agreement for US dollars 200 million for construction of affordable housing and social infrastructure projects was signed between the State Investment Committee of Uzbekistan and the EXIM Bank in January 2019. India has also conveyed an offer for additional USD 800 million as Line of Credit/Buyers Credit to Uzbekistan. A Joint Centre for Information Technology was set up in 2006 and upgraded in 2014 with Indian assistance. An India-Uzbekistan Entrepreneurship Development Centre (EDC) was inaugurated on 24 December 2018 in Tashkent. An Indian expert has been deputed at EDC for training and capacity building of Uzbek entrepreneurs. India has offered grant assistance for implementation of High Impact Community Development Projects to Uzbekistan. Two MOUs were signed in Tashkent on 11 December 2021 at the cost of about USD 2.5 Million under India's grant assistance.[28]

A significant part of the relationship is based on India focusing on areas of its strength small businesses, digital enterprise etc since India's partnership would be dependent on how it deploys its soft power by offering cooperation and capacity building, knowledge transfer, people to people contacts and humanitarian assistance.[29] It is argued that from a perspective of connectedness as the basis of development there are for instance, several industries where regional value chains could be developed in and between Central and South Asia: (a) fresh and chilled fruits and vegetables (b) processed foods (c) agricultural raw materials; (d) herbs and spices (e) precious and semi-precious stones (f) other non-ferrous and ferrous metals (g) slabs of marble and other stones (h) garments (i) carpets and (j) pharmaceuticals and herbal medications. The selection of these industries is based on a number of factors like the number of countries having an advantage in the industries and the benefits of diversifying industries across resource-intensive, labour-intensiveand technology-intensive industries like those of food and textiles. Natural resource intensive industries in minerals and fabricated metal products generally support government revenue-generating objectives particularly in Central Asia. And technology-intensive industries like those of pharmaceuticals create opportunities for market development. India is one of the largest producers of bulk pharmaceuticals and other countries like Tajikistan and Uzbekistan could form part of regional value chains.

Conclusion

India's prioritization of her neighbourhood through the Neighbourhood First Policy should reflect on continued attention on an extended region that covers her continental and maritime vicinity and takes note of multiple facets of the relationship through sustained engagement. Here, proactive outreach through non traditional diplomats whether they be private conglomerates or think tanks would facilitate engagement at various levels. This would involve taking strategic advantage of India's soft power through policies that involve new partners and utilizing their knowledge and influence to the best advantage of Indian diplomacy. India's natural geographic advantages, economic complementarities and shared heritage puts her in a position to re-evaluate her Asian connects despite China's growing footprints in Asia. With growing recognition of the significance of regional connects and the fact that regional stability and peace is crucial for everyone there have in recent times been some indications of prioritizing connectivity rather than disconnects. And here certain digital technologies could play a significant role in determining the nature of bilateral and multilateral relationships in the coming years.

End Notes

1 Olubukola S Adesina, "Foreign Policy in an era of Digital Diplomacy", *Cogent Social Sciences,* Vol 3, 2017, https://doi.org/10.1080/23311886.2017.1297175

2 Nazia Hussain, "Inida's G20 Presidency: Towards a Digital Diplomacy Strategy", *RSIS Commentary,* No 094 July 2023.

3 Anita Sengupta, "Introduction: Image, Influence and Legacy", in Symbols and the *Image of the State in Eurasia,* p. 2.

4 Sengupta, "Introduction: Image, Influence and Legacy", in *Symbols and the Image of the State in Eurasia,* p. 3.

5 Sengupta, " 'Incredible India' and the Brand State"

6 Ilan Manor, "What is Digital Diplomacy and How is it Practiced Around the World? A Brief Introduction" November 2016, originally published in *The 2016 Annual Review* of the Diplomatist Magazine http://www.diplomatist.com/dipoannual2016/index.html?pageNumber=36

7 Sengupta, "Introduction: Image, Influence and Legacy", in *Symbols and the Image of the State in Eurasia,* p. 4.

8 Wally Olins, Branding the Nation—the historical context. *The Journal of Brand Management,* 9 (2002, April). www.wallycollins.com.

9 Simon Anholt, *Places, Identity, Image and Reputation.* Houndmills, Basingstoke, Hampshire: Palgrave Macmillan. (2010).

10 This argument is borrowed from Anita Sengupta, " 'Incredible India' and the Brand State", https://www.asiainglobalaffairs.in/reflections/incredible-india-and-the-brand-state/

11 Sengupta, " 'Incredible India' and the Brand State".

12 Sengupta, " 'Incredible India' and the Brand State".

13 "Present dimension on the Indian Foreign Policy", Address by Foreign Secretary Shyam Saran at the Shanghai Institute of International Studies, Shanghai, January 11, 2006.

14 For a detailed analysis, see C. Raja Mohan, *Crossing the Rubicon: The Shaping of India's New Foreign Policy* (New Delhi: Viking, 2003).

15 Raja Mohan, *Crossing the Rubicon.*

16 Sengupta, "Perceptions and Strategies".

17 For a detailed discussion Sengupta "India's Evolving Relations with Kyrgyzstan ", *Diplomacy and Beyond*, Special Publication CIS at 30, 2021.

18 See for instance Zhang Zhexin, "The Belt and Road Initiative: China's New Geo-Political Strategy", https://www.worldscientific.com/doi/pdf/10.1142/S2377740018500240

19 This segment benefitted from a Focus Group Discussion organized as part of the project on "Afghanistan at Crossroads" on 31 August 2021 and discussions during an online international seminar on *The Current Dynamics of India Central Asia Cooperation: New Opportunities and Challenges*jointly organized by Jindal School of International Affairs, O P Jindal University, New Delhi, University of Central Asia Kyrgyzstan, University of World Economy and Diplomacy, Tashkent Uzbekistan and Al Farabi Kazakh National University, Kazakhstan on 10 February 2022.

20 Sengupta, Situating Indian Studies on Central Asian Narratives".

21 Situating Indian Studies on Central Asian Narratives".

22 Sengupta, "Situating Indian Studies on Central Asian Narratives".

23 Sengupta, "Connectivity as Influence".

24 Sengupta, "Connectivity as Influence".

25 Nirmala Joshi (ed.), Preface to *Reconnecting India and Central Asia: Emerging Economic and Security Dimensions* (Washington, Stockholm: Central Asia-Caucasus Institute and the Silk Road Studies Program, 2010).

26 Sengupta, ""Logistical Spaces VI:

27 India-Uzbekistan, Ministry of External Affairs, https://mea.gov.in/Portal/ForeignRelation/India-Uzbekistan_15_June_22.pdf

28 India-Uzbekistan, Ministry of External Affairs, https://mea.gov.in/Portal/ForeignRelation/India-Uzbekistan_15_June_22.pdf.

29 Bhavna Dave, "Resetting India's Engagement in Central Asia: From Symbols to Substance", *RSIS Policy Report*, January 2016.

4

India-Uzbekistan Cultural Relations

Dr Rashmini Koparkar

Culture transcends borders! It is deep-rooted as well as long-lasting. It binds people in a more organic way that goes beyond political and business connections. Culture creates bridges connecting hearts and minds of the people. Therefore, cultural relations prepare a foundation for establishing diplomatic relations between any two nations. Moreover, cultural relations flourish at a greater scale if the diplomatic relations are sound.

Being an ancient civilisation, India has nurtured strong cultural, commercial, intellectual, and spiritual linkages with the surrounding regions. Throughout the history, Indian subcontinent and Central Asia have seen exchanges of men, materials, and ideas, leading to mutual enrichment of our cultures. Age-old cultural links between India and Uzbekistan have prepared a solid basis for the contemporary relationship. Even today, as in the past, cultural and people-to-people contacts form one of the strongest pillars of the bilateral relations. This cooperation has seen qualitative as well as quantitative intensification in recent years because of a diplomatic push.

As India-Uzbekistan relationship deepens, this is an opportune time to take a stock of cooperation in various areas. This article is an attempt to assess the partnership mainly in the field of cultural relations.

Conceptual Framework

In simple words, culture means the way of life of a particular population developed through generations. It includes tangible things like cuisine, clothing, jewellery, rituals, festivals, arts, music, theatre, architecture, as well as intangible things like language, religion, ideas, manners, values, and philosophy. English anthropologist Edward Burnett Tylor defines culture as the "...complex whole which includes knowledge, belief, art, morals, law, custom, and any other capabilities and habits acquired by man as a member of society."[1] Culture is a broad term encompassing various aspects of human life. On one hand, culture is deeply rooted in the past; but on the other hand, it is dynamic. Cultural patterns keep evolving slowly but constantly.[2]

Culture has been a part and parcel of international relations since time immemorial. Nevertheless, it has assumed the centrality of the field in recent years. There is no universally accepted definition of cultural relations. But it generally refers to cultural interactions between two or more nations with an aim of enhancing inter-cultural dialogue. Cultural relations play an important role in promoting peace, security, stability, and prosperity. Moreover, they take international relations beyond the realm of diplomatic, military, and economic considerations.

It is very difficult to list out the attributes of cultural relations as they are all-encompassing. However, they generally operate at two broad levels: direct and indirect. Direct level interactions take place between peoples and objects of various cultures, including dresses, cuisines, languages, art forms, music, and dances. Indirect level denotes subtle influences involving ideas, values, beliefs, and philosophies.[3] This distinction is at the broad level for the sake of understanding; however, there cannot be a watertight compartmentalization in actual interactions.

Cultural interactions are mostly driven by the people; and therefore, governments have a limited role to play in developing such relations. Despite this, in contemporary international relations, governments have taken initiatives to promote cooperation in the cultural arena. When governments initiate or sponsor such relations, it becomes cultural diplomacy.[4] Although the two concepts are often used interchangeably, there is a difference between cultural relations and cultural diplomacy. There is a hint of mutuality and reciprocity in the former; while later has an element of self-interest.[5] To put it differently, Cultural relations are wider and multi-dimensional; whereas cultural diplomacy is narrow and unidirectional. Cultural diplomacy is mostly aimed at promoting national culture in foreign countries.

Evolution of India-Uzbekistan Cultural Relations

India and Uzbekistan have always enjoyed vibrant cultural relations, which are based on the civilizational, commercial, cultural, intellectual, and spiritual links that go back for centuries. There has been a constant flow of people, goods, and ideas between these two regions leading to emergence of their unique cultures. In ancient times, '*Uttar Path*' or the Northern Route connected Indian cities like Varanasi, Pataliputra, Kannauj, Ujjaini with Central Asian cities of Samarkand and Bukhara.[6] Various references in ancient literature substantiate these links. As a matter of fact, the land where modern-day Uzbekistan is situated played the role of a bridge connecting India with rest of the world. It is well-documented that Indian travelers, merchants, traders, moneylenders, translators played an important role in the Silk Road trade. Indians were present in large numbers in Central Asian cities;[7] and were settled in separate quarters known as the '*Hindistani Mohallas*'.

The trade and commercial links of those times also facilitated transmission of cultures, ideas, and values. This was the time when Buddhism travelled from India to Central Asia and further to China and East Asia. Central Asian age of scientific enlightenment was deeply influenced by Indian mathematics, medicine, astronomy and philosophy. Three outstanding personalities of the Central Asian golden period, namely Al Khworezmi, Al-Beruni and Ibn Sina were inspired by the ancient Indian knowledge systems.[8] The political, commercial and cultural interactions intensified after the establishment of Mughal rule in India, which left lasting impact on Indian languages, literature, music, clothing, cuisine and architecture.

During the Soviet era, political relations between India and Uzbekistan mainly operated via Moscow. Nevertheless, warm friendship between India and the Soviet Union played an important role in bringing these cultures closer. In 1970s, Tashkent started to emerge as a center of *Indology* and Indian languages. Significant exchanges were facilitated between the scholars, students, writers, artists, historians, and archeologists. Indian movies were translated and shown in theatres and on television, and were widely watched. The pair of Raj Kapoor-Nargis had become very popular.[9] This was the time when love for Hindi cinema and songs became a household phenomenon creating a lot of goodwill towards India and the Indian people.

India-Uzbekistan Cultural Relations after 1991

Uzbekistan became independent in 1991 as a result of the Soviet disintegration. India was one of the first countries to recognize Uzbekistan's independence. Formal diplomatic relations were established between the two nations in 1992; and the Consulate in Tashkent was instantly upgraded to the level of an embassy. Since the very beginning of the bilateral relations, governments have acknowledged the importance of cultural cooperation. The 1994 agreement on cultural cooperation was the first step towards deepening ties. This agreement covered arenas like art, cinema, television, broadcasting, science, education, sports, youth activities, press and publications.[10] Its validity was initially for the period of five years, but was later renewed by both the sides. Interestingly, since 1992, culture has occupied significant space in all the high-level visits, meetings, and talks. Number of agreements and MoUs have been signed between the two sides covering vast expanse under the cultural umbrella.

Bilateral relations between the two nations received a quantum jump after Shri Narendra Modi became India's Prime Minister (PM) in 2014 and Mr Shavkat Mirziyoyev became Uzbekistan's president in 2016. The leadership from both sides gave a boost leading to expansion of cooperation in various fields, including culture and people-to-people relations. The Cultural Exchange Programme for the year 2021-25 was signed by the governments of India and Uzbekistan in 2021. This agreement is comprehensive; and facilitates exchanges between musical ensembles, theatre performances, classical and folk-dance troops, archaeologists, art exhibitions, publications; and encourages participation in festivals, conferences, seminars, and joint research.[11] In addition, governments have brought several new initiatives to promote cultural cooperation. Joint Working Groups (JWGs) have been established to deal with several arenas like pharmaceuticals, tourism, agriculture, textiles, information technology (IT), education, and healthcare.

Study of Indology and Indian languages has been prevalent in Uzbekistan since Soviet times. After independence, the Uzbek government has also promoted this; as a result of which several new centres of Indian studies have come up. During his visit to Tashkent in 2015, PM Narendra Modi said, "Few countries can match Uzbekistan in nurturing Hindi and Indian culture". He also held a meeting with leading Indologists and Hindi linguists during this visit.[12] Three educational institutes in Tashkent teach Hindi language from primary to the PhD level.[13] Each year, two Uzbek students are selected under the Indian Council for Cultural Relations (ICCR) fellowships for training in Hindi at the Central Institute of Hindi in Agra.[14] The popularity of Hindi language among Uzbek students has seen an upper trajectory in recent years, which underscores the everlasting Indian influence on the Uzbek youth.

Knowledge of Uzbek language has been limited in India, even though there are thousands of common words between Uzbek and Indian languages. *Jamia Millia Islamia* University has an Uzbek language centre, which conducts graduation course of Uzbek language since last many years. In 2021, centres for Uzbek language were also inaugurated in Jawaharlal Nehru University (JNU) and Delhi University, offering one year certificate course in Uzbek.

India is one of the leading partners of Uzbekistan in the fields of education and skill development. Recently, Amity University and Sharda University have opened their campuses in Tashkent and Andijan respectively. Number of Uzbek students come to India for higher education every year; some of whom receive the government of India scholarships. Uzbekistan is also a partner in Indian Technical and Economic Cooperation (ITEC) programme since 1993. As many as 2500 Uzbek students have received training in IT, English language, and mass media under ITEC fellowships. Likewise, number of Indian medical students has risen in recent years. In 2022, Uzbekistan provided 2000 seats in its medical colleges for Indian students who had to halt their medical education in the wake of the Ukraine Crisis.[15]

University of World Economy and Diplomacy in Tashkent hosts the India Chair since 1996. Recently, India classrooms have been opened in some universities in Samarkand, Bukhara, and Termez. Indo-Uzbek IT centre named after first Prime Minister Jawaharlal Nehru was opened in Tashkent in 1998. Number of universities and educational institutes from both sides have signed memorandums, and interact on regular basis. Uzbekistan's first president Islam Karimov was awarded with an honorary doctorate by Jawaharlal Nehru University.[16]

Indian culture is extremely popular in Uzbekistan through movies, television serials, dances, music, cuisine, and Yoga. Mr. Dilshod Akhatov, former ambassador of Uzbekistan to India in an interview stated, "India is well-known in Uzbekistan ... as the country with rich history and unique culture; the country with which Uzbek people are connected with centuries-old cultural, trade, and economic relations, and, above all – with bonds of sincere friendship."[17]

The Lal Bahadur Shastri Centre for Indian Culture was established in Tashkent in 1995. It has emerged as the epicentre of Indian cultural activities within Uzbekistan. It functions under the ICCR of the Ministry of Culture of India. It conducts regular classes of Hindi language, *Kathak*, *Tabla* and Yoga. The Yoga classes have been receiving very high enrolment in recent years. It also organizes weekly programmes like film screenings, dance shows, music concerts, *Mehendi* workshops, art exhibitions, public lectures, and seminars. Creative activities like quizzes on India, singing of Indian songs, recitation of Hindi poetry, and essay writing invites enthusiastic participation from the Uzbek side.[18] The Centre also organizes programmes on occasions like Indian Independence Day and Republic Day, International Yoga Day, Hindi Divas, and Mahatma Gandhi's birth anniversary. Festivals like Diwali, Holi and Navratri are celebrated with great zeal. As part of its outreach activities, the Indian Cultural Centre facilitates visits of its *Kathak* dance and Yoga Students to different provinces of Uzbekistan.[19] Indian community readily participates in centre's activities; however, its success can be measured through the enormous response it receives from Uzbek people, especially the youth.

ICCR regularly facilitates the visits by music and dance troops to Uzbekistan. The Indian cultural events are met with magnificent response in cities like Tashkent, Samarkand, Bukhara, Fergana, and Andijan. Indian musical troops have been participating in the *Sharq Taronalari* (Oriental Tunes) international music festival held in Samarkand biannually since 1997.[20] On the other hand, Uzbek singers like Kakhramon Gulomjanov have earnedfame by signing Indian songs in concerts organized under his band, *Havas Guruhi*.[21] Hindi broadcasting on the Uzbek Radio completed60 years in 2022. The *'Namaste Hindiston!'* programme went on for years on the radio, popularizing Indian culture, festivals, and songs.[22] Indian movies are regularly translated in Uzbek language and are shown in cinema halls and television. TV serials are also shown in Uzbek, which have become popular especially among women in Uzbekistan. In last couple of years, many Indian filmmakers have shot their movies at various locations in Uzbekistan.

Tourism is another sector in which cooperation between India and Uzbekistan has expanded. Although, mainly related to economic activities, tourism does promote cultural give and take. India is one of the leading countries in terms of Uzbekistan's inbound tourism. Number of Indian tourists has seen a significant rise recently. Uzbek government has extended e-Visa facility for Indian tourists. In the year 2017, around 40000 Indians visited Uzbekistan for tourism purpose.[23] The JWG on Tourism was formed in 2018between the two countries to promote tourism from both sides. Number of Uzbek tourists travelling to India is still negligible. Nevertheless, Uzbekistan is an important source of medical tourism to India, with average 8,000 Uzbeks seeking medical treatment in India annually.[24]

The popularity of Uzbek culture within India has been limited. However, because of the recent efforts by Uzbekistan's embassy in New Delhi, various facets of Uzbek culture have received recognition. In September 2018, Uzbek Embassy and ICCR jointly organized the Uzbekistan Culture Day in New Delhi, which was marked by the Uzbek dance performances, display of handicrafts and serving of Uzbek national Uzbek food. In 2019, Uzbek government appointed fashion designer Ritu Beri as the first Cultural and Tourism Ambassador of Uzbekistan in India;[25] and was invited to participate in the Kokand International handicrafts festival in the same year.[26] Ritu Beri has displayed in many fashion shows clothing ranges using Uzbek textiles, '*Adras*'.

Uzbekistan regularly participates in Surajkund International Crafts Mela as a partner country, with stalls displaying Uzbek ceramic pottery, puppets, and cloths. In 2019, the Surajkund Crafts Mela signed an agreement with Kokand International Handicrafts Festival for mutual participation and cooperation in respective events. Uzbekartisans and craftsmen have exhibited their work also in the *Vibrant Gujrat* summit. During President Mirziyoyev's visit to New Delhi in October 2018, sister city agreement was signed between Agra and Samarkand. Similarly, through an MoU, state of Gujrat and the Andijan region of Uzbekistan have taken many initiatives towards mutual exchanges and cooperation. These initiatives signal at the expansion of bilateral cultural cooperation beyond capitals.

Conclusion and Way Forward

After an in-depth analysis of India-Uzbekistan cultural relations, one can conclude that these contacts are solid, multi-layered, and diverse. They cover variety of areas like music, dance, films, television, cuisine, education, science, Yoga, tourism, and so on. Nevertheless, the common theme running behind these kind of relations is the mutual trust and respect for each other's cultures and traditions. There is considerable love and goodwill amongst Uzbek people towards India and Indians. The cultural commonalities in cuisine, arts, architecture, and languages play a positive role in bringing these cultures closer.

Cultural cooperation forms the strongest link in the contemporary bilateral relation. However, there is still a lot of scope for expansion and improvement from both sides. Firstly, Indian government and universities can organize specialized campaigns to attract Uzbek students. Symposiums and seminars can be arranged in Tashkent and other cities whereby common Uzbek students can gather information about higher education opportunities in India. In the wake of the new National Education Policy (NEP) in India, more academic collaborations, joint courses, exchange programs, and joint research projects can be promoted. Secondly, promotion of Uzbek language studies in various Indian cities can be helpful in strengthening contacts. Thirdly, youth delegations from both sides should be encouraged to create better understanding of each other's societies and cultures. Lastly, there is a need to create awareness about Uzbekistan amongst common Indians. Films festivals, road shows, exhibitions, literary fests, concerts can be organized in the tier-II and tier-III cities in India.

In 2022, India celebrated the 75th anniversary of its independence; similarly, 30 years of India-Uzbekistan diplomatic relations were also celebrated simultaneously. This is an opportune time to take a stock of existing relations and expand the relations by opening new vistas. After all, sky is the limit when it comes to cultural relations.

End Notes

1 Edward Burnett Tylor, *Primitive Culture: Researches into the Development of Mythology, Philosophy, Religion, Language, Art and Custom*, London: 1871, John Murray Publication.

2 Cultural characteristics and the roots of culture, Social Sciences LibreTexts, URL: https://socialsci.libretexts.org/Courses/Pueblo_Community_College/GT-SS3%3A_Intercultural_Communication/02%3A_Cultural_Diversity_and_Context/2.01%3A_Cultural_Characteristics_ and_the_Roots_of_Culture, Accessed 24 Oct 2023.

3 Akira Iriye, Cultural Relations and Policies, URL: https://www.americanforeignrelations.com/A-D/Cultural-Relations-and-Policies.html, Accessed 24 Oct 2023.

4 *Ibid.*

5 Alasdair Donaldson, "The Value of Cultural Relations", *British Council*, February 2018, URL: https://www.britishcouncil.org/research-policy-insight/insight-articles/value-cult-relations, Accessed 24 Oct 2023.

6 *India-Uzbekistan Relations*, Ministry of External Affairs-Government of India, Jan 2017, URL: https://mea.gov.in/Portal/ForeignRelation/Uzbekistan_Jan_2017.pdf, Accessed 27 Oct 2013.

7 Scott C. Levi, *Caravans: Punjabi Khatri Merchants on the Silk Road*, 2015, Portfolio-Penguin, pp. XIII.

8 D P Srivastava, "India-Uzbekistan Relations: New Opportunities", *Vivekananda International Foundation*, 13 Nov 2017, URL: https://www.vifindia.org/article/2017/november/13/india-uzbekistan-relations-new-opportunities, Accessed 17 Oct 2023.

9 J.N. Roy and B.B. Kumar, *India and Central Asia: Classical to Contemporary Periods*, 2007, Delhi, Astha Bharati Publications, pp. 85-87.

10 *Agreement between India and Uzbekistan on Cultural Cooperation*, Ministry of Culture, Government of India, 1994, URL: https://indiaculture.gov.in/sites/default/files/Cultural%20Agreement/CA_UZBEKISTAN_1994-15-09-21.pdf, Accessed 17 Oct 2023.

11 *Cultural Exchange Programme between the government of The Republic of India and the government of the Republic of Uzbekistan for the years 2021-2025*, URL: https://indiaculture.gov.in/sites/default/files/cultural_rel/CEP_Uzbekistan_2021-2025_20_10_2021.pdf, Accessed 25 Oct 2023.

12 *PM's Statement to Media during the Joint Press Briefing with President of Uzbekistan in Tashkent*, 6 July 2015, URL: https://www.narendramodi.in/gu/text-of-pm-s-statement-to-media-during-the-joint-press-briefing-with-president-of-uzbekistan-at-tashkent-182579, Accessed 27 Oct 2023.

13 *India-Uzbekistan Relations*, Ministry of External Affairs-Government of India, Jan 2017, URL: https://mea.gov.in/Portal/ForeignRelation/Uzbekistan_Jan_2017.pdf, Accessed 27 Oct 2023.

14 *Lal Bahadur Shastri Centre for Indian Culture*, Tashkent, Uzbekistan, Indian Council for Cultural Relations, URL: https://www.iccr.gov.in/indianculturalcenter/lal-bahadur-shastri-centre-indian-culture-tashkent-uzbekistan, Accessed 27 Oct 2023.

15 "Uzbekistan relocating 2,000 Indian medical students from war-torn Ukraine", *Business Standard*, 14 Oct 2022, URL: https://www.business-standard.com/article/current-affairs/uzbekistan-relocating-2-000-indian-medical-students-from-war-torn-ukraine-122101301247_1.html#google_vignette, Accessed 27 Oct 2023.

16 List of honorary degrees awarded by the university, Office of the Controller of Examinations, Jawaharlal Nehru University, URL: https://www.jnu.ac.in/Academics/HonoraryDegreesToDignitaries.pdf, Accessed 27 Oct 2023.

17 Dilshod Akhatov, "Uzbekistan – India: Close Friendship and Strong Partnership", *Diplomacy and Beyond Plus*, 20 Jan 2022, URL: https://diplomacybeyond.com/uzbekistan-india-close-friendship-and-strong-partnership/, Accessed 26 Oct 2023.

18 Lal Bahadur Shastri Centre for Indian Culture, Tashkent, Uzbekistan, Indian Council for Cultural Relations, URL: https://www.iccr.gov.in/indianculturalcenter/lal-bahadur-shastri-centre-indian-culture-tashkent-uzbekistan, Accessed 27 Oct 2023.

19 *Ibid.*

20 Dilmurod Ernazarov, "Some notes on the history of development of cultural relationship between Uzbekistan and India", Aug 2016, URL: Some_notes_on_the_history_of_development_ of_cultural_relationship_between_Uzbekistan_and_India_PDF, Accessed 29 Oct 2023.

21 "Listen to this Uzbekistan family band belt out popular Kollywood numbers", *Times of India*, 5 Jan 2018, URL: https://timesofindia.indiatimes.com/city/coimbatore/listen-to-this-uzbekistan-family-band-belt-out-popular-kollywood-numbers/articleshow/62372907.cms, Accessed 29 Oct 2023.

22 "Namaste Hindiston connecting Uzbekistan with India", *Economic Times*, 18 Sept 2013, URL: https://economictimes.indiatimes.com/namaste-hindiston-connecting-uzbekistan-with-india/articleshow/22698228.cms?from=mdr, Accessed 27 Oct 2023.

23 India-Uzbekistan Relations, *Embassy of India*, Tashkent, Uzbekistan, URL: https://eoi.gov.in/tashkent/?2615?000, Accessed 27 Oct 2023.

24 *Ibid.*

25 "Designer Ritu Beri becomes first Indian to be appointed as Cultural and Tourism Ambassador of Uzbekistan in India", *News18*, 18 Mar 2019, URL: https://www.news18.com/news/lifestyle/designer-ritu-beri-becomes-first-indian-to-be-appointed-as-cultural-tourism-ambassador-of-uzbekistan-in-india-2069357.html, Accessed 27 Oct 2023.

26 "Fashion designer finds inspiration in the arts and crafts of Uzbekistan", *The Sunday Guardian*, 28 Sept 2019, URL: https://sundayguardianlive.com/culture/fashion-designer-finds-inspiration-arts-crafts-uzbekistan, Accessed 29 Oct 2023.

5

Roadmapping India-Central Asia Ties

Prof P.L. Dash

Introduction

No sooner did the new political dispensation in New Delhi assume power than questions were raised about addressing India's cooperation with its immediate neighbours and deal with the security concerns. The "Neighbour First Policy" was unfolding. As a good will gesture to India's neighbours, the new Prime Minister, Narendra Modi, extended an Olive Branch by inviting leaders from the neighbouring countries associated in the regional grouping called SAARC.

Three Layered Ring

Along the Af-Pak corridor, new permutations were appearing on the contours of regional security complex, where there are three clear layers of security concerns were to be addressed. The first one ran along India's borders with Pakistan that had remained ever tense, the second one is along the Afghanistan Pakistan borders that also remained equally disturbing and the third one is the Afghanistan-Central Asian borders in the extended neighbourhood of India, where cooperation matters more than confrontation.

It is the ambience of this cooperation that would usher in a phase of fruitful regional synergy in various realms of human activities. Depending on the intensity and magnitude of cooperation, countries of the region would veer towards progress and prosperity and eschew the path of hostility now

Acronyms

APEC	:	Asia-Pacific Economic Cooperation
ASEAN	:	Association of South-East Asian Nations
BIMSTEC	:	Bay of Bengal Multi Sectoral Economic Cooperation
CACO	:	Central Asian Cooperation Organization
CAEC	:	Central Asian Economic Community
CAOP	:	Central Asia Oil Pipeline
CAREC	:	Central Asian Regional Economic Cooperation
CARs	:	Central Asian Republics
CAS	:	Central Asian States
CAU	:	Central Asian Union
CICA	:	Conference on Interaction and Confidence Building Measures in Asia
CIS	:	Commonwealth of Independent States
CPSU	:	Communist Party of the Soviet Union
CRDF	:	Collective Rapid Deployment Force
CST	:	Collective Security Treaty
CSTO	:	Collective Security Treaty Organization
EBRD	:	European Bank for Reconstruction and Development
ECO	:	Economic Cooperation Organisation
ECOSAN	:	Ecological Sanitation
EEC	:	Eurasian Economic Community
EU	:	European Union

EURASEC	:	Eurasian Economic Community
FDI	:	Foreign Direct Investment
FIEO	:	Federation of Indian Export Organisations
GDP	:	Gross Domestic Product
HuT	:	Hizb-ut-Tehrir
ICRC	:	International Committee of the Red Cross
IGC	:	Inter-Governmental Commission
IMT	:	Islamic Movement of Turkistan
IMU	:	Islamic Movement of Uzbekistan
INSTC	:	International North-South Transport Corridor
IPCC	:	Inter-Governmental Panel on Climate Change
IRP	:	Islamic Revival Party
IRPT	:	Islamic Renaissance Party of Tajikistan
IRPU	:	Islamic Renaissance Party of Uzbekistan
ISAF	:	International Security Assistance Force
ISI	:	Inter-Services Intelligence
ITEC	:	Indian Technical and Economic Cooperation
JUI	:	Jamiat-i-Ulema Islami
JWG	:	Joint Working Group
MoUs	:	Memorandums of Understanding
NA	:	Northern Alliance
NGO	:	Nongovernmental Organisation
NIDA	:	National Islamic Movement of Afghanistan
NPT	:	Non-Proliferation Treaty
ODA	:	Official Development Assistance
OIC	:	Organisation of Islamic Cooperation
OSCE	:	Organisation for Security and Cooperation in Europe
RATS	:	Regional Anti-Terrorism Structure

RFE/RL	:	Radio Free Europe/Radio Liberty
SAARC	:	South Asian Association for Regional Cooperation
SCO	:	Shanghai Cooperation Organisation
TACIS	:	Technical Assistance to Commonwealth of Independent States
TRACECA	:	Transport Corridor Europe-Caucasus-Asia
UBTIC	:	Uzbek-British Trade and Industry Council
UN	:	United Nations
UNAMA	:	United Nations Assistance Mission in Afghanistan
UNDP	:	United Nations Development Programme
UNESCO	:	United Nations Educational Scientific and Cultural Organisation
UNICEF	:	United Nations International Children's Emergency Fund
USSR	:	Union of Soviet Socialist Republics

wrecking the present. This paper highlights an overall roadmap for India's cooperation with the five Central Asian countries in India's extended neighbourhood – a neighbourhood troubled by the ferocity of terrorism. Located at the juncture connecting South Asia with Central Asia, the regional challenges, emanating from the Af-Pak security complex, need to be juxtaposed with India's synergetic ties with Central Asian countries. If the first and second layers of the security rings in the periphery of India are seemingly fruitless, it is obviously on the third ring the focus should be laid.

The Central Asian region has emerged as the most challenging region in the past three decades. Lack of real information despite many books and articles published in English and Russian drives us to be information hungry and seek grassroots information, which is unavailable. The other handicap is the language barrier. Most scholars do not know native Central Asian languages; as a result, existing research outside the Central Asian domain are based on secondary and tertiary data sources. These two problems put together impede the research process on Central Asia worldwide; India included.

Thus, while making efforts to forge out relations, many challenges facing Central Asia are considered paramount. India's relations with Central Asian countries have largely remained a riddle: on the face of it, all countries are professing and espousing close ties with India; but in reality, relations are not growing strong enough as desired. As a result, pronouncements are mismatching with practice, making us to ponder of a roadmap, looking into the future to focus on areas we consider important.

Areas of Intense Engagement

The first area of focus ought to be capacity building in Central Asian countries that encompasses many other related fields in all branches of economy and society. India is better poised technologically and economically to extend a helping hand in health, education, banking, entrepreneurship development and in many other areas. Particularly Central Asian countries that have embarked upon a massive project of state building could look to India for sharing experiences forging as much a governance model as for a developmental model. The help of India to Central Asian countries in the following areas would be central and tangible.

1. All Central Asian countries without exception have been pursuing a great desire to learn the English language. Some countries like Uzbekistan have made it recently compulsory in school curriculum right from the first standard to teach English. Indian teachers through our CBSC system could be deputed to various cities to train students in all Central Asian capitals and open the access of enrollment not only to children of our mission staff, but also native pupils on pay and study basis? The Americans have successfully experimented such a system by introducing American school system. And if we can provide less expensive education as per CBSC syllabi, that would open up a path-breaking area of business cooperation in the realm of education.
2. Medical education and healthcare system is underdeveloped in all Central Asian countries. By equipping the hospitals with technology will not help; there has to be trained cadres to operate those technologies and trained doctors to correlate the findings to treatment. Technology training facilities in the medical sector are inadequate. Technology application and governance are adequately taken care of while treatment side is lagging behind because doctors require to be adequately trained. Skill development is a component that is lacking and these countries cannot do that by themselves. No country can produce an experienced doctor overnight and all the experienced medical experts have fled the regional medical hub- the Tashkent Medical Academy (TASHMI) in post- Soviet years. In the light of this situation, Central Asian countries need help and India could help them do so. Some doctors like cardiologist, Dr. Trehan, have been shuttling between Tashkent and Delhi to help Central Asians get treated. As a result, patients are thronging him in Delhi for heart surgeries, while other disciplines are ignored. Trehan's has been an individual initiative, which can be taken up in an organized manner to set up multispecialty hospitals as joint ventures where Central Asian specialists could be trained. Based at TASHMI, we could open one such multi-specialty hospital to train medical and paramedics from interested Central Asian countries with high skill and provide capacity enhancement facilities. In ten years, we could help them build a pool of Indian trained specialists in all medical fields, who can be dispersed

across Central Asia to treat and train their own tertiary care cadres. This deserves special attention elsewhere in this paper.

3. Pharmaceutical is a corollary to the healthcare system. A great many opportunities could be availed there in this field to set up joint ventures and production facilities. Efforts should be made to create a regional pharmaceutical hub, produce various medicines and injections and distribute them across the region to needy medical centers.
4. The ITEC programme for skill enhancement is going on with all Central Asian countries for many years now. India has been providing this sort of training at its own expenses as a goodwill gesture to our Central Asian friends and innumerable participants of the ITEC programme have benefitted immensely. It has been a successful unilateral experiment with no reciprocal gestures from the other side. Could we devise a way so that we set up computer training centers in joint collaboration with each Central Asian countries, at least one Centre in each country, as a pilot project and motivate youngsters to avail of such facility? A three-month computer crash course training followed by a subsidized trip to India for a week or a fortnight to get a feel of India would be worthwhile in addition to the existing ITEC programme.
5. Banking sector is a virgin field where India could train Central Asian specialists to work at various levels in the banking and financial realms. There is so much to be done in this sector and India has so much experience in the sector to share with any developing country that an effort is worthwhile. In the stock market only, government stocks such as oil and gas, gold and metal are registered and listed; and all of them are in the state sector. So, the state controls production, the state is enlisted in the stock exchange and state is the controller of finances. As a result, there is no competition in the stock market. Since 60 million people in Central Asia buy everything and produce almost nothing worthwhile for consumption, there is a possibility of great stock of goods exchanging hands. Would it be worthwhile to invite a Central Asian apex level delegation to learn Indian financial system including banking and stock market systems? Groups of Russians were getting trained in Pune some years ago at the Institute of banking.

The same experience may be replicated, should Central Asians are interested to learn from India. No study about the banking sector operations in Central Asian countries have been done in India and that is a big black hole in our domain of knowledge about Central Asia. We can also organize a week or two long training programme in Delhi, Kolkata, Mumbai or Chandigarh for a group of Central bankers to make them aware of the Indian banking system and its institutional linkages. Digital banking is a remote possibility, when people exchange dollars in the street and take local money in gunny bags to pay fees for a course they intend to pursue. Most people do not operate bank accounts.

6. Central Asia is famous for growing cotton but textile production has been lagging behind. Seven decades of Soviet rule has not resulted in technology transfer in this field; as a result, when the Soviets left, the textile factories became dysfunctional. Alone in and around Tashkent – capital of the largest cotton producer in Central Asia – six textile factories are in such dilapidated condition; none of them fully functional even after three decades of Soviet exit. As a result indigenous textile production is negligible, uncompetitive, highly cost consuming, consequently,native apparel industry suffers from anemia. Finished products are imported from Turkey and China and the local markets are flooded with cotton and synthetic products from both these countries – both cloths and readymade apparel. Cooperation in this sector could be of paramount importance to exchange production and business experience so that Central Asia could benefit from India's experience. Textile technology transfer could also be considered as a modicum of cooperation.
7. Cooperation in the energy sector is of crucial importance for India. Given India's growing need for energy, availability of all forms of energy – gas, oil, hydropower and uranium – in the neighbourhood of Central Asia is an opportunity to be tapped. The efforts of the past two decades have not yielded desirable results while China and Western countries have laid pipelines to connect their territories to get gas and oil piped out from the region. Caspian energy reserves, Kazakhstan's uranium and gas, Uzbekistan's oil and gas, Turkmenistan's gas and Tajikistan's

hydropower potential have to be tapped in India's interest; if need be in collaboration with China and Iran. Although interests of the concerned countries – both buyers and suppliers are clashing with prevalent geopolitical realities of the region, persistent efforts may yield fruits in future. TAPI and IPI are yet to materialize ever after decades of efforts. Therefore, various combinations and formulations have to be explored through consistent endeavour.

This is an energy realm where intense competition is on with involvement of big players such as Russia, The EU and the US and China. India's place is currently marginal. The Western world has succeeded in laying pipeline BTC and BTE and going ahead with Nabucco, while China has succeeded in ensuring investment in Kazakhstan's energy sector to safeguard its own energy interests in the region. Russia as a supplier of energy has ensured its own interest by taking the responsibility of providing an outlet to supplying Central Asian energy to the outer world. India has so far been largely sidestepped from the picture, whereas there is an urgency to ensure its presence, given the enormous opportunities in the field.

8. The New Silk Road concept is conceptualization of the link between the past and the present, tracing the ancient shenanigans along the route covering Central and South Asia. This concept also advocates a crisscross of connectivity between three Asia- South, Central and West. The concept also brings to its embrace the north south transport corridor, the Eurasian continental bridge as well as the northern transport corridor. Taken together they provide good road and surface infrastructure to communicate with one another for facilitation of trade and commerce. It is presumed that cooperation along the new Silk Road would bring about a drastic paradigm change in the mindset in favour of cooperative peace in the region by bringing people and product to transact through a corridor bound by common interest. India ought to play a proactive role in this project and get her fair share of pie in the ongoing geopolitical jockeying. The September 2023 G-20 Delhi initiative of India Middle East Europe Corridor (IMEEC) to devise a route map alternative to China's OBOR may be fruitful way of cooperation in the years to come in the field of

geopolitics and geoeconomics.

9. Security is a tangible realm for mutual cooperation both on bilateral and multilateral plains. Central Asia is in South Asia's immediate neighbourhood and numerous agreements have been signed between India and all Central Asian countries to curb various nefarious activities stemming from growing Islamism, narcotic trafficking and arms smuggling from the Af-Pak corridor. Initiatives are so far fair enough but what lacks is a regional security architecture in which all stakeholders would have a decisive say in resolving problems facing the region. India is one of the major stakeholders and her voice must match the efforts she undertakes in this regard. The huge investment in infrastructure building in Afghanistan, the initial line of credit to Central Asian countries and a benign approach to all countries of the region are babysteps in this direction to be augmented by vigorous efforts to involve all concerned in the security interface including regional and non-regional powers.
10. India has been training some military cadres from Central Asian countries at its military training facilities, including at Khadakvasla. The basket has to be widened and more slots be allotted to countries which are significant to India from the security viewpoint. Possibility has to be explored whether Central Asian countries who are interested to pay and study instead of getting things for free. Military to military exchanges would be more rewarding than stationing a military attaché in our mission, who does not know the local language and cannot even read local military journals and cannot communicate with the locals. Security cooperation needs a recast and a more proactive agenda must be worked out after considerable discussion.
11. Training in computers and Information Technology is a concrete area where India could extend tangible help to Central Asian countries. India has been spending a lot of money to donate computers to institutes dealing with IT sector in Uzbekistan and other countries. The donation of computers to the TUIT worth $350,000 is a worthwhile effort. Side by side, manpower training programs are to be initiated. These donated computers in the hands of untrained personnel would otherwise go waste. Have we studied their manpower

capability before donating computers to Tashkent University of Information Technology? Or just donated them because they are an IT institution? Since capacity building refers first of all to manpower training, a deep thought has to be put on the manpower aspect before venturing into gifting something to a country, particularly a Central Asian country. As a pioneer in the field of information technology, India has the exclusive preserve of helping Central Asia compared to other countries of the region, including China

Proposal for a Healthcare Pilot Project

Among the areas of bilateral cooperation, the realm of healthcare comes to the fore for significant collaboration. Given that all Central Asian states have had a typical Russian healthcare system entirely funded by the state. After two decades of public-private partnership system what is extant in many places across the region is a decadent Soviet system where the state endeavours to pump in money but fails to revive or restructure the entire system into a modern functional healthcare system. Herein the role of India comes to help modernize the healthcare system in Central Asia. How to go about is the question. One could attempt at the following two models as pilot project in healthcare.

Ad hoc Model

There are two ways of going ahead: 1) follow an Ad hoc model or 2) follow a tangible model of cooperation. What India has done at the government level or Indian doctors have done at their personal level are all ad hoc measures that help erect a cooperative model- agreed and operated bilaterally. That has partially addressed medical need of the population at various levels. This has largely been possible through personal contacts and created the semblance of a public-private partnership for which the state support has remained crucial. However, such arrangement has no permanent mechanism to train native Central Asian medical cadres so they take over from Indian doctors after a few years. In some cases, for example the state allots a dysfunctional or malfunctioning hospital mostly in a city and rarely in primary healthcare centre in a village to revive the hospital through foreign collaboration and modernize it to provide good primary, secondary and tertiary healthcare to the population.

The ad hoc arrangements could be a modus operandi to set up primary healthcare centers across the region with diagnostic facilities made available to the patients at their place of residence from where complicated cases could be referred to specialized centers. Local doctors alongside Indian doctors will work together at each of these centres supplementing and complementing his/her knowledge for the benefit of the people.

The US Department of State has tried such method, set up hospitals, identified English speaking local doctors to work while the overall supervision, fee structure and treatment methods are run by foreign doctors from the US and other European countries. As result under one roof we find a Kyrgyz or Uzbek doctor treating patients under overall guidance of a foreign specialist, a physiotherapist from Spain undertaking post-stroke rehabilitation process and a minor surgery getting performed. However, these are not big-ticket programs, they do not make a sizeable pool of native specialists and consequently cater to the diagnostic needs of patients. The clients of such medical centers are elite patients from foreign missions and foreign business houses, operating only in the capital or in big cities. Major surgeries and complicated cases are referred to and performed in big hospitals, largely run by native doctors in state- and privately-run hospitals and medical centers. The ad hoc method excludes teaching and training cadres, providing tertiary care to patients. They largely perform as daycare centers, while the need is for a permanent solution through setting up of a chain of modern hospitals – equipped with technology and cadres.

Tangible Model

A permanent solution lies in training native Central Asian medical and paramedical cadres by Indian medical experts to prepare them to take over in a few years to teach and train their native specialists in various medical disciplines. Bilateral cooperation is essential in this regard since none of the Central Asian countries could make a mark by themselves. Areas such as Laporoscopic and minimal invasive surgeries, areas of high-end ophthalmic surgeries, cardiovascular surgeries and advanced diagnosis need particular attention. Establishment of AIIMS type super specialty, multi-specialty hospital may be the answer. The AIIMS model could be replicated in all Central Asian capitals, provided the host country acquiesce to India's proposal. What is currently lacking in the region is super specialization and a hospital of a new type could fill this gap.

The efforts could internationalize the medical education system by elevating it from isolation and over dependence on Russia. As the Russian trained doctors are on their way out due to aging, the new generation, trained once again in the Russian method, but trying to break away from it, would replace the existing system by introducing a new system that would be the amalgam of Russian and Anglo Saxon system of medical education. India is therefore best suited to provide affordable medical education and through it a healthcare system the Central Asians would love to embrace.

While the AIIMS model could be set up in the capital, a miniature model could be replicated in Velayat headquarters akin to our government medical colleges and hospitals in district headquarters across India. Currently, the Central Asians do not visualize any viable model of Medical system for them. Their policy makers are averse to change or to emulate anything foreign other than Russian. They should be persuaded to understand effective western model or Indian model before venturing into cooperation with foreign countries.

Since medical set up involves huge investment, cost sharing and profit-sharing arrangements must be agreed upon to avoid future hassles. Ideally based on percentage pattern of 50-50 or 60-40, the entire gamut of cooperation ought to be finalized bilaterally before any further advancement is made. Aside from medical education, two other aspects are important: treatment and hospital administration. Central Asian countries do not have courses on hospital administration and doctors are manning the administrative jobs even on those positions, which do not require specialized medical education. This is an area where India could train Central Asian personnel in hospital administration either in India or in their respective countries by deputing Indian teachers. The beneficiaries have to bear the expenses for such courses and training.

On the cadre-training front, apart from making arrangements to train new batches of doctors, there is requirement for periodic refreshers courses to upgrade the doctors' knowledge about technology application and new treatment methods. In a nutshell, institutional training mechanism is absent and it has to be put in place to undertake urgently such activities at periodic intervals. Discipline-wise courses are to be introduced to take care of such refreshers courses. Most hospitals do run such courses, but they are putting old wine in new bottles – the same people, the same story, the same Russian method and the same old technique. Take for example the refreshers courses in English language. The classes are conducted, enrolled students pass out exams with excellent marks and the result is: none of the pass-outs can write a few correct sentences, let alone speak fluently. There is a malaise in mindset across the board that ought to be removed. We have to devise a way to upgrade human resources in a country that conducts retraining programs for doctors where they are hardly trained

Therefore, setting up of a multispecialty hospital would push things ahead significantly. Under one roof it could provide all facilities – training, retraining, refreshing and upgrading knowledge in all medical disciplines plus good medical facilities for treatment of patients.

A significant realm of bilateral cooperation could be in pharmaceuticals. The Central Asian countries do not have their own pharmacopeia so far, and a very feeble pharmaceutical industry. Production of essential drugs, antibiotics and other medicines is a prerequisite for developed healthcare. Joint collaboration could help the Central Asians to involve pharmaceutical multinationals, which are active in India and open their door to map and tap and access Central Asian drug market. This is a significant area of cooperation to be explored. Some companies have ventured in the past like Ajanta Pharma, but were forced out of business when local taxation laws slapped cases against them. Companies must learn how to turn challenges to opportunities.

Conclusion

Clearly, there is a great potential to foster India's friendship with Central Asian countries as great opportunities for Central Asian countries to better their ties with India. It is also clear that there is a mismatch between practice and potential. It is also clear that many of these fields where we visualize relations to surge ahead are based on mutual benefit and realms of reciprocity. It is also clear that development, prosperity and cooperative peace in the region are interlinked with sustainable security for which regional cooperation is a tangible instrument. It makes sense to conclude that all countries of the region must create the ambience conducive for their foray into a prosperous future. Where is then the hitch to peace and cooperation, harmony and prosperity?

It always needs two hands to clap. But the two hands never join or join with caution. And India's efforts in the last three decades have been largely unilateral in this regard. It has been taking initiative such as the Connect Central Asia, when some countries are not allowing even to hold a conference on their territory, although they do not have to spend money on that account.

In the industrial sector from small and medium business to the energy sector the opportunities are as wide as the competition from other interested parties. Nobody is today talking about the Turkish model in Central Asia, but the penetration of Germany and China to the construction sector, Turkey and China to the textile and energy sectors are widely visible. While Russia has withdrawn, China has crept in. And India cannot easily perform in the internal markets across Central Asia without competition with China. Russia however remains a potential competitor, fairly a large absorber of Central Asia's raw material. Its endeavour to embrace Central Asia through various regional trade blocks such as Customs Union and Eurasian Union are designed to insulate the region from outside competition and keep it forever as a Russian backyard. We must posit ourselves in the midst of this intense competitiveness and find our way to Central Asia wherever we could make a dent.

Indian Prime Minister Narendra Modi's maiden official visit to five Central Asian countries and Ufa in the Russian Federation in the first week of July, 2015 has had significant bearing on bilateral and multilateral relations among and between these countries. The earlier presumptions that Modi is unclear about Central Asia is set aside by the very range and magnitude of coverage his visit received from different quarters in all these countries. This has been beautifully depicted by the Prime Minister's Office at *centralasiaebook.narendramodi.in* – a pictorial website that has detailed Modi's sojourn. The biggest achievement of the visit is that what was unclear earlier has become clear and transparent now to safely mould a Modi doctrine for Eurasia. Foundations have been laid and his personal chemistry would extend beyond unimaginable horizon in the years to come. The fact that he took National Security Advisor and Foreign Secretary in his entourage is noteworthy. He received field inputs from Indian Ambassadors in all these countries to evolve a clear Eurasia strategy for India. Thus, dozens of Foreign Service officers spent sleepless nights to formulate a clear Modi vision, which was earlier lacking.

References

1. First Track Diplomacy: A Public Diplomacy Initiative of the Ministry of External Affairs, New Delhi. 2014.
2. Challenges of South Asia, *World Affairs*, Vol. XVI, No. 3, Autumn (July-September, 2012. (The whole Issue)
3. India and her Troubled Neighbourhood, *World Affairs*, Vol. XVII, No. 1, Spring (January-March, 2013, Whole Issue.
4. Rashpal Malhotra, P.L. Dash, Sucha Singh Gill, Murat M. Bakhadirov (Editors), South and Central Asia: Quest for Peace and Cooperation, A joint Publication of CRRID, Chandigarh and UWED, Tashkent, 2013.
5. Ramakant Dwivedi, Indo-Kyrgyz Relations: Challenges and opportunities, (Ed.) Pentagon Press LLP, New Delhi, 2023.
6. Shekhar Adhikari and Sanjeeb Bhadauria (Editors),India's National Security in the 21st Century, Pentagon Press, New Delhi, 2014.
7. Ashok Malik, Geopolitical Geoeconomics, *The Economic Times*, Mumbai, 18 September, 2023.

6

The Importance of Being Al-Beruni Then and Now

Prof Rashmi Doraiswamy

Introduction

Al-Beruni was born in Khwarazm (present-day Khiva in Uzbekistan) in Kath in 973 CE. He died in Ghazni in Afghanistan after 1050.[1] He was a polymath, who specialized in astronomy, mathematics, geography, history, philology and pharmacology, among other disciplines. He is credited with having written 146 books of which only twenty three have survived. These include *Chronology, Tahdid, Densities, Shadows, Canon, Gems,* and his book on India.

He was a linguist who knew his mother tongue Khwarazmian, as also Arabic, Persian, Turkic Sanskrit and Greek. He was a student of the Khwarazminian astronomer and mathematician, Abu Nasr Mansur.

Al-Beruni, as a consequence of historical events, travelled to many cities and shifted base several times in his life, returning to his homeland whenever he could. He had to flee Kath in 995 when Prince Abu Nasr who was the ruler was killed by the Emir of Jurjaniyya. Edward Kennedy points out that "Beruni's pursuit of truth was not confined to the written or spoken word. He had a strong penchant for firsthand investigation of natural phenomena, exercised at times under very trying circumstances. Along with this went an ingenuity in the devising of instruments and a flair for precision in observations."[2]

Surrounding Khwarazm, was the empire of the Samanids with its capital in Bukhara (ruled by King Mansur II from 997). To the west of this was the Buwayhid empire that stretched from the Caspian Sea to the Persian Gulf. Between the Samanid and the Buwayhid Empires was the Ziyarid state in Gurgan. All these empires were taken over by Sultan Mahmud of Ghazna from what is today Afghanistan. Son of a Turkish slave, he built an empire that stretched from Iran to the Gangetic plain. Al-Beruni had a difficult relationship with the Sultan. According to Julio Samso, "Al-Biruni's relationship with Mahmud was always cold and none of his writings were dedicated to the Sultan. He does mention Sultan Masud, Mahmud's son and successor, to whom he dedicated his most important astronomical work, *al-Qanun al-Masudi* (the Masudic Canon). Al-Biruni reports that he was able to determine the latitude of Ghazna from observations made between 1018 and 1020 using a graduated astronomical ring, which al-Biruni called the Yamini ring in honour of Mahmud."[3]

As a result of his travels, he engaged with other polymaths of the time such as Al Khujandi, the astronomer in the Buwayhid Empire and corresponded with Ibn Sina, who was then still in his teens on the nature of heat and light. He also found support and patronage: his *Chronology*, for instance, was dedicated to the King Qabus of the Ziyarid Empire. He was also feted by the Khwarazmshahs whenever he came back to his native land. Under the patronage of Sultan Mamun he set up the *Shahyiye* ring in Jurjaniyya.

By 1010 CE Sultan Mahmud of Ghazna had taken over Multan and Bhatinda in the Indian subcontinent, by 1022, the Ganges Valley, finishing in 1026 when he carried off huge bounties from India. Sultan Mahmud died in 1030. His conquests and extension of his empire provided Al-Beruni the opportunity to travel to India.

Al-Beruni was well acquainted with Indian thought on astronomy and mathematics before he came to India. He was the first Muslim scholar to undertake the study of the *Puranas*. Edward Sachau notes that "His description of Hindu philosophy was probably unparalleled. His system of chronology and astronomy was more complete and accurate than ever before given. His communications from the *Puranas* were probably entirely new to his readers, as also the important chapters on literature, manners, festivals, actual geography and the much quoted chapter on historic chronology."[4] Sachau also points out that the body of his chapters usually consists of three parts: an introduction; the beliefs of the Hindus usually with references from books in Sanskrit; and a comparison with Greek or other systems of thought. "In general it is the method of our author, not to speak himself, but to let the Hindus speak, giving extensive quotations from their classical authors. He presents a picture of Hindu civilization as painted by the Hindus themselves."[5]

Al-Beruni's book on India, *Tahqiq ma li-l-hind min maqulahmaqbulah fi al-aqlawmardhulah* (*Verifying all that Indians Recount, the Reasonable and the Unreasonable*), completed in 1030, is unique in the annals of writings by a scholar on a land that is not his own. He is known as the Father of Indology because this is the first book that provides detailed information on Indian society with a historical perspective. He has dealt with festivals, borders, gods, idol worship, ancient texts, the caste system, Indian system of numbers, astronomy, the notion of time according to ancient Indian texts, marriages, places, their distance and location, eating habits, the status of women and concepts of justice. The sources available on ancient India are mostly religious or literary texts, along with a few political ones such as Kautilya's *Arthashashtra* or Kalhana's *Rajatarangini*. There are few others by writers who were from other lands such as Megasthenes or Huen Tsang. This book, however, is one written after studying the texts and sources in Sanskrit and in translation and observing Indian society first hand. Al-Beruni uses the comparative method to place the documentation in a larger theoretical context, without allowing his own beliefs and views to colour the text. As Al-Beruni himself says in the Preface to his own book, "This book is not a *polemical* one. I shall not produce the arguments of our antagonists in order to refute such of them as I believe to be in the wrong. My book is nothing but a simple historic record of facts. I shall place before the reader the theories of the Hindus exactly as they are, and I shall mention in connection with them similar theories of the Greeks in order to show the relationship existing between them."[6]

The Golden Age of Islam

As is evident from this brief outline of Al-Beruni's life and works, there was a great deal of mobility and travels in his life that gave him access to several worlds and perspectives. The empires and their shifting contours due to the wars and conflicts of succession, caused the scientist to flee as well as opened new vistas for thought and writing. This immediate context of dynasties and kingdoms was embedded in a larger context of what has been termed as the Islamic Golden Age or the Asian Renaissance that lasted from the 8th to the 12th centuries, till the Mongolian conquest. This was an age of the extraordinary leaps in science and philosophy, brought about by successive generations of scholars from the Islamic world that stretched from Central and West Asia to North Africa, Spain and parts of Southern Europe. Many of these great scientists and philosophers – like Al-Beruni – were polymaths and specialists of a whole range of disciplines.

The Arab conquest of Persia and Central Asia, in particular, opened the doors to civilisational influences from China, South Asia, Central Asia, Persia and the Mediterranean region. This was not new in the Eurasian region, because the network of trade routes that ran from China to the Mediterranean, retrospectively named the Silk Road by Ferdinand von Richtofen in the late XIX century, had facilitated civilizational encounters for 17 centuries from the 2nd century BCE to the 15th century CE. These routes had served for the exchange not only of goods, but of ideas, technologies, religions, languages, empires across the vast and geographically varied expanses of the continent. As Julio Samso points out, "The Islamic world came into contact with the great civilisations of antiquity during the eighth and ninth centuries. The scientific knowledge of not only Greece but also India and Persia, was then assimilated by its scholars in a two-stage process. First, all the sources were translated into Arabic, and then during the ninth and tenth centuries, their contents were held up to critical analysis."[7]

Due to the spread of Islam and the territorial expansion of the Abbasid Caliphate new social classes came into being. The new empire based on a comparatively new religion wanted theology and philosophy to develop so as to overtake Byzantine. New cities developed and older ones that had been active nodes on the Silk Road also witnessed tremendous intellectual activity. Samarkand, Bukhara, Tashkent, Nishapur Maragha, Damascus, Isfahan, Cairo, Cordoba, Seville and Toledo all became centres of political, economic, spiritual and intellectual exchanges. The second Abbasid Caliph, al-Mansur shifted the capital to Baghdad from Damascus in 762 and this became one of the greatest cities in the world in a few decades. According to Bernard Lewis, the civilization that flourished in these centuries is called 'Arabic' due to the language and faith followed, but was a hybrid creation of many people that included the Egyptians, Persians and many others. It also had people from other religions, such as Christianity, Zoratrianism, Judaism etc.[8]

One of the spectacular achievements of this period is the enterprise of translation that develops with great rapidity. The technique of making paper travelled from China to these parts around 751 CE. The boom in translation starts in 775, speeds up under Haroun al-Rashid and peaks under al-Mamun. Private and public libraries were established in cities thanks to the co-incidence of all these historical, cultural and technological factors. Al-Mamun set up the famous library 'The House of Wisdom'. Astrolabes and observatories were set up in these cities and the march of science could not be stopped. Manuscripts were scouted for and came from Greece, Persia, India, many in a fragile deteriorating condition. The translators were from many faiths and languages. They included Greeks from the Byzantine empire and Christian scholars as well. The latter wrote Syriac, the language the Bible was originally written in. The texts and manuscripts, scouted from the farthest corners of the Abbasid empire were often first translated into Syriac and then Arabic.

This was an age that lasted four centuries, when a great confluence of ideas and civilisations took place, leading to innovations in diverse disciplines through the works of polymaths such as Al Kindi, Al Farabi, Ibn Sina, Averroes, Omar Khayyam, etc. Al-Beruni belongs to this great age of churning and discovery. "The Islamic world came into contact with the great civilisations of antiquity during the eighth and ninth centuries. The scientific knowledge of not only Greece but also India and Persia, was then assimilated by its scholars in a two-stage process. First, all the sources were translated into Arabic, and then during the ninth and tenth centuries, their contents were held up to critical analysis."[9]

Astronomy and mathematics in particular, saw immense development during this period. Many reasons have been given for the extraordinary development of science during these centuries. The study of stars in the sky arose out of practical needs. Navigational aids were required by trading caravans that had to cross deserts and by travellers seeking to cross vast empires. The need was religious, too, since the Muslim call for prayer five times a day had to be done punctually in an era when there were no watches and shadows and the position of the sun along with the direction of the *qibla* was important for the prayers. Muslims also follow the lunar calendar. Al-Mamun was interested in the traditions of astronomy from India and Greece and *Sindhind* and Ptolemy's *Almagest* were translated during his reign. Al-Beruni's own translations, including *Samkhya* and *Patanjali* from India, must be viewed in the context of a milieu where even scientists undertook translation, because it was seen as a valuable tool to learn, further one's knowledge and offer critiques.

When the Abbasid Caliphate began to lose power in the second half of the tenth century regional rulers emerged as representatives of the Caliph who was now a religious rather than a political authority. The regional rulers continued the practice of patronizing scientists and scholars. Science and innovation continued to flourish despite the changes in empires and political structures. It is therefore possible to state that the entire Central and West Asian region had, on the one hand, a homogenizing milieu of religion and scientific pursuits, but on the other, was multicentric and decentred in the diverse intellectual outcomes of polymaths all across the region.

Though the scientific movement of the Golden Age was centred in Baghdad under the reign of the Abbasids, the Fatimids in Cairo in the 11th century were equal them in their patronage of learning and the sciences. In 11th and 12th century Spain, too, under the Umayyad the sciences flourished and a magnificent court was established in Cordoba. Later, the sciences found immense development in Samarkand and Maragha. Thus, the entire region from Central Asia to northern Africa to western Europe was interconnected, with each of the courts serving as a node in a network, through which scientific and other knowledge kept getting exchanged and developed.

Al-Beruni can be seen as an important figure who worked through the late tenth century and the first half of the eleventh century, connecting Central and South Asia. Since there is no definitive source chronicling Al-Beruni's own life, his movements across Central and South Asia are deduced from the discoveries of latitude and longitude of places that he fixed, through his own observation and scientific knowledge. Edward Kennedy, for instance, states that "Regardless of where he had been, Biruni was back in Kath by 997, for on 24 May of that year he observed the lunar eclipse there…, having previously arranged with Abul-Wafa that the latter should simultaneously observe the same event from Baghdad…. The time difference so obtained enabled them to calculate the difference in longitude between the two stations."[10] He contributed significantly and in many cases, came up with surprisingly accurate figures to some of the problems that polymaths of the age were trying to solve. Hillel Ofek points out that "One of al-Biruni's most accurate accomplishments was the near-accurate measurement of the Earth's circumference using his own trigonometric method; he missed the correct measurement of 24,900 miles by only 200 miles."[11]

Area Studies and Travel Literature

Al-Beruni was not only a colossus of the times he lived in, but his work has significance for many new fields of study that have come up in contemporary times. His book on India, *Kitab al-Hind*, for instance, reaches out across the millennium to provide insights into the pre-history of Area Studies. This is a field of knowledge that dates from the period of the Second World War which was established through the joint effort of government agencies, funding foundations and academic institutions, first in the US and later in many countries of the world. Its aim was to create a body of interdisciplinary knowledge covering the politics, history, economics and culture of areas being studied. The objectives for the existence of Areas Studies in various countries differed from the set of aims that the US had when it pioneered this field.

If a pre-history of Area Studies could be charted it would include cartographic projects since ancient times when the first maps of how the world was imagined to be were drawn and later how the world was discovered to be were charted. Travellers accounts, too, of unknown lands as well as Orientalist Studies would also be part of this pre-history.

Al-Beruni's *Kitab al Hind* is one of the forerunners of this field of knowledge, since it can also be considered as 'travel literature'. Armed with knowledge of the ancient language of the region, the ability to read texts in the original, the felicity of having translated texts, wide ranging knowledge that we would term 'interdisciplinary', along with a methodology that made objectivity and respectful distance as its main principles – all these are the methods enshrined in the contemporary study of specific areas and regions. His preface to his own work begins with an outlining of the pros and cons of hearsay and being an eyewitness. His association with Sultan Mahmmud of Ghazna facilitated his 'field-trip' to India, although he was never swayed by the Sultan's own view of and attitude towards the subcontinent and its people.

Historians Alam and Subrahmanyam state that "A thousand years ago, a great Muslim intellectual and polymath, native of the Central Asian region of Khwarizm, embarked on a study of distant and exotic matters, namely matters Indian. A contemporary and sometime correspondent of Avicenna, ... this intellectual was no armchair scholar but came to derive his knowledge of India from first-hand experience and travel, related in large measure to his association with Sultan Mahmud of Ghazna ...who raided Northern India on several occasions."[12]

Alam and Subrahmanyam point out that for the West Marco Polo and his travels remain the template for travel accounts. The closest a non-European comes to Marco Polo is the Moroccan traveller Ibn Batuta. While it is true that travellers and travel accounts are part of the larger Orientalist thinking, Al-Beruni does not fit any of these paradigms. He travelled to India with a fairly deep prior knowledge of the subcontinent and wrote his account of Indian society after close observation and deep understanding. This is a travel that is fuelled by an entire milieu in which the subcontinent is recognized as a neighbouring civilization, with specific inputs to offer in the larger quests for knowledge. Travellers travelling within Asia, whether Fa Hein, Huen Tsang, Al-Beruni or others, do not seem to be fueled by the lure of visiting exotic lands with extraordinary riches, but of gaining knowledge of Buddhism (as in the case of the Chinese travellers), or knowledge of other societies and their sciences (astronomy, mathematics, philosophy, and so on) as in the case of Al-Beruni. There is in the case of Al-Beruni a unique understanding of 'difference' and 'otherness' and the methodological frameworks needed to overcome it, all the while tempered with tolerance towards this 'otherness'.

Some writers like Hillel Ofek have pointed out that since Al-Beruni, unlike Ibn Sina, Al Farabi or Averroes, was not translated into Latin, he was not widely known outside the Arabic world. Alam and Subrahmanyam, underlining the Orientalist bias of the West wryly note that, "We are often reminded that his work on India (unlike his works on mathematics and astronomy) was little read for nearly two centuries after it was written, until it was discovered by the Persian historian Rashid-ud-Din (d. 1318).... The fate of the *Kitab al Hind* thus seems to lead paradoxically to the ineluctable conclusion of an Oriental lack of enterprise and curiosity, confirming the cliches that so many leading scholars of Islam have long sustained. One al-Biruni can hardly be thought to be representative of anything besides his own extraordinary genius."[13] Alam and Subrahmaniam are critical of this 'Orientalist' view. To this critique we may add that Al-Beruni was one scientist and philosopher amidst a whole galaxy of thinkers who adorned the firmament of Central and West Asia for several centuries. He was a great polymath who made inventions and discoveries across a range of disciplines that stood the test of time. His life and works offer us insights into the intellectual milieu of an important period of history in Central and South Asia. More importantly, his works speak to us across the centuries, shedding light on many new areas and methods of study that have emerged in the contemporary world.

End Notes

1 See Edward Kennedy's entry on Al Biruni for debates on the date of death in *The Dictionary of Scientific Biography*, Charles Coulston Gillispie (ed.), Vol II, Charles Scribner's Sons, NY, p. 148.

2 Ibid, p. 155.

3 'The First Golden Age of Islamic Science', Julio Samso, https://inference-review.com/article/the-first-golden-age-of-islamic-science#:~:text=Arabic%20science%20was%20 now%20 beginning,half%20of%20the%20tenth%20century.

4 Preface, *Alberuni's India*, Edward C Sachau, Rupa and Co, New Delhi, 2002, p. xl.

5 Ibid, p. xxvii.

6 Author's Preface, *Alberuni's India*, Rupa & Co, New Delhi, 2002, p. lix.

7 Julio Samso, op. cit.

8 For more on this, *The Arabs in History*, Bernard Lewis, OUP, Oxford, 2002.

9 Julio Samso, op. cit.

10 *The Dictionary of Scientific Biography*, Charles Coulston Gillispie (ed.), Vol II, Charles Scribner's Sons, NY, p. 149.

11 'Why the Arabic World Turned Away from Science', Hillel Ofek, https://www.thenewatlantis.com/publications/why-the-arabic-world-turned-away-from-science

12 *Indo-Persian Travels in the Age of Discoveries, 1400-1800*, Muzaffar Alam, Sanjay Subrahmayam, Cambridge University Press, London, 2007, p. 1.

13 Ibid, p. 2.

7

Regional Cooperation in Central Asia: Past, Present and Future

Prof Sanjay Kumar Pandey and Rahul Gupta

ABSTRACT

A new wave of regionalism is sweeping Central Asia. Considered a failure by some scholars earlier, the new-found enthusiasm for regional cooperation in the region is underpinned by several important changes within Central Asian republics and in their external environment. As a result, the leaders of five Central Asian countries are meeting more often, speaking in one voice on multilateral platforms and articulating their common interests on the global fora. There is a realisation that they no longer can be divided and played against each other. This paper evaluates some recent trends in regional cooperation in Central Asia, especially since 2016 when the push came, first from Uzbekistan and subsequently from Kazakhstan and others, for upgrading the level of cooperation in the region. However, significant challenges remain in the form of inter-state issues, such as unresolved borders, disagreements over the sharing of water resources among the region's states, and governance challenges, among others.

Keywords: *Regional Cooperation, Central Asia, Afghanistan, Eurasian Economic Union, Shanghai Cooperation Organisation, Silk Road, Organisation of Turkic States, Consultative Meeting of Heads of State.*

Introduction: Central Asia's Significance as a 'Region' in Contemporary Times

Modern Central Asia sits at the juncture of Europe and Asia, connecting the East with the West and the North with the South, and forms the core of the

Eurasian landmass. The region has historically acted as the meeting ground of major world civilizations, absorbing their cultural influences, political systems, and technological inputs, yet retaining its unique features. In the past it was known by such names as *Ma Wara an-Nahr* by the Arabs, *Turan* by the Iranians, *Transoxiana* by Westerners, *Turkestan* by Imperial Russians and *SrednayaAziya* by the Soviets. The Great Silk Road that passed through the region made it an important hub of trade and commerce throughout the late ancient and early medieval period.[1] During different periods of history, Central Asia witnessed relative decline and rise in importance. Several factors make modern Central Asia a crucial region in the world: rich availability of natural resources – most prominently hydrocarbons and minerals; geopolitical location among such regional behemoths like China and Russia; proximity to Afghanistan-Pakistan, with concerns relating to international terrorism, drug trade and human trafficking; along with the interests of powers like the US, EU, India, Turkey and Iran.[2]

The standard definition of Central Asia includes the five post-Soviet states of Uzbekistan, Kazakhstan, Tajikistan, Kyrgyzstan, and Turkmenistan, but the normative limits of the region stretch beyond the conventional boundaries and include parts of Iran, Afghanistan, Caucasus, China, Mongolia, and even India.[3] For the purpose of this article, Central Asia comprises the five post-Soviet states, though Afghanistan, which shares historical and ethnic commonalities with neighbouring republics, except for the shared Soviet past, can be included within the region's definition. Moreover, if one looks at the recent past, geopolitical developments in Afghanistan, for instance, the rise, decline and resurgence of the Taliban, directly impact stability and regional security in Central Asia.

Another debate is whether Central Asia, commonly understood as the five 'stan' countries, forms a coherent region. Most analysts who study the region agree that due to geographical contiguity, landlockedness, as well as shared history and culture, Central Asia is one region. Moreover, a century and a half of Russian and Soviet rule created strong economic interdependencies throughout the region, most notably in the areas of energy, water usage arrangements, and transport infrastructure.[4] An early instance of the region's unity and cooperation potential was the decision in 1993 by leaders of the five newly independent Central Asian states to give the name *Tsentralnaiia*

Aziiya to describe themselves, including Kazakhstan.[5] It was justified because in a way regions are also 'political communities' as their boundaries are not fixed and are the outcome of a complex interaction between the structures of the international system, the political as well as the ideological struggles among states and social actors, and their conscious strategies in response to global changes.[6]

Need for Regional Cooperation in Central Asia

Since Central Asia serves as a strategically important land bridge between Europe and Asia, there is broad agreement that economic integration and political stability in the region are critical not only for the well-being of seventy-five million inhabitants of the region but also for Central Asia's neighbours. A critical prerequisite for long-term economic growth and stability is successful economic integration backed by effective regional cooperation.[7] A UNDP report published in 2005 claimed that greater regional cooperation among the Central Asian countries would usher in huge gains by slashing trade costs, boosting remittances from migrant workers, and improving water and energy use patterns.[8] It suggested that with greater cooperation, Central Asia could become an attractive destination for foreign direct investment, if neighbours treat one another as trading partners, lift formal and informal tariff barriers and improve institutional and political structures to facilitate mutual cooperation.

The report further highlighted that the costs of non-cooperation could be much higher, in the form of lost opportunities, natural disasters, environmental degradation, as well as conflict and insecurity, whereas regional cooperation alone could double the size of the regional economy in ten years. According to Lyaziza Sabyrova, Director for Regional Cooperation in Central Asia at the Asian Development Bank, Central Asia faces intertwined challenges of climate change-induced hardships, food insecurity, and economic repercussions of geopolitical conflicts. Regional cooperation and integration can remedy many of these hardships by ensuring sustainable food production in the long term, and helping countries in the region transition to clean energy. It's crucial that the Central Asian countries coordinate their efforts to manage their common water resources of the Amu and Syr Darya rivers and share knowledge about modern, climate-resilient technologies to maximise agricultural productivity.

In this regard, the existing institutional mechanisms such as the Asian Development Bank-backed Central Asia Regional Economic Cooperation (CAREC) Program can provide the necessary platform for countries to address common challenges.[9]

Another vital reason that necessitates greater regional cooperation among the Central Asian countries is their long history of inter-dependence, which can be partly attributed to the relatively small size of their population and economies as well as their landlocked location due to which the region has historically fallen prey to great powers surrounding it. While Russia colonised the region during the eighteenth and nineteenth centuries, China annexed the Easternmost parts of Central Asia, or the Xinjiang region, also known as East Turkestan. Despite parts of the region coming under the suzerainty of neighbouring great powers, there was flow of populations, goods and ideas. The region greatly benefited from trade by acting as transit-trade hub for the larger Eurasian landmass. There is little doubt that the region can regain that centrality in world politics with a greater level of cooperation and economic integration.

Regional Cooperation in Central Asia: The Soviet Legacy and Post-Independence Scene

The roots of intra-regional cooperation in Central Asia can be traced back to the Soviet economic planning and forms of dependency created by Moscow to put the region firmly into Soviet orbit. A semblance of intra-regional integration was visible ever since the 1920s as Central Asia was treated as a single economic subdivision within the 'unified economic complex' of the USSR.[10] Major economic activity was directed from Union ministries based in Moscow which resulted in exceptionally high levels of intra-union trade. But the Soviet rule forced a peculiar economic system on Central Asia, marked by centralised economic planning, collectivised agriculture, cotton monoculture and sector-specific industrialisation.[11] The region's water and energy resources were distributed according to need through an integrated, centrally controlled grid infrastructure, where hydropower was supplied to the network by Tajikistan and the Kyrgyz Republic, whereas hydrocarbon-generated power was supplied by Kazakhstan, Turkmenistan and Uzbekistan. Integration of Central Asia in the Soviet System for over six decades did not however translate into increased regional cooperation following 1991 and intra-regional trade, along with political cooperation, fell drastically in subsequent years.

The five Central Asian countries gained independence in 1991 following the Soviet dissolution, but it was somewhat reluctantly accepted as all of them depended heavily on the Soviet Union's more industrialized regions for their economic survival. Resource flows from Moscow to the region's small economies attest to their total economic dependency, which caused severe disruption once they became independent and had to fend for themselves.[12] This however did not prevent the newly independent Central Asian republics from finding ways to cooperate with each other, and as opposed to the popular notion that regionalism in Central Asia was a failure unless backed by prominent external actors, these republics did in fact manage to set-up some institutional mechanisms almost immediately after independence, not to forget the frequent statements from the top political leadership claiming their shared Central Asian cultural heritage.

The first indication of a budding sense of unity came from within the region when, in 1993, the presidents of Uzbekistan, Kazakhstan, Turkmenistan, and Kyrgyzstan and the chairman of Tajikistan's parliament convened in Tashkent and declared the region would henceforth be known as *Tsentral'naia Aziia* (Central Asia) rather than by the Soviet-era term *Sredniaia Aziiai Kazakhstan* (Middle Asia and Kazakhstan), reclaiming Kazakhstan as an integral part of the region. This might seem a semantic exercise, but to those gathered, it was a statement of unity and a declaration that they share a common space and future.[13] The next more concrete initiative towards regional cooperation came in 1994 when Uzbekistan, Kazakhstan and Kyrgyzstan created the Central Asian Union (CAU), effectively forming a common economic space among themselves. In 1995, it decided to create a joint Council of Defense Ministers to consider issues of regional security and joint military exercises, adding a security angle.[14]

This was followed by the signing of a 'Treaty of Eternal Friendship' between Kazakhstan, Kyrgyzstan and Uzbekistan in 1997 where the leaders highlighted their common 'Turkic heritage' and pledged to form a Central Asian peacekeeping battalion and conduct joint military exercises.[15] The same year, Central Asian states declared their intent to form a Nuclear Weapons Free Zone in Central Asia and signed the 1997 Almaty Declaration. The following year, CAU transformed into the Central Asian Economic Union (CAEC), and Tajikistan joined it as an observer. By 2001, the CAEC became the Central Asian Cooperation Organisation (CACO) which later opened membership to other post-Soviet States, but as events unfolded, Russia first joined CACO and later engineered its merger in 2005 with the Eurasian Economic Community formed in 2000. Surprisingly, none of the four Central Asian states that had formed CACO objected to Russia's proposal and decided to let go of Central Asian integration in favour of Eurasian integration.[16] In hindsight, it can be argued that the efforts at regional cooperation in Central Asia never really took off because of several factors, including Turkmenistan's non-participation in the CAU/CAEC structure, civil war in Tajikistan and other intra-regional disputes resurfacing now and then among member-states, and, most important of all, Russia dominated Eurasian integration projects subsuming Central Asian integration projects.

Regional Cooperation in the Twenty-First Century: Role of External Actors

In many ways, CACO's merger with the Eurasian Economic Community was a hindrance in the path of Central Asia-led, Central Asia-owned regional cooperation. From 2005 onwards, institutional frameworks of cooperation in Central Asia were increasingly provided by powerful neighbours, mainly China and Russia, and sometimes the United States, European Union, and Turkey in recent years. The countries of the region however continued to take initiatives to foster dialogue on ensuring regional peace and security: in 2006 they unanimously signed the 'The Central Asian Nuclear-Weapon-Free Zone (CANWFZ) Treaty' at Semipalatinsk in Kazakhstan. Informally known as the 'Semipalatinsk Treaty,' it is a legally binding agreement that created a nuclear weapons-free zone in Central Asia, whereby signatory states renounced any plans to build or possess nuclear weapons in the future.

The first regional organization that Central Asia's newly independent republics joined was the Commonwealth of Independent States (CIS) established shortly after the Soviet disintegration in 1991. More than self-choice, joining Russia-led CIS was a necessity as the newly independent Central Asian republics were historically dependent on Moscow. The CIS failed to show any meaningful progress, and its relevance came under doubt within a decade of its founding.[17] Its efficacy as a regional organization has repeatedly come under scrutiny as it has a weak decision-making system and lack of normative supranational acceptance, unlike other successful regional initiatives like the European Union. Other institutional weaknesses emanating from its shaky legal-political foundation have hollowed its political command and control structure.[18]

Another Russia-backed organization in which two Central Asian countries participate is the Eurasian Economic Union (EEU), founded on May 29, 2014, by a treaty that came into force on January 1, 2015. Its members include Russia, Belarus, Kazakhstan, Kyrgyzstan and Armenia. The EEU was the result of Russia's vigorous attempts to forge closer economic partnership in the post-Soviet space by emulating the European Union model and was in fact a successor of the Eurasian Economic Community (EEC) founded in 2000 and the Eurasian Customs Union formed in 2012. The Eurasian Economic Commission and the Court of the Eurasian Economic Union are modeled along EU institutions, but their effectiveness in resolving disputes and streamlining policy directives is questionable. Moreover, only two of the five Central Asian countries are members of the EEU, whereas talks with Uzbekistan for acceding to it have faltered, suggesting limited scope for the EEU to provide the necessary framework for regional cooperation among Central Asian countries.[19]

China's rising economic and political heft is mirrored by its ambitious integration efforts in Central Asia, the best example of which is the Shanghai Cooperation Organization (SCO).[20] The SCO was founded in 2001 as a successor to the Shanghai Five, a forum that facilitated coordination between China, Russia and Central Asian countries for delimiting borders, ensuring security and demilitarisation along the border regions. Initially comprised of six states – China, Russia, Kazakhstan, Kyrgyzstan, Tajikistan and Uzbekistan – its membership and political profile have increased manifold, with India and Pakistan joining it in 2017, and Iran in 2023. Among all the Eurasia-centred regional intergovernmental organizations, SCO can be said to be the most comprehensive in terms of agenda, membership, and formal legal structures. It is the only non-Western Central Asia-centred regional organization that has seen its membership expand. However, despite its foundational focus on Central Asian regional security issues, it remains a China-backed/dominated group, something evident by its name. The SCO has also failed to deliver any significant result in terms of regional economic cooperation, as promised.[21]

Another Chinese-led initiative that has made Central Asia its core focus is the Belt and Road Initiative (BRI), also known as the One Belt One Road (OBOR) initiative. Initially floated in 2013 during Chinese Premiere Xi Jinping's state visit to Kazakhstan, the BRI "aims to build a web of infrastructure, including railways, telecommunications, energy pipelines and ports, to facilitate development across Asia, Europe and Africa" and has a land and sea component: an overland Silk Road Economic Belt and a Maritime Silk Road.[22] The BRI assumes significance for Central Asia as President Xi Jinping chose Kazakhstan to unveil the BRI in 2013, and China's trade with the region has surpassed Russia's coinciding in the years following the launch of BRI. Concerns, however, have been flagged about China employing BRI-related financing to create economic dependencies in Asia and Africa. Low public approval in countries participating in the BRI, especially in Central Asia about the nature of Chinese engagement with the local economies, has called into question BRI's viability for catalysing economic integration of Central Asia with the world.[23]

Compared to Russia and China, the collective West – here, the European Union and the United States – has faltered in providing regional cooperation mechanisms to Central Asian countries. This is partly due to the fact that neither of them share a border with any of the Central Asian countries nor have they historically been linked to the region. The United States floated the New Silk Road[24] initiative in 2011 to integrate Afghanistan with Central Asia by announcing that it would fund transit-transport corridors, but that didn't materialise due to unclear objectives and the rapidly deteriorating security situation in Afghanistan. If one observes closely, initiatives like the New Silk Road or CASA-1000 (another Western-backed initiative to supply electricity from Kyrgyzstan and Tajikistan to Afghanistan and Pakistan) are Afghanistan-centric, which makes them less attractive to Central Asian states. Moreover, Western initiatives are more about policy directives, than having real institutional content. Lack of funding commitments, unclear political objectives and concerns about financial sustainability hamstrung Western efforts at providing Central Asia with effective regional cooperation structures.

Turkey-backed Organisation of Turkic States (OTS) is a non-Western, non-Russian and non-Chinese dominated regional organisation that has gained prominence in recent years. The OTS traces its origin to the Summit of Heads of State of Turkic Speaking States starting in 1991. The leaders came together in 2009 to sign the Nakhchivan Agreement that established the Cooperation Council of Turkic States (Turkic Council). At the Istanbul Summit held on November 21, 2021, the Turkic Council gave itself a new name – the OTS. It has five full members – Azerbaijan, Kazakhstan, Kyrgyzstan, Turkey and Uzbekistan, and three observer states – Hungary, Turkmenistan and the Turkish Republic of Northern Cyprus.[25] With the primary motive of developing wide-ranging multilateral cooperation among Turkic-speaking countries, the OTS "aims to serve as a new regional instrument for advancing international cooperation in the Eurasian continent, particularly in Central Asia and the Caucasus."[26] The rise in the political profile of the OTS has led to concerns that it promotes 'Pan-Turkism' and 'Pan-Islamism' and can potentially challenge China and Russia in Central Asia.[27] However, a more grounded analysis suggests that OTS doesn't have that much heft, given member-states' limited economic potential.

Recent Trends in Regional Cooperation in Central Asia

Many observers who had earlier written off regional cooperation in Central Asia are surprised by the renewed regionalism in Central Asia since 2016. A host of interconnected factors explain this positive trend of regional cooperation among Central Asian countries. The first factor that has incentivized greater cooperation in the regions is the increasing trade between Europe and Asia. Central Asian states realize that they can reap the full benefits of this transit-trade only by coordinating their economic and custom policies, and resolving long-standing political issues. Domestically, positive developments in Central Asia's two largest states, Uzbekistan and Kazakhstan, with new leadership initiating comprehensive reforms and boldly opening up to the outside world, has given an impetus to regional cooperation. This is led by Uzbekistan, whose president Shavkat Mirziyoyev – assuming power in 2016 after – has embarked on an ambitious reform agenda spanning every sector, including foreign relations, focussing on neighbourhood first policy. Another factor is that Central Asian states' approach towards Afghanistan has undergone a change. They increasingly view Afghanistan as a country with deep links to them and as essential for their well-being and for forging closer links with South Asia.[28]

Consultative Meeting Format of Heads of State of Central Asian Countries since 2018

Due to the above factors and new-found confidence, Central Asian States are enhancing the level of dialogue and taking their states on the path to accelerated regional cooperation and greater economic integration. The first Heads of State level summit held in 2018 in Astana was a milestone as it was after a lull of two decades that the Heads of State convened to give new direction to inter-state relations in Central Asia. Unlike the previous heads of state summits, which were limited to one or more topics, this time around the consultative summit meeting was open to deliberations on a wide range of issues.[29] It was also the first such initiative launched without the support or participation of external powers. It offers a renewed hope that Central Asian states can collectively address common challenges such as natural resources governance, delimitation of borders, climate change, low connectivity and poor infrastructure.[30]

In light of new domestic and international developments that have profound implications for Central Asia, the first Consultative Meeting of Heads of State of Central Asia in 2018 was a significant achievement. The idea was mooted by Shavkat Mirziyoyev of Uzbekistan in 2017, and the first meeting was hosted by Kazakhstan's Nursultan Nazarbayev the next year. It was followed by events that bolstered Central Asian attempts at regional cooperation. On June 22, 2018, three months into the first consultative meeting, the United Nations General Assembly passed a resolution titled 'Strengthening Regional and International Cooperation to Ensure Peace, Stability and Sustainable Development in the Central Asian Region.'[31] Introducing the draft in the General Assembly, Uzbekistan's representative stated that its primary purpose was to garner the support of the international community in favour of Central Asian states' efforts to foster closer collaboration and ensure peace and stability in the region.[32] The draft lauded the first heads of state consultative meeting and encouraged Central Asian countries to promote the peace process in Afghanistan and assist Kabul in its social and economic development.

Building on the sense of mutual trust generated after the first meeting in

Astana, the second Consultative Meeting of Heads of State of Central Asian countries was held in Tashkent, Uzbekistan in November 2019. This time Turkmenistan's president, Gurbanguly Berdimukhamedov participated in the meeting, unlike the Astana meeting in 2018 where he had sent the speaker of parliament, his son Serdar Berdimukhammedov. The joint statement released at the time acknowledged that the consultative meeting format at the heads of state level was happening after two decades – the last such happened in 1998 in Ashgabat. It further "underscored the need to strengthen political trust and mutual understanding among Central Asian states" and called for "expanding the trade-economic, transport-communication and cultural-humanitarian ties" among them. The joint statement reiterated that "Central Asia's stable development is linked to achieving stable and long-term peace in Afghanistan."[33]

The third Consultative Meeting of Heads of State of Central Asia was scheduled for 2020 but was postponed to 2021 due to coronavirus-induced lockdown measures. This led to suspicion in some quarters, but it was successfully organised by Turkmenistan in August 2021, dispelling concerns that region-wide disturbances might disrupt it. The meeting itself was a positive signal since Turkmenistan earlier had maintained distance from regional cooperation forums due to its longstanding policy of 'permanent neutrality.'[34] Several significant events were set in motion by the time heads of state of Central Asian countries gathered in Cholpon-Ata, Kyrgyzstan in July 2022 for the fourth edition of the consultative meeting. Some negative developments had created uncertainties: the destructive impact of the coronavirus pandemic, Russia's war with Ukraine since February 2022, the Taliban taking over Kabul by blitz, and Kazakhstan and Uzbekistan faced with challenges in 2022.

Speaking at the same meeting, President Shavkat Mirziyoyev noted "the difficult situation the region was facing in light of the rapid transformation of the international order" and the "breaking of traditional logistical supply chains, growing inflation, and rising energy and food security risks." President Mirziyoyev further called on Central Asian countries to coordinate and improve the effectiveness of multilateral cooperation in the framework of consultative meeting format and promote such initiatives as joint industrial cooperation projects, development of transport and energy infrastructure, and digitalization of the region's economies.[35] Another significant outcome of the summit was the signing of the 'Treaty of Friendship, Good Neighbourliness and Cooperation for the Development of Central Asia in the 21st Century' proposed by Kazakhstan's new President Kassy-Jomart Tokayev. Kyrgyzstan and Uzbekistan readily signed the treaty, but Turkmenistan and Tajikistan deferred signing till they completed the required internal legal process.[36]

The fourth Consultative Meeting of Heads of State of Central Asia was shortly followed by a resolution in the United Nations General Assembly on July 20, 2022. Introduced by Turkmenistan, the resolution declared "Central Asia as a zone of peace, trust and cooperation."[37] This was somewhat similar to the UN resolution proposed by Uzbekistan which was passed months after the first consultative meeting, supporting the process of regional cooperation in Central Asia. Appreciating that regional cooperation has been steadily strengthening since the first consultative meeting in 2018, Kazakhstan's president, Kassym-Jomart Tokayev proposed that foreign ministers of Central Asian states must meet every six months to develop coordinated approaches to key regional and international issues. Among other important outcomes, the heads of state adopted the Joint Statement of the Cholpon-Ata consultative meeting, a Roadmap for the Development of Regional Cooperation for 2022-2024, the Green Agenda, and the Concept of Interaction of Central Asian States in multilateral formats.

The fifth edition of the Consultative Meeting of Heads of State of Central Asia was hosted by Tajikistan in Dushanbe in September 2023. The bulk of the initiatives proposed in the fifth meeting came from Uzbekistan and Kazakhstan, suggesting their leadership position in the format proceedings. Despite several good discussion points, including climate change, creating a free-trade zone, and engaging Taliban-led Afghanistan, the meeting did not revisit the previous year's regional treaty proposed by Kazakhstan and signed by others, except Turkmenistan and Tajikistan. The border conflict between Tajikistan and Kyrgyzstan was not taken up for discussion.[38] The meeting instead focused on issues related to the governance of water and energy resources, general directions for youth policy, connectivity and transit routes, etc. The meeting saw several new developments such as the participation of Azerbaizan's President Ilham Aliyev, indicating future expansion of the consultative meeting format, adoption of documents on youth policy, a WHO-backed plan for health and well-being in the region for 2022-2025, and an agreement on strengthening connectivity through land transport in Central Asia.[39]

A closer look at the proceedings and outcomes of the five Consultative Meetings of Heads of State of Central Asia held so far suggests that there are some recurring issues that have been discussed so far. Among them are promoting the shared cultural heritage of the region, ensuring regional security by peaceful resolution of intra-state conflicts in accordance with the principles of good neighbourliness and friendship, establishing cross-border trade and industrial hubs for incentivizing joint production and intra-regional economic integration, and closely working with Afghanistan to ensure its socio-economic stability and to prevent it from becoming a hub of trans-national security threats. Working towards decarbonization goals, creating a green economy and digitalization for the region are some of the recent agendas that have seen the light of the day.

Regional Cooperation in Central Asia: Substance or Rhetoric?

That Central Asia's economic, political, and security interests are intertwined, and solutions must come from within the region is now a widely acknowledged fact within and outside the region. Doubts have however been cast on the future of regional cooperation in Central Asia. In post-Soviet period, despite the forward march of globalisation, Central Asia retreated into one of the world's most disintegrated and disconnected regions. Some blame the nature of political systems in the region,[40] others, who dwell on the puzzle of the so-called 'failure of regionalism' in Central Asia, emphasize external factors, such as the extra-regional economic dependence of the region's economies and the impact of external powers in the region for the failure of regionalism in Central Asia.[41] It is true that regionalism in Central Asia backslid in the decades following independence due to the above-listed factors, but the situation has been rapidly changing in recent years, and, for good.

Uzbekistan-Kazakhstan Ties as the Bedrock of Regional Cooperation in Central Asia

While earlier regional efforts at cooperation were hampered by competition between Uzbekistan and Kazakhstan, there is an increasing realisation of the necessity of providing joint leadership in the face of regional and global geopolitical challenges. The rapprochement between Uzbekistan and Kazakhstan is partly the result of domestic political transitions in both countries. In Uzbekistan, a reformist president, Shavkat Mirziyoyev, took charge in 2016 whereas in Kazakhstan, Kassym-Jomart Tokayev took over from the long-time president Nursultan Nazarbayev, consolidating power ever since and has pushed for regional cooperation. On its part, Kazakhstan had always prized its distinct 'Eurasian' identity, but in the more recent past, it has attempted to drift away from Moscow's sphere of influence by positioning itself as an integral part of Central Asia.[42]

Following the strengthening of Kazakhstan-Uzbekistan relations, the two signed a 'Treaty on Allied Relations' and an 'Agreement on Border Demarcation' during Kazakh President Tokayev's state visit to Uzbekistan in December 2022.[43] Both parties signaled a desire to give a strategic character to their relationship and bury old differences. The reformist regimes and change in leadership in Central Asia's two largest countries have removed many of the roadblocks to regional cooperation and incentivized other neighbours to similarly open up to each other. The heads of state meeting format and the 'C5+1' format are just some of the successful regional cooperation mechanisms that have manifested in recent years as a result of greater trust between Uzbekistan and Kazakhstan.

Rise in Intra-regional Trade

Central Asian countries have made significant economic progress since the dawn of the twenty-first century, but there's scope for increasing intra-regional trade, leading to greater economic prosperity and macroeconomic stability for the region. A cursory look at the region's economic profile suggests that in the last twenty years, the region's GDP has grown by an average of 6.2 per cent in real terms, reaching $347 billion. Kazakhstan is the region's leader when it comes to trade and constitutes 80 per cent of the total mutual trade whereas Uzbekistan, the second largest economy in the region, is Kazkahtsan's largest trade partner, with bilateral trade between both touching $5 billion in 2022.[44]

As Central Asia's largest economies, Kazakhstan and Uzbekistan have taken the lead in initiating regional economic projects, followed by Turkmenistan, which has proposed selling more of its natural gas to the countries of the region. There is an atmosphere of loosening up of impediments to intra-regional trade as trade barriers have come down, supported by the fact that there are now more border crossings for the movement of labour, reduction in visa grant timings in Uzbekistan and Kazakhstan, and better air connectivity between major Central Asian cities. The most significant development is in intra-regional trade turnover, which increased to $225 billion between 2016 and 2022.[45] In fact, mutual trade between Central Asian countries is growing even faster than their total foreign trade, with the share of mutual trade between Central Asian countries in their total trade turnover having reached 9.9 per cent by 2021. Nevertheless, the countries of the region need to overcome key structural challenges including dependence on hydrocarbons and low level of development of the financial sector, lack of coordination in the management of water and energy resources, and climate change, to foster greater economic growth and integration.[46]

Cooperation in Education, Science and Technology

On June 18, 2021, the ministers of education of Kazakhstan, Kyrgyzstan, Turkmenistan and Uzbekistan signed the 'Turkestan Declaration' to create a unified higher education area in the Central Asian region. The declaration appreciated the Bologna process in Europe and the role of the European Union in integrating its higher education system. It recognised the need to follow the principles set by it and declared the creation of the Central Asian Higher Education Area (CAHEA) to enhance cooperation in higher education in Central Asia. This was significant because Central Asian countries have a dynamic and large higher education sector that has undergone rapid transformation since their independence. There are intra-regional differences in the quality of higher education, but several common features persist.

Global experience shows that regional integration of higher education systems can be an effective instrument to solve similar challenges and ensure long-term growth across industries. The quality of higher education in Central Asia can be improved by fostering regional cooperation, knowledge sharing and pooling resources among the region's universities. Towards this end, a high-level conference was organised by the World Bank and the Ministry of Higher Education of Uzbekistan in Tashkent to foster dialogue and cooperation between Central Asian countries in higher education. The conference resulted in a World Bank report 'Towards Higher Education Excellence in Central Asia: A Roadmap for Improving the Quality of Education and Research through Regional Integration.' It offers a roadmap to stimulate cooperation across three priority areas: to improve access, quality and relevance of higher education; advance instruments for an integrated regional higher education area; and strengthen research and innovation capacity.[47]

Afghanistan Factor

Central Asian countries have a history of dialogue with Afghanistan, but recent developments in the country have given a new sense of urgency to coordinate policy on Afghanistan. This is paralleled by a greater propensity to treat Afghanistan as a part of the region, not just due to historical socio-political linkages but also because of Afghanistan's strategic position as a critical land bridge connecting Central Asia with South Asia. In 2021, riding on the wave of enthusiasm and external support for regional cooperation, Uzbekistan hosted a conference in Tashkent on fostering connectivity between South Asia and Central Asia via Afghanistan.[48] However, the Taliban's capture of power in Kabul within a month of the conference came as a setback to Uzbekistan's plan to integrate Afghanistan within the framework of South Asia-Central Asia connectivity.

The Taliban-run Afghanistan poses a tricky new reality for Central Asia where some countries such as Uzbekistan and Tajikistan face more uncertainty than others since they share borders with Afghanistan, and past experience with the Taliban was anything but pleasant.[49] Nevertheless, the rapidly deteriorating security and human rights situation in Afghanistan has not let Central Asian states' focus away from this war-ravaged country. It is important to mention here that while no Central Asian state has given full recognition to the Taliban regime in Afghanistan, except Tajikistan the other four Central Asian states have resumed trade ties with it, and are willing to reintegrate the country into the regional economy. Kazakhstan and Uzbekistan have further taken the lead in providing humanitarian aid and sponsored talks with Taliban officials to stabilise the political situation in the country. Gathering at consultative meetings and C5+1 format summits, Central Asian leaders have repeatedly made clear their stand that regional security and prosperity in the region are linked to stability and an inclusive government in Afghanistan.

Speaking as 'One': The C5+1 Format

Another significant manifestation of the rising trend of regional cooperation in Central Asia is that in the last few years, these countries have expanded their interaction with major powers in the 'C5+1' format, whereby they speak in one voice in dealing with major powers and are articulating their interests in a more concerted manner. The origin of Central Asian countries speaking in one voice when dealing with influential external powers can, however, be traced to the 'Central Asia plus Japan' dialogue mechanism that started in 2004. While the dialogue-level mechanism still exists and runs successfully at the foreign ministers level with Japan, Central Asian countries have inaugurated a new multilateral mechanism at the highest political level in recent years, the Summit format – whereby Heads of State of the five Central Asian countries gather biennially, sometimes annually, with the Head of State/Government of another major power.

'C5+1' format summits now exist with India – starting from January 2022, China – from May 2023, the European Union – from June 2023, the Gulf Cooperation Council – from July 2023, the United States – from August 2023, and Germany – from September 2023. Clearly, the 'C5+1' Summit mechanism has ushered in a new phase of diplomacy in Central Asia. The Central Asian countries now have a sense that their interests are better taken care of when they speak in one voice, despite the intra-regional contestations and pressure points. This also signals a nuanced instrumentalization of their 'multi-vector' foreign policies as a way to balance the external influence of great powers, especially China and Russia.[50]

Obstacles to Regional Cooperation in Central Asia

There is little doubt among those who study Central Asia that regional cooperation and economic integration will deliver significant benefits to the region. However, there are several obstacles, some immediate and others systemic, that need to be tackled before the region's countries can realize the true potential of their economies and integrate the region with the world's major economic powerhouses.

Among the region's political challenges, managing inter-state conflicts ranks prominently. Whereas the recent progress in border delimitation between Uzbekistan and Kyrgyzstan, and, between Kazakhstan and Uzbekistan, has reduced distrust and largely settled Soviet-era borders among them, the process of border delimitation and demarcation has hit roadblocks in the case of Kyrgyzstan and Tajikistan. A year has passed since Kyrgyzstan and Tajikistan fought a brief but bloody war over their disputed border. The two mountainous Central Asian republics are locked in a cycle of violence and have engaged in sporadic shootings along disputed parts of their border, most recently in April 2021[51] and again in September 2022.[52] The last two rounds of fighting have claimed over 150 lives, injured thousands, and internally displaced more than 1,30,000 people in Kyrgyzstan's Batken province alone.

Much of the border conflict has occurred in and around the politically volatile Ferghana Valley, where long-time inter-ethnic rivalries have dominated the region's politics. The growing scarcity of water and land resources has been aggravated by the absence of new institutional structures since the dissolution of the Soviet Union.[53] The territorial disputes between these relatively new republics have at times aggravated as their competing versions of history become ever more deeply ingrained in their national consciousness. This is happening since their populations, unlike in the Soviet days, have much less contact with one another, either due to lack of a common language or due to unpleasant lived experiences.[54]

Additionally, all five Central Asian countries face significant governance challenges even after three decades of independence from the Soviet Union. They have struggled to adopt indigenous governance models and stabilize their economies long pegged to Moscow. Moreover, deceleration of economic diversification still present challenges in creating cooperative regional mechanisms. Other external pressures have likewise accelerated in the face of heightened geopolitical competition surrounding the region and present tough choices.

More pressing are the challenges concerning climate change-induced resource scarcity, especially sharing the region's already scarce water and land resources, which explain many of the conflicts in the region. One can observe that the growing scarcity of natural resources in the region has led to intense competition and acquired socio-economic and political dimensions. Climate change-induced resource scarcity is further squeezing the region's already fragile water availability which is further hampered by existing economic problems, socio-political instability, population growth, and limited institutional and infrastructure capacity in the region.[55] The disagreements over the sharing of water resources and the construction of dams have long acted as irritants in normalizing inter-state relations between upstream Tajikistan and Kyrgyzstan and downstream Uzbekistan, Kazakhstan and Turkmenistan. Many such disagreements have been resolved in recent years, but it might take time to fully resolve them as climate change worsens resource availability in the region.

Conclusion

Central Asia, a landlocked region with a long and rich history, has been a meeting ground of various cultures and the focal point of trade routes during ancient and medieval periods. From the eighteenth-nineteenth century, it came under Russian/ Soviet rule and became isolated from the rest of the world. The region witnessed significant growth under the Soviet Union, which created an integrated economic model heavily dependent upon Moscow. In the post-Soviet period, there was disruption of this system and the region became less integrated. Despite some early efforts by the Central Asian states at regional cooperation, due to a variety of reasons, it did not go very far. External actor-led integration efforts have had better success, especially those led by Russia, the main security provider, and China, the increasingly dominant economic player in the region. The states of the region, however, have limited say in these organisations, which creates a type of dependency.

In the last few years, some external and internal developments led to a realisation among the leaders of these states, especially the two dominant actors – Uzbekistan and Kazakhstan – about the need for greater regional cooperation. It induced a number of initiatives, most notably the Consultative Meeting of the Heads of States, and an overall growth in regional trade and connectivity. This has the potential to lead to a more institutionalised framework for regional cooperation and integration. Though there are challenges, but the the recent efforts are in the right direction and give hope for a prosperous and regionally integrated Central Asia.

End Notes

1 Mansura Haidar, "The Silk Road and the Surrounding Regions," in Central Asia: Introspection, eds. Mushtaq Ahmad Kaw & Aijaz A Banday, Centre of Central Asian Studies, 2016.

2 Mirzokhid Rakhimov, "Internal and External Dynamics of Regional Cooperation in Central Asia," *Journal of Eurasian Studies*, Vol. 1 Issue 2, July 2010.

3 See definition of Central Asia in Federico Mayor, "The Dawn of Civilization, Earliest Times to 700 B.C.," in History of Civilization in Central Asia, eds. A.H. Dani et. al. Vol. 1, Paris: UNESCO Publishing.

4 Martha Brill Olcott, "Rivalry and Competition in Central Asia," Eurasia Emerging Markets Forum, January 23-23, 2010.

5 Martha Brill Olcott, "The Myth of Tsentral' naiaAziia," The Asian Interior, 1994.

6 Kato Lambrechts & Chris Alden, "Regionalism & Regionalisation," in Palgrave Advances in Development Studies, ed. J. Hynes, Palgrave Macmillan, 2005.

7 Johannes F. Linn, "Central Asian Regional Cooperation and Integration: Reality of Mirage?," EDB Eurasian Integration Yearbook, 2012.

8 See report, "Central Asian Human Development Report: Regional Cooperation for Human Development and Human Security," UNDP, 2005.

9 Lyaziza Sabyrova, "Q&A: Addressing Intertwined Challenges in Central Asia and the Caucasus through Regional Cooperation," Asian Development Bank, May 3, 2023.

10 Martin C. Spechler, "Regional Cooperation in Central Asia: Promises and More Promises," *The Fletcher Journal of Development Studies*, Vol. XVI, p. 2, 2000.

11 See Richard Pomfret, "The Economies of Central Asia," Princeton University Press, 1995.

12 R.G. Gidadhubli, "Economic Transition in Central Asia," *World Affairs: The Journal of International Issues*, Vol. 2, No. 1, June 1993.

13 Martha Brill Olcott, "The Myth of Tsentral' naiaAziia," The Asian Interior, 1994.

14 Roy Allison, "Regionalism, Regional Structures and Security Management in Central Asia," International Affairs, Vol. 80, No. 3, 2004.

15 NarynbekIdinov, "Central Asia: Three Presidents Sign Friendship Treaty," Radio Free Europe, January 7, 1997.

16 Farkhod Tolipov, "CACO merges with EEC: The Third Strike on Central Asia's Independence," The Central Asia Caucasus Analyst, October 19, 2005.

17 Richard Sakwa& Mark Webber, "The Commonwealth of Independent States, 1991-1998: Stagnation and Surviva'," *Europe-Asia Studies*, Vol. 51, No. 3, May 1999.

18 Kemal Baslar. "The Commonwealth of Independent States: Decayed Within A Decade," Turkish Year Book, May 1, 2001.

19 Kataryna Wolczuk, Rilka Dragneva & Jon Wallace, "What is the Eurasian Economic Union," Chatham House, July 15, 2022.

20 See Chapter 5, "Beijing's Strategy: The SCO, Xinjiang and China's Great Leap Westward," in Great Games, Local Rules: The New Great Power Quest in Central Asia by Alexander Cooley, Oxford University Press, July 2012.

21 Johannes F. Linn & Oksana Pidufala, "The Experience with Regional Economic Cooperation Organizations: Lessons for Central Asia," Wolfensohn Center for Development Working Paper No. 4, October 2008.

22 Y.Y. Chang, "Understanding the Belt and Road Initiative: An Initiative to Make China Great Again?," *European Journal of East Asian Studies*, 7-35, 2019.

23 AkbotaKaribayeva, "Public Attitudes Toward China in Central Asia," Special Report by the Caspian Policy Center. Also see book discussion, "China's Belt and Road Initiative and its impact in Central Asia," Voices on Central Asia, January 19, 2018.

24 See the document "U.S. Support for the New Silk Road," Bureau of South and Central Asian Affairs (Archived Content), U.S. Department of State. The CASA-1000 regional electricity

grid is supported by the U.S. as part of its New Silk Road initiative, along with funding from the World Bank.

25 Aidana Baktybek, "Importance of Organisation of Turkic States from the perspective of Uzbekistan," Ankara Center for Crisis and Policy Studies (ANKASAM), November 22, 2022.

26 See homepage "Organization of Turkic States," official website of the Organization of Turkic States.

27 Nurettin Akcay, "Does the Organization of Turkic States Worry China and Russia?," *The Diplomat*, November 23, 2022.

28 Svante E. Cornell & S. Frederick Starr, "Modernization and Regional Cooperation in Central Asia," Silk Road Studies Program, Central Asia-Caucasus Institute, November 2018.

29 Bruce Pannier, "Why This Central Asian Summit Could Be Different," Qishloz Ovozi (Archive), Radio Free Europe, March 14, 2018.

30 Akram Umarov, "How Rising Great Power Tensions WIll Affect Central Asia," Eurasia Program, Foreign Policy Research Institute, April 8, 2021.

31 See proceedings of the 72nd session of the United Nations General Assembly, "Document: A/RES/72/283: Strengthening regional and international cooperation to ensure peace, stability and sustainable development in the Central Asian region," General Assembly of the United Nations, United Nations.

32 "General Assembly Adopts Resolution On Strengthening Cooperation in Central Asia," United Nations Regional Centre For Preventive Diplomacy For Central Asia, June 25, 2018.

33 See Joint Statement of the Consultative meeting of the heads of state of Central Asia, Embassy of Uzbekistan in New Delhi, November 30, 2019.

34 Askar Nursha, "Central Asia Moves Towards Greater Regional Cooperation After Successful Third Consultative Meeting," *The Astana Times*, August 9, 2021.

35 See the address by President of the Republic of Uzbekistan Shavkat Mirziyoyev at the fourth Consultative Meeting of the Heads of State of Central Asia, Embassy of Uzbekistan in New Delhi.

36 See the speech by President Kassym-Zomart Tokayev at the Fourth Consultative Meeting of Heads of State of Central Asia, Official Website of the President of the Republic of Kazakhstan, July 21, 2022.

37 See proceedings of the 76th session of the United Nations General Assembly, "A/RES/76/299: Zone of Peace, Trust and Cooperation in Central Asia," General Assembly of the United Nations, United Nations, July 2022.

38 Gavin Helf, "New Central Asian Leaders Look to Balance Relations with Major Powers," United States Institute of Peace, September 28, 2023.

39 See "Press Release: Fifth Consultative Meeting of Heads of State," Ministry of Foreign Affairs of the Republic of Tajikistan, September 15, 2023.

40 Luca Anceshi, "The Resurgence of Central Asian Connectivity," *The Diplomat*, December 1, 2017.

41 Sebastian Krapohl & Alexandra Vasileva-Dienes, "The region that isn't: China, Russia and the failure of regional integration in Central Asia," *Asia-Europe Journal*, May 28, 2019.

42 Annette Bohr et.al, "Kazakhstan: Tested by Transition," Chatham House, November 27, 2019.

43 Dana Omirgazy, "Kazakhstan, Uzbekistan Sign Treaty on Allied Relations, Agreement on Border Demarcation to Foster Strategic Partnership," *The Astana Times*, December 23, 2022.

44 Nurlan Kulbatyrov & Aida Haidar, "Five Trends in central Asian Connectivity," *The Astana Times*, June 26, 2023.

45 Akramjon Nematov, "Central Asian countries are gradually developing a sustainable

architecture of regional cooperation," Institute for Strategic and Regional Studies under the President of the Republic of Uzbekistan, September 18, 2023.

46 See report "The Economy of Central Asia: A Fresh Perspective," Eurasian Development Bank, 2022.

47 See "Regional Cooperation on Higher Education in Central Asia to Improve with World Bank Support," Press Release No. 2024/ECA/012, The World Bank, September 21, 2023.

48 Navbahor Imamova, "Uzbekistan Promotes Connectivity to Enhance its Regional Connectivity," South & Central Asia, VOA, July 13, 2021.

49 Kate Mallinson, "Afghanistan creates tricky new reality for Central Asia," Chatham House, August 27, 2021.

50 See "Dynamics of Regional Development in Central Asia and the Format of Multilateral Cooperation 5+1," Central Asian Bureau of Analytical Reporting, 2021.

51 See Charles J. Sullivan, "Battle at the Border: An Analysis of the 2021 Kyrgyzstan-Tajikistan Conflict," Asian Affairs, Vol. 52 Issue 3, 2021 for an in-depth analysis of the 2021 border clash.

52 Alys Davies, "Kyrgyzstan-Tajikistan border clashes claim nearly 100 lives," *BBC*, September 19, 2022.

53 Gulzana Kurmanalieva, "Kyrgyzstan and Tajikistan: Endless Border Conflicts," Institut fur Europaische & Centre International de formation europeene, February 2019.

54 Martha Brill Olcott, "Rivalry and Competition in Central Asia," Eurasia Emerging Markets Forum, January 23-25, 2010.

55 Timur Idrosov, "Climate Change and Water Resources in Central Asia: Growing Uncertainty," Central Asian Bureau For Analytical Reporting, January 12, 2023.

8

Engaging with Uzbekistan: India's Foreign Policy Achievement

Prof Tabasum Firdous and Dr Fozia Jan

ABSTRACT

Over the past few decades, India's aspirations and actions in its neighbourhood have been in sync with the broader regional and global environment. Indian foreign policy framework has become more vibrant and robust. Moreover, adopting proactive and pragmatic diplomatic strategies to engage with the world has helped India to emerge as a resurgent global actor. India's global footprint is scripting the narrative about India from an underdeveloped third-world country to an influential and promising economy. Diplomacy has gained a go-getting edge. India is the initiator, leader, and agenda seeker. Focusing on diverse horizons of foreign policy engagements, India regards connectivity as a subtle but essential element of the contemporary foreign policy framework. Overcoming the challenges from the new geopolitical and geo-economic realities, India has managed to survive the regional objectives by rejuvenating its foreign policy. One of the trials in front of Indian foreign policymakers was Central Asia. Assuming the importance of the Central Asian Region, India has always stressed encouraging mutual relations with the Central Asian Republics. With the introduction of the foreign policy initiative by India, 'Connect Central Asia Policy-2012,' the ties between India and the Central Asian States were expected to be diversified but could not reach the expected standards. However, soon after assuming office as Prime Minister of India, Narendra Modi stressed rejuvenating foreign relations. The geostrategic and security implications arising from China's ambitious projects in the region, like the China-Pakistan Economic Corridor (CPEC), One Belt and Road Initiative, and the widening presence of global players in the area have raised fears for India to reframe its foreign policy towards the Central Asian Region (CAR). Direct access to Central Asia enables India to assert itself as a competent player in the New Great Game. It allows India to counterbalance and check China's presence in the region. And one of the promising partners among the Central Asian Republics' is Uzbekistan. India-Uzbekistan relations have reached a strategic segment through mutual efforts and engagements. This paper explores the defence and strategic ties between India and Uzbekistan. The report aims to highlight the achievements of this bilateral partnership over the years.

The Central Asian Region

With a notable history, Central Asia has remained one of the critical areas of global affairs. One cannot eliminate the imprints of the Silk Road imprints or the Great Game of the 1990s. The former showcases the linkages between Central Asia, China, and the region in between, and the latter emphasizes the great power rivalry in the form of the competition between the Russian and British Empires for power and influence. As the Central Asian Region is part of a geostrategic space of Eurasia encompassed by China, Russia, Iran, and Turkey (Sikri, 2009), India regards this region as an essential element of contemporary India's vision for the future. From a strategic location to a momentous historical manifestation, the region has far-reaching geostrategic implications and significance for India. Central Asia had been India's Principal route connecting to the rest of the world. Throughout history, this region has been essential. Central Asia has deeply influenced India across land or maritime frontiers, from polity to culture, religion to economy. India has emerged directly or indirectly from its connections with the historic Silk Route. People-to-people ties and religious transformations are the principal elements, and Central Asia has been part of long traditional linkages of India's foreign engagements. Northern India had a Central Asian character, while the Himalayan belt seamlessly showcases glimpses of links via Tibet, Xinjiang, and Afghanistan. Ladakh is an example of such a linkage. Also, historically, Islam and Central Asian cultural patterns have been transmitted to Kashmiri culture and character (Peter Krasnopolsky, 2022).

India was the first to accord recognition to Central Asian Republics after the disintegration of the Soviet Union. The geopolitical realities extensively defined the initiatives and strategies of India. Acknowledging the regional aspirations, energy dependency and economic adventures, India has maintained highly positive behaviour while engaging with the Central Asian Countries.

The region of Central Asia is rich in minerals and hydrocarbon resources scattered around all the five Republics. Kazakhstan contains the world's second-largest reserves of uranium; Uzbekistan has gas, uranium, and gold reserves; Turkmenistan is the fourth-largest producer of natural gas; Tajikistan comprises a vast hydroelectric power potential; Kyrgyzstan has significant gold reserves. However, Due to inter-state issues like water disputes, Uzbekistan emerged as a potential leader in its tough neighbourhood (i.e., Tajikistan and Kyrgyzstan). And Kazakhstan competes to become a dominating power in the region.

Among the five, Uzbekistan is strategically pivotal to India's Foreign Policy. It is a potential ally to serve as a vital foothold as it shares its border with Afghanistan and is militarily strong. It thus can serve India's security ends, and both nations have already strengthened their bilateral strategic partnership for security, connectivity and counter-terrorism initiatives. Besides being one of the biggest exporters of uranium, gas and gold, Uzbekistan is a crucial player in India's plan to produce nuclear fuel to create a strategic uranium reserve. Importantly, Uzbekistan supports India's United Nations Security Council membership bid.

India-Uzbekistan Bilateral Relations

Through centuries of socio-political and economic changes, India and Uzbekistan have remarkably survived their rich inheritance of civilisation and historical connections (Roy, 2005). The emerging contours in the bilateral relations between Uzbekistan and India are defined by the convergence of interests, growing economic opportunities, current challenges, and shared foreign policy objectives. The formal diplomatic relations between India and Uzbekistan have been materialised in 1992. Since then, various ministerial and diplomatic visits have been carried out to imbibe rhythm and substance in bilateral relations.

There is convergence of approaches between India and Uzbekistan on various issues of regional or international character. The anti-terrorism agenda is an issue where both nations follow similar actions on regional and international platforms. Both India and Uzbekistan assert the necessity of a 'global comprehensive fight against terrorism' and believe that global combat against terrorism should essentially address those involved in the instigation, assistance and acquiescence equally to the perpetrators of terrorism. A global effort against Weapons of Mass Destruction (WMD) and Drug Trafficking has been an essential foreign policy agenda of both India and Uzbekistan. Both nations have signed several agreements over the years regarding such concerns. For instance, Uzbek President Islam Karimov visited India in 2001 and signed an extradition treaty and a legal assistance agreement with India to strengthen bilateral criminal scrutiny.

There has been continuity in bilateral diplomatic efforts between India and Uzbekistan in Information Technology, innovation, and technical expertise. In 2003 and 2004, India and Uzbekistan signed the Memorandum of Understanding (MOU) on mutual assistance in software, technical expertise, network equipment, and so on (Roy, 2005). Both nations have maintained prospectus strategies to engage with each other on defence, commerce and energy collaboration. High-level visits of senior officials, parliamentarians, corporations and academicians have substantiated mutual efforts to further the bilateral relations.

The continuity in commitment has been materialised by the ministerial visits from both sides to explore the bilateral partnership beyond the conventional ties. Besides the government-to-government channels, both nations have been encouraged to establish relations based on the soft power capabilities of both. Therefore, business and corporate sector communication, academicians and cultural features are welcomed by both the Indian and Uzbek governments (MEA, 2022).

However, the bilateral ties between India and Uzbekistan witnessed a gradual but slow pace. The significant hindrances were a lack of connectivity, the commitment of both nations to enrich the partnership, low trade and commerce activities between the two, and China's growing influence in the form of its economic standoffs.

2015: The Turning Point

With the formation of the National Democratic Alliance (NDA) led government in 2015, there was a significant reshuffle in the framework of Indian foreign policy. One of the critical features of the foreign policy of

Prime Minister N. Modi has been to build India on its glorious past but with modern content (Stobdan, 2016) and by making a 6-day integrated tour of Central Asia PM Modi in June 2015 covering all the five Central Asian Republics proved not only symbolic feat for Indian Diplomacy but also a strategic move that cemented the route for overcoming dilemmas that have so far thwarted India's outreach to this strategically important region in its locale. Moreover, the bilateral relations now encompass a broader canvas covering security and defence, trade and commerce, banking and investment, energy, agriculture, education, science and technology.

Significant Milestones in the India-Uzbekistan bilateral partnership include:

- PM-President (Mr Narendra Modi & Mr Shavkot Mirziyoyev) Virtual Summit, held on 11th December 2020
- India-Central Asia Summit (virtual) held on 27th January 2022
- Regular exchange of visits by the respective governments' Foreign Ministers to date
- Connect Central Asia Vision by the Indian Government to re-energise and expand the bilateral ties between India and all the five Central Asian Republics.

Current Scenario

Today, India is one of the key players in international politics. India has become a part of the economic chain, not just as a market but as a *factory of the world.* Contemporary India is living in a demographic dividend phase wherein initiatives like *Atmanirbhar Bharat, Young India, Make in India*, and others are employed to make India an influential nation globally. These initiatives elevate India's domestic position and make it a significant international player. Moreover, India's efforts to engage with Uzbekistan have been remarkable, reflected in their 30 years of partnership. India has cherished its age-old connections with Uzbekistan and has viewed it as a strategic partner in the region. The significant dimensions of this partnership include:

1. Military and Defense Cooperation:
   - To encourage bilateral engagements in the military field, '***Dustlik***' – a 1st ever joint military exercise was held in 2023 in Uttarakhand, India.

- Uzbekistan has set up an Indian Room at its Armed Forces Academy in Tashkent to mark and recognise its commitment to cordial relations with India.
- India is involved in the assistance in training and capacity building of Uzbek security agencies.

2. Trade and Investment:
    - There has been an increase in bilateral trade from 247 million USD in 2019-20 to 342 million USD in 2021-22, showing growth of 38.5 per cent
    - India and Uzbekistan are working on widening investment in pharmaceuticals, amusement parks, automobile parts, and hospitality.
    - To promote the Start-up ecosystem in Uzbekistan, Indian initiatives like ***icreate*** have been introduced to train entrepreneurs.
3. Education:
    - Bilateral initiatives of student exchange programmes
    - Opening of campuses of Amity University and Sharda University in Tashkent
4. Tourism:

- ***E-Visa*** facility extended by the Uzbekistan government to tourists from India.
- Medical tourism has been a flourishing dimension of the contemporary bilateral partnership between India and Uzbekistan. India is known for its medical facilities, and around 8,000 Uzbek nationals annually seek medical treatment in India.

5. Solar Energy:
    - Uzbekistan's interest in joining the International Solar Alliance has added to the contours of their bilateral relations.
    - India is also working on its participation in developing the solar power sector through competitive bidding in Uzbekistan.
6. Bilateral and Multilateral Initiatives:
    - To encourage continuous collaboration and administer the

implementation of mutually agreed projects and initiatives, India and Uzbekistan have set up a *National Coordination Committee.*

- A dialogue initiative, '***India-Central Asia Business Council***' has been constituted with a multilateral feature where Business Councils of all five Central Asian Republics mutually work to take trade and investment initiatives forward and focus on energy, pharmaceuticals, automobile, Urban infrastructure, civil aviation, IT, etc.
- India has initiated a multilateral dialogue platform, '***India-Central Asia Dialogue***,' to enable avenues for emancipating the cooperation between India and five Central Asian Republics in politics, economy, digitalisation, culture, and human rights.

To encourage a suitable environment for mutually coordinated efforts for the betterment of the world health scenario, India upheld its vaccine diplomacy worldwide. Under the COVAX initiative, The Serum Institute of India delivered around 600,000 Covid-Shield doses to Uzbekistan. At the same time, Uzbekistan also provide 100 oxygen concentrators and 2000 injections of Remdesivir to India in 2021.

As a token of care and commitment to bilateral partnership, India sent Hydroxychloroquine (HCQ) and Paracetamol tablets to Uzbekistan, including other essential medicines to counter the impact of COVID-19 in the country. India also conducted E-ITEC programmes for capacity building of medical professionals of Uzbekistan during the COVID-19 pandemic. India gifted HCQ and Paracetamol tablets sought by Uzbekistan, along with the lifting of essential medicines to counter the grip of COVID-19. Besides, India also conducted e-ITEC programmes for the capacity building of medical professionals from Uzbekistan. 600,000 CovidSheild doses were delivered from the Serum Institute of India to Uzbekistan under the initiative of COVAX on 17th March 2021. Also, Uzbekistan provided 100 oxygen concentrators and 2000 injections of Remdesivir to India on 1st May 2021.

Convergence of interests between India and Uzbekistan

In the global sphere of affairs, all nations are interconnected and interdependent in one or the other way. That is where foreign policy and international relations play a crucial part. While dealing with each other, nations put forward the reflections of their national interests through foreign policies. Similarly, the bilateral relations between India and Uzbekistan depend on their respective foreign policies and national interests. The convergence of interests and approaches brings magnetism between two nations to engage with each other. Rajiv Sikri, a renowned foreign policy analyst of India, points out the foreign policy perspective on the lines of the primary 'four arcs': the Arc of prosperity, the Arc of energy, the Arc of instability, and the Arc of communication. Here, we apply the concept of arcs for drafting out the convergence of interests between India and Uzbekistan and the implications thereof.

Arc of Prosperity

India represents South Asia as an influential regional player and an essential link in the proportion of global trade. Moreover, India is expanding its economic aspirations beyond the conventional stakeholders. Uzbekistan, a young aspiring republic in Central Asia, aims to encourage its economic linkages with India and the subsequent region. India and Uzbekistan are part of a strategic region stretching from the Himalayas and the Pacific. Therefore, the convergence of economic aspirations is the result.

Arch of Energy

The Republic of Uzbekistan is at the crossroads of the Arc of Energy that begins from the Persian Gulf Region and passes through the Mediterranean and the Caspian Sea. Three-fourths of the world's oil and natural gas reserves are here. Thus, this region constitutes a strategic arena where major global powers' interests intersect. For India, Uzbekistan signifies a vital connection on the lines of this Arc regarding its growing energy dependence and search for bargaining stakeholders.

Arc of Instability

India aspires to a secure neighbourhood from all of its borders. This region's already complex traditional geopolitics, marked by energy geopolitics, created enormous tension and potential conflicts. Therefore, India's primary foreign policy objective is to stabilize its relations with major, regional and global powers, for which India aims to develop a strategic connection and consensus on strategic and security issues. Similarly, the region's countries are dealing with fundamentalist activists. Therefore, both nations are equally interested in encouraging a secure security apparatus in the area and beyond.

Arc of Communication

We are well versed with the outcomes of globalisation, where communication plays a crucial role in channelling information, resources, cultures, trade, etc. The Persian Gulf and Sea Lines Communications (SLOs) between Europe and Asia exist at the pivotal junction of the Arc of Communications wherein all nations near or remote stand affected. India and Uzbekistan are equally involved and influenced by it. India's objective of connecting Central Asia is essential for a specific foreign policy engagement with the Central Asian Republics. While Uzbekistan is a doubly landlocked country, it is immensely interested in growing its connectivity for building infrastructure and evolving a reliable communication system. This fact was evident in Uzbekistan's interest in joining the Indo-Iran Chabahar Port Project in Iran.

The convergence of interests thereof:

1. *Based on the Arc of Prosperity:* both nations are interested in growth by expanding bilateral economic engagements in trade and investment and diversification of elements of business beyond conventional areas.
2. *Based on the Arc of Energy:* both nations are involved in building reliable apparatus for encouraging cooperation in energy and related sectors, for instance, solar energy.
3. *Based on the Arc of Instability:* both nations are interested in eradicating Terrorism, Weapons of Mass Destruction (WMD), and Drug Trafficking. Both countries have shared commitment to non-violence and negotiation at various international forums like UNO.
4. *Based on the Arc of Communication:* both nations are interested in secure connectivity, developed infrastructure and peaceful trade, reflecting each other's foreign policy objectives. India needs economic involvement in Central Asia and aims to evolve its regional strategic presence and influence. For Uzbekistan, India can be a strategic partner in encouraging regional integration and cooperation.

India's presence in Central Asia will check regional power play and thus allow India to situate its foreign policy goals. The Central Asian Republics can simultaneously engage their economic, infrastructural, and energy interests. Rajiv Sikri points out, 'if India is to protect its vital national interests in Central Asia, it has to be on an equal footing with other major players like the US, Russia, and China'.

Future Ahead

India's geostrategic aspirations have altogether witnessed a revision over the years. India's future policies are directly linked with the global system, and India needs to survive the challenges and evolve a foreign policy that is robust and influential. Similarly, India's Vision for Central Asia also reflects its strategic interests and national goals. India's Private Sector can explore the possibilities by taking advantage of bilateral agreements and initiatives by implementing joint investment projects in multiple areas. Besides, India and Uzbekistan need to increase mutual trust by encouraging convergence between each other. As said, Uzbekistan is essential to India's Central Asia Policy. India's presence in Central Asia signifies a geostrategic check in the regional power play, thus enabling India to situate its foreign policy goals, and the Central Asian Republics can engage for their economic, infrastructural, and energy interests simultaneously. Rajiv Sikri points out, '*if India is to protect its vital national interests in Central Asia, it has to be on an equal footing with other major players like the US, Russia, and China.*' The scholars need to explore and research the relevance of both nations for each other, considering concerns like energy politics, cyber-crime, geopolitical challenges of the region and the role of regional players like Russia and China.

References

1. Krasnopolsky, P. (2022). *China, Russia and Central Asian Infrastructure*. Palgrave Macmillan: China
2. Ministry of External Affairs. (2022). *India-Uzbekistan Bilateral Brief - 2022*
3. Montgomery, D.W. (2022). *Central Asia: Contexts for Understanding*. The University of Pittsburgh Press: USA
4. Roy, M.S. (2005). India-Uzbekistan: Emerging Partnership, in Himalayan & Central Asian Studies. *Journal of Himalayan Research and Cultural Foundation*, ECOSOC: UNO. Vol. 9:1-2, pp. 98-128
5. Sayfullayev, B.D. (2022). Development of Bilateral Political Relations Between Uzbekistan and India. *International Journal of Novel Research in Advanced Studies (IJNRAS)*, Vol. 1:3, pp. 54-56.
6. Sikri, R. (2009). Challenges and Strategy: Rethinking *India's Foreign Policy*. SAGE: India

9

Navigating Geostrategic Frontiers: India-Uzbekistan Relations in the Contemporary Global Context

Ramanshi Dwivedi

In the twenty-first century, bilateral ties between India and Uzbekistan are seen as essential components of global collaboration. The two nations have strong socio-economic links that date back to the time when the Silk Road was first used for trade and commerce. This demonstrates the deep geo-cultural affinities that existed between the two nations, which are further reinforced now by common beliefs about security, stability in the region, culture and the economy. This potent coordination creates a positive foundation for India to carefully explore new opportunities in Central Asia. India and Uzbekistan have adopted a geostrategic enrichment approach that is reciprocal and involves a wide range of joint endeavours.

Tracing the Foundation

During the Soviet Union's leadership, Uzbekistan experienced a certain amount of isolation. However, India kept up its cordial relations with Uzbekistan, hosting representatives from Tashkent at the inaugural Asian Relations Conference in 1947. From then on, there were frequent bilateral exchanges between the two countries, encompassing everything from trade deals to joint declarations. The Joint Declaration of Principles of Relations was the outcome of Uzbekistan's President Islam Karimov's 1991 visit to India. Uzbekistan emerged as India's most active partner among the five Central Asian nations. President Karimov of Uzbekistan and then-Indian Prime Minister Manmohan Singh's subsequent trips increased a number of opportunities to expand cooperation. As a result, the Joint Declaration of Strategic Partnership was signed in 2011. Bilateral ties were reinforced after Narendra Modi became Indian Prime Minister. The goal of eradicating radicalism and extremism through defense advancements, improved funding, and the creation of commercially viable avenues for collaboration received unanimous attention. India-Uzbekistan partnership can be better understood by focusing on the conceptual ideas developed via ingrained political, economic, and cultural exchanges, which further indicate to the expanding cooperation between India and Uzbekistan, given the substantial convergence of interests.

Political Diplomacy

On April 7, 1987, the Consulate General of India was formally established in Tashkent. The Protocol on Diplomatic and Consular Matters was signed on March 18, 1992. High-level contacts between the two nations over the ensuing era included regular visits by the Prime Ministers of both nations, which persist to this day. When both nations integrated their capacity development efforts with the goal of enhancing security, the issue of security and regional stability began to gain speed. India and Uzbekistan have long shared views and goals, ranging from cross-border terrorism to religious fanaticism. This made it clear from the beginning that Uzbekistan is an important stabilizing partner for India in its efforts to reduce the violent unrest in Afghanistan, which has a detrimental effect on other Central Asian countries as well. In order to promote operational effectiveness in light of the growing unpredictability in Afghanistan, India decided to hold multiple bilateral security discussions. Over time, India hopes to strengthen its geopolitical position in the area in order to meet the evolving needs of its own national security.

Frequent political meetings between the Indian and Uzbek foreign ministries have resulted in mutually beneficial partnerships and productive dialogues. Shavkat Mirziyoyev visited India in 2018 following his resumption as President of Uzbekistan. During his tour, 17 agreements pertaining to space exploration, science, agriculture, and the military were inked (Mann, 2018). The Vibrant Gujarat Global Summit in 2019 resulted in an agreement that included provisions for a long-term supply of uranium ores, boosting India's energy resources and providing a new impetus in the bilateral relationship.

Cultural Convergence

The Indian Cultural Centre, sponsored by the Indian Council for Cultural Relations, opened in Tashkent in 1995. It was established to foster cultural diversity and boost bilateral collaboration between India and Uzbekistan. As a proactive member of the Indian Technical and Economic Cooperation (ITEC), Uzbekistan has included training in fields such as languages, information technology, remote sensing, management, and education based on humanitarian principles. Agreements were struck to attain consensus in the domains of art, music, culture, tourism, and mass media, ensuring that both countries' citizens benefit equally and mutually. In the past, Indian painting masters have routinely attended cultural gatherings known as "Sharq taronalari" in Samarkand. Music, literature, and movies have been exchanged on a continual basis, followed by sports competitions that have extended the perspectives of both India and Uzbekistan, allowing them to culturally mature and generate additional peace and tranquility. In 2019, the inaugural India-Uzbekistan International Congress of Guides was held. It determined the influx of tourists from India to Uzbekistan while also tracking the flow of human resources into the country. This program strengthened bilateral cultural relations between the two countries by highlighting and promoting diverse historical heritages and strong cultural standards. Thus, India and Uzbekistan strive to strengthen their ancient cultural linkages through contemporary visions and agreements, productive talks, and policy execution.

Economic Horizons

India and Uzbekistan's economic ties are managed by a bilateral trade and commerce agreement dating back to 1993. This agreement aims to produce reciprocal benefits through methods such as Most Favoured Nation (MFN) treatment, scientific and technical collaboration, promotion of economic and industrial training, and the participation of small and medium-sized businesses. The aforementioned prospect finally served as a source of diversity in the two countries' bilateral economic relations. Bilateral trade between the two countries, on the other hand, was hampered due to issue of geographical inaccessibility. However, trade practices began to gain traction over the last two decades, accelerating through a balanced import-export cycle. Though trade was heavily lopsided in favour of Uzbekistan, India's foreign commerce expanded following economic liberalization. However, certain trade barriers remain, revealing the absence of a long-standing plan to increase financial power. Limitations include a lack of geographical affinity, making it difficult to direct resources between the two countries. This impedes transit and hence reduces output. Despite these limitations, both countries have agreed to begin steady negotiations through a Preferential Trade Agreement – and to increase efficiency through the India-Uzbekistan Entrepreneurship Development Centre, which aims to cater to small-scale and private industries in order to promote bilateral economic activities. Through this conversation, Uzbekistan chose to take a major step toward economic liberalization and attracting foreign investment, particularly from Indian enterprises. This will also boost Indian markets with a multi-pronged strategy to reinforcement. Uzbekistan is a significant cotton grower (and exports raw cotton), has piqued the interest of Indian textile industries, as well as the pharmaceutical industry. It is worth noting that Uzbekistan is looking for new ways to realign its market economy, as well as peaceful, reciprocal relationships. Uzbekistan's petrochemical sector appeals to Indian investors and transit lines with easy cargo patrol imply smooth economic activity. This provides another motive for India to strengthen its presence in Central Asia. Furthermore, Uzbekistan established various Free Trade Zones (FTZ), and it is expected that through bilateral talks, profit margins from specific nations can be repatriated (Ishapani, 1989).

Strategic Frontiers: Central Asia's Crucial Role in India's Foreign Policy

Central Asia has an important place in Prime Minister Narendra Modi's foreign policy. India intends to explore new avenues of interaction. The India-Central Asian Dialogue was conducted on January 13, 2019 in Samarkand. It involved the establishment of strong economic and cultural ties in order to investigate ways to improve connection between Central Asian Republics and India. To highlight multilateralism, India was included in the Ashgabat Agreement, which established a transit corridor and made it easier to transport products and services between the two countries. India, on the other hand, involved

Uzbekistan in the development of Iran's Chabahar Port, which helped Uzbekistan in part because it gave convenient access to a seaport. It also enabled India to transport its oil purchases and connect Central Asia, Eurasia, and Afghanistan. The International North-South Transport Corridor (INSTC) for smooth connectivity intends to boost efforts in science and technology, medicine, and education, sports, and tourism through investments, innovations, and communication channels. This has also been viewed as a multimodal transit corridor connecting the Indian Ocean, Persian Gulf, and Caspian Sea. According to the leaders participating, this will help to avoid confrontation and conflicts of interest among the world's major nations. The sector of pharmacy also experienced significant growth and reciprocal benefits for both countries. Joint ventures such as "Novafarm", "Ultra Health Care", "Bravo Pharm", and others allowed Uzbekistan to rely on the Indian pharmaceutical sector while also allowing India to establish marketable chains throughout the Central Asian region (India-Uzbekistan Relations, 2019). Uzbekistan is even mentioned as Central Asia's major military force, India signed three Memorandums of Understanding (MoUs) to improve military training and defense cooperation. This has resulted in the launch of a combined military exercise called "Dustlik 2019" aimed at combating cross-border terrorist activity. It was presided over by Indian Defence Minister Mr. Rajnath Singh of India and General Bakhodir Kurbanov of Uzbekistan.

India considers Uzbekistan as a critical gateway to Central Asia due to key factors such as, Uzbekistan's strategic location distinguishes it from other Central Asian Republics. Uzbekistan's connectivity with India through a transport corridor via Afghanistan can promote smooth trade relations. Additionally, Uzbekistan's vast energy resources will assist India in meeting rising energy demands. Uzbekistan is the only state that shares borders with all four Central Asian countries as well as Afghanistan. These arguments demonstrate that Uzbekistan has become India's crucial partner and a gateway to Central Asia. This interaction was not harmed by the present global pandemic. India did not forget its staunch friend; it sent hydroxychloroquine medications and even rescued trapped Indians from Uzbekistan. Though the socioeconomic sector has been severely impacted by the crisis, diplomats and frontline workers from both nations are working collaboratively to ensure a speedy recovery; the death toll in Uzbekistan has been fairly low. Despite

India's vulnerability in terms of Coronavirus cases, New Delhi maintained to provide a consistent supply of necessary medicines to Uzbekistan's most vulnerable parts. This gesture has strengthened trust and confidence between the two countries.

Forging a Path Forward

The relationship between India and Uzbekistan has progressed significantly. Both countries are seeking to strengthen their partnership through prospective development projects. India sees Uzbekistan as a critical ally in establishing solid relations with Central Asian Republics, given its geopolitical strategic importance. Uzbekistan maintains cordial and progressive political, economic, and cultural relations with India. From nuclear collaboration to institutional economic reforms, both countries have increased their growth and prosperity in the past, prompting India to offer a concessional line of credit to support infrastructure projects in Uzbekistan, as well as initiatives to strengthen the diaspora. In order to achieve the modern-day notion of power maximization and strategic autonomy, which is a critical goal for India, it is envisaged that India-Uzbekistan relations will establish a new standard in the worldwide realm of bilateral interactions through realistic discussions. The aforementioned elements demonstrate a stable foundation of cooperation between India and Uzbekistan, which is equally important for Central Asia and is heavily dependent on transparency and accountability. Looking ahead, the future holds promising opportunities for enhanced bilateral interactions, paving the way for mutual prosperity and stability in the region.

References

Embassy of India in Uzbekistan. (2023). Bilateral Agreements between India and Uzbekistan. Tashkent: Embassy of India.

Gupta, S. (2016). India's Strategic Interests in Central Asia: Focus on Uzbekistan. *Central Asian Affairs*, 3(2), 189-204.

Indian Council for Cultural Relations. (1995). Annual Report: Activities in Uzbekistan. New Delhi: Indian Council for Cultural Relations.

India-Uzbekistan Relations, *Embassy of India.*

Karimov, I. (1991). Joint Declaration of Principles of Relations between the Republic of Uzbekistan and the Republic of India. New Delhi: Ministry of External Affairs, Government of India.

Kumar, A. (2020). India-Uzbekistan Relations: Challenges and Opportunities. *Central Asian Survey*, 39(4), 543-561.

Mann, K. (2018). India-Uzbekistan Relations: A Comprehensive Analysis. *International Journal of Political Science and Diplomacy,* 3(2), 65-78.

Mirziyoyev, S. (2018). Speech at the Joint Press Briefing with Indian Prime Minister Narendra Modi. Tashkent: Government of Uzbekistan Press Office.

Santhanam, Krishnan, & Dwivedi, Ramakant. (2004). India and Central Asia: Advancing the Common Interest. New Delhi: *Institute for Defence Studies and Analyses.*

Singh, R. P. (2017). Dynamics of India's Engagement with Central Asia: A Case Study of Uzbekistan. *Strategic Analysis,* 41(5), 447-460.

10

India: A View from Central Asia

Amb A. Khaydarov

ABSTRACT

The purpose of this study is to analyse India's contribution to the development of world civilisation. The author focuses on the main spheres to which Indian scientists of antiquity made a significant contribution, which served as one of the foundations for the development of modern human civilisation. In particular, the achievements of ancient India in the field of astronomy, medicine, mathematics, philosophy and other sciences are shown. At the same time, the modern achievements of India since the declaration of independence and the adoption of the Constitution in 1950 are reflected. The current foreign policy of India, bilateral Uzbek-Indian relations, problems of connectivity of Central and South Asia, as well as the place and role of India in world politics and economy are revealed. The work is based on the study of historical material, chronicles of events of the last decade and the author's personal observations. The author concludes that the basis of India's successes is the Constitution, which created a legal framework for the processes of democratisation and economic development.

Keywords: *Science, civilisation, medicine, mathematics, astronomy, foreign policy, diplomacy, cooperation, Constitution.*

Indian civilisation is one of the oldest civilisations in the world, India has a long history and is home to brilliant philosophers and modern scientists who have made significant contributions to world scientific knowledge and culture. These contributions include numerous ideas and methods developed by the ancient Indians that have served as a starting point and helped to create and strengthen the foundations of many areas of modern science and technology. Touching upon this subject, one cannot but quote the words of the great American writer Mark Twain, who, assessing India's contribution to world civilisation, noted very succinctly: "India is the cradle of the human race, the birthplace of human speech, the mother of history, the grandmother of legends and the great great grandmother of traditions. Our most valuable and most instructive materials in the history of man are treasured up only in India."[1]

The contribution of ancient Indian mathematicians is invaluable. The Indians invented zero and the number system, one of the greatest innovations in history. The decimal system, the value of pi, algebra, trigonometry, calculus and many mathematical concepts were born in India. The largest number Greeks and Romans used was 10 to the power of 6; well before 5000 B.C., Indians used numbers as big as 10 to the power of 53.[2] The concepts of zero, the number system and decimalisation are fundamental to modern mathematics.

The contribution of Indian healers to medicine is undeniable. As early as 5000 BC, India developed a comprehensive healing methodology called Ayurveda. Ayurvedic healing methods have been documented in books and have been used by many generations of Indians and are still practised today. The origins of modern cosmetic surgery also go back centuries and its origins date back more than 2500 years. During the sixth century BC, an Indian sage known as Sushruta – the "father of surgery" – documented more than 1,100 diseases, catalogued the use of various medical herbs, and wrote directives for performing surgical procedures including rhinoplasty and skin grafts.[3]

Indian ancient thinkers made a significant contribution to the development of astronomy as a science. Today, the world knows the names of ancient Indian astronomers like Aryabhatta (476-550), Varahamichira (505-587 AD), Brahmagupta (598-668 AD), Bhaskara-1 (600-680 AD), and Bhaskara-2 (1114-1185). These ancient scholars developed the fundamental principles of astronomy, including the centric concept of the Earth's rotation around the Sun, predicted lunar and solar eclipses, and the movements of the planets. Their sophisticated astronomical theories were adopted by Greek and Arab astronomers. These principles are fundamental in nature and form an important step in the advancement of astronomy and contribute to our understanding of the modern Astronomy and the methods of Celestial Mechanics that are used in the space Programme.[4]

The creations of the ancient Indian architects, who created the most beautiful structures, cannot be ignored. These structures and sculptures have their own history, from the ancient Indus Valley civilisation to the present day. The growth of Indian architecture and art reflects the rise and fall of large empires, the invasion of foreign rulers who gradually became indigenous, the fusion of many cultures and styles, and so on.[5] The beginning of Indian architecture dates back to the advent of Buddhism in India. It was during this period that a large number of magnificent buildings came into existence. Some of the highlights of Buddhist art and architecture are the Great Stupa at Sanchi and the rock-cut caves at Ajanta.[6] The magnificent temple complex at Khajuraho in central India is particularly beautiful. The methods and styles of construction of large structures by ancient Indian architects and engineers have influenced the development of modern architecture.

During the medieval period, after the invasion of muslim rulers, a new architectural style developed in India, Indo-Islamic architecture of which the medieval period architecture can be divided into two main categories, such as the imperial style and the Mughal architecture.[7] The Taj Mahal is undoubtedly the most famous and greatest achievement in Mughal architecture. A little later, as a result of the colonisation of India, another style of architecture developed, which was called Indo-Saracenic.[8] It combines features of Hinduism, Islam and Western elements.

The contribution of Indian sages and rulers to the development of ancient Indian political thought and diplomacy is particularly noteworthy. Among the most significant and well-known ancient Indian sources, the Manu Smriti (the Code of Sacred Writings or the Laws of Manu) stands out as a treasure trove of information on the social, judicial and political life of that period.[9] The collection of Manu's laws was compiled by the priests of one of the Brahmanical schools around the 2nd century B.C. and had a significant impact on the development of political thought and issues of state administration in ancient India.[10] These laws also directly addressed issues of interstate relations, as well as the functions and privileges of ambassadors. In particular, the laws of Manu spoke of the sanctity and inviolability of ambassadors. They laid down useful rules of behaviour to be observed towards them.

Another major Indian thinker who left a significant mark in the history of Indian and world diplomacy is a legendary Indian Brahman named Kautilya, who compiled the ancient Indian political and economic treatise Arthashastra. It contains valuable information on the state, political and economic structure of ancient India. According to Kautilya's views, practicality was to be the basic principle of foreign policy.[11] This treatise is an outstanding monument of political, diplomatic, economic, legal and philosophical thought of ancient India.

In turn, ancient Indian philosophy had a profound influence on the development of modern thought, especially in the field of ethics, morality and spirituality, which formed the basis for the views of Mahatma Gandhi, one of the greatest political and spiritual leaders of the 20th century and the founder of independent India.

India has made tremendous progress in its socio-economic and political development, becoming one of the most influential members of the world community since independence. Today India plays an important role in the world politics and economy due to a number of objective factors. Firstly, there is the favourable demographic growth that keeps India at the first place in the world in terms of population. The Indian economy is also one of the largest, ranking fifth in terms of gross domestic product and third in the world in terms of purchasing power parity gross domestic product (PPP GDP).

The tangible advances in India's economic development over the past decade are attributed to the election of Narendra Modi as Prime Minister in 2014, who has been pursuing a policy of economic modernisation aimed at improving the nation's well-being and prosperity. This policy has been informally labelled as 'modinomics' in several countries. New Delhi's technological capabilities, especially in the field of computer programmes, are also undeniable.

The country has emerged as an important player in the global technology industry, with a flourishing startup ecosystem, a thriving IT sector and a growing bias towards digital connectivity. The government's Digital India initiative[12] aims to harness technology for inclusive growth, transforming the landscape of governance and public service delivery. India continues its successful growth and development of software and IT services.[13] The country is home to a vibrant IT industry with companies such as Tata Consultancy Services (TCS), Infosys and Wipro making a global impact. India has also become a centre for tech outsourcing due to its large pool of skilled IT professionals and engineers.

India's significant achievements are noteworthy in the field of space technology. The Indian Space Research Organisation (ISRO) has achieved significant results, including the successful Chandrayaan and Mangalyaan missions to explore the Moon and Mars, respectively. These missions have demonstrated India's capabilities in space exploration and its commitment to technological innovation in aerospace.[14]

In the health sector, India is using technology to increase access to health services and improve the delivery of health care. Telemedicine and e-health have found widespread use, especially in rural and remote areas, allowing patients to consult health professionals and receive medical advice from a distance. India has also pioneered the development of affordable medical technologies and pharmaceuticals, serving both domestic and international markets.

India's commitment to sustainable development and environmental protection has gained prominence both nationally and internationally. The country has made commitments towards renewable energy, combating climate change and sustainable urban development. With initiatives such as the International Solar Alliance[15] and efforts to increase forest cover, India has endeavoured to balance industrial growth with environmental conservation. Today, the Indian government's efforts are focused on further developing the country's economic potential, with an emphasis on areas such as electronics, semiconductors and green energy.

India's foreign policy has also undergone significant changes, with a growing bias towards participation in strategic alliances, economic diplomacy and global leadership. The country's participation in international forums such as the G20, BRICS, SCO, engagement with neighbouring countries and involvement in global initiatives have shaped the contours of its foreign policy. India's quest for a permanent seat in the UN Security Council and aspirations for a greater role in world governance underline its ambitions as a leading global player.[16] As India steps into the future, the mutual interplay of socio-economic progress, technological innovation, political evolution and global engagement will continue to shape its development. India's commitment to technological advancement, coupled with its rich history of innovation, creates a promising future as a leading technological power.

India's markedly increased economic potential and its active involvement in the global economic and political world order have led to the formation of new strategic interests that encompass the Central Asian region as well. The India-Central Asia dialogue, established in January 2019 in Samarkand at the meeting of the Foreign Ministers of Central Asia and India, aimed at expanding friendly and mutually beneficial relations between the two in bilateral and multilateral formats. This has been successfully developing. The ongoing dialogue between the two regions represents a renewed focus on enhancing cooperation in various spheres to promote meaningful cooperative partnerships and strengthen regional stability.

India, through its "Connect Central Asia" policy,[17] has emphasised its desire to strengthen relations with the Central Asian region. This is particularly important in light of the evolving dynamics of international relations and the increasing role of Central Asia in world affairs. The region's rich energy resources, its strategic location and importance for initiatives such as the International North-South Transport Corridor (INSTC),[18] make it a key partner for India. Similarly, Central Asian countries are keen to diversify their international partnerships and see India as a potential ally for economic cooperation and strategic engagement.

From an economic perspective, the India-Central Asia dialogue offers many opportunities for multilateral cooperation. Trade linkages, infrastructure development and energy cooperation are key areas where both regions can benefit from deeper engagement. The development of transport corridors, including roads, railways and air routes, is critical to ensuring efficient trade and people-to-people exchanges. Efforts to simplify trade rules and strengthen financial cooperation can also enhance economic cooperation between the two regions.

Constructive nature is inherent in the current bilateral Uzbek-Indian relations. The development of these relations is facilitated by the proximity or coincidence of our positions on the most important problems of international relations and regional security issues, in particular on combating international terrorism, countering illicit trafficking in narcotic drugs, as well as the commitment of the States in reducing and eliminating weapons of mass destruction. The parties continue to focus on the difficult situation in Afghanistan, preventing the humanitarian crisis from worsening and promoting the peace process in the country. Uzbekistan views India as one of the leading partners in the region and the world.

A powerful impetus to the development of bilateral relations was given by the summit meetings between President of Uzbekistan Sh. M. Mirziyoyev and Prime Minister of India N. Modi in September-October 2018 and January 2019. President Shavkat Mirziyoyev's participation in the first India-Central Asia summit in January 2022 in the videoconference format made a significant contribution to the development of bilateral relations. This summit considered strategic priorities and concrete proposals to promote practical cooperation between India-Central Asia.

The two sides have achieved considerable success in trade and economic, scientific, technical and humanitarian cooperation. In recent years, the trade turnover between Uzbekistan and India has doubled, and the number of joint ventures has increased, reaching 400. Agreements have been reached on the implementation of 50 investment projects worth about $3 billion. Together with Indian partners, work has been completed on the construction of a technopark of advanced information technologies in Tashkent. Branches of India's leading higher education institutions – Amity University in Tashkent and Sharda University in Andijan – have been opened in the country. Major investment projects are being implemented.

As noted above, the lack of a direct land transport link between India and Central Asia remains a major constraint to the dynamic development of our economic relations. In this regard, the development of a new corridor through the Chabahar port could become a key link in the framework of the North-South International Transport Corridor project. All this suggests that both sides are interested in further development of long-term partnership, utilisation of untapped potential, expansion of cooperation in political, economic, investment, cultural and humanitarian spheres.

In general, contemporary bilateral Uzbek-Indian relations are a dynamic and multifaceted partnership covering political, economic, cultural, humanitarian and strategic aspects. The depth of their interaction reflects the common aspirations of both states for prosperity, stability and cooperation. Further deepening of existing ties and exploring new avenues of cooperation will contribute to regional harmony and global progress.

This fruitful cooperation of India at the bilateral level and generally within international structures has been made possible by India's commitment to international peace and security, support for just and respectful relations between States and respect for international law as enshrined in the fundamental law of the land.

The Constitution of India was drafted with the participation of various social, cultural and political groups in the country, which is reflected in its democratic and pluralistic character.[19] It also reflects the principle of secularism.[20] The Constitution of India also contains the principles of social justice and equality to addness social and economic inequalities. It guarantees the rights of children, women, and the right to education and environmental protection.

In addition, the Indian Constitution also contains mechanisms to protect the fundamental rights and freedoms of citizens, including the rights to freedom of speech, freedom of assembly and association, the right to religious belief and the free exercise of cultural and linguistic identity. It also places special emphasis on the protection of the rights of minorities and vulnerable segments of society. The Constitution, adopted in the middle of the last century at a time of national liberation and political independence, embodies the unique spirit of pluralism and tolerance forged by India's long history and inherent in the multi-ethnic and multi-religious society of this fascinating country.

Thus, the Constitution of India serves not only as the foundation of the country's legal system but also reflects the rich diversity of India's cultural, religious and social traditions. As a fundamental document, the Constitution of India continues to play a pivotal role in shaping and protecting democratic values and principles, in creating a just and inclusive society, contributing to India's stable and peaceful development. The Constitution has ensured the rule of law in the country for the past more than 70 years, which has led to the successful development of the largest democracy in the world, ensuring the preservation and continuity of the achievements of many generations of the Indian people.

The enactment of the fundamental law of the country and the proclamation of the Republic of India on 26 January 1950 marked the beginning of a new era in the history of one of the world's earliest civilisations.

End Notes

1 Idia's contribution to the world. https://shreegauranga.org/indias-contribution-to-the-world/

2 How ancient India laid modern society's foundation. Tejraj M. Aminabhavi. January 22, 2014. https://asia.nikkei.com/Business/Science/How-ancient-India-laid-modern-society-s-foundation

3 History of medicine in ancient India. Keerthana Kalla. Seattle, Washington, United States. https://hekint.org/2021/08/27/history-of-medicine-in-ancient-india/

4 Q.3437: Contribution of ancient astronomers. https://idsa.in/resources/parliament/q3437Contributionofancientastronomers

5 Gopakumar Nair. The ancient architecture of India. https://medium.com/@gopakumarnair/the-ancient-architecture-of-india-94e2f025e09

6 Ibid.

7 Ibid.

8 Gopakumar Nair. The ancient architecture of India. https://medium.com/@gopakumarnair/the-ancient-architecture-of-india-94e2f025e09

9 Dr Mousumi Das. Political Thoughts of Manu. http://www.rbu.ac.in/home/avz9s6ve0gq6/public_html/ckfinder/userfiles/files/MousumiDas_BA6-DSE6_1_09062020.pdf

10 Ancient Indian political thought. https://tripurauniv.ac.in/Content/pdf/StudyMaterialsDetail/MA%20Political%20Science%201st%20Semester/POLS-701C-Ancient%20Indian%20Political%20Thought.pdf

11 Aabid Majeed Sheikh1, Saima Rashid. Kautilya, the Indian Machiavelli; On War and diplomacy in Ancient India. https://papers.ssrn.com/sol3/papers.cfm?abstract_id=3648416

12 Digital India A programme to transform India into a digitally empowered society and knowledge economy https://www.meity.gov.in/sites/upload_files/dit/files/Digital%20India.pdf

13 Building capabilities in the software service industry in India: Skill formation and learning of domestic enterprises in value chains https://www.ilo.org/wcmsp5/groups/public/--dgreports/--inst/documents/publication/wcms_315673.pdf

14 India's space triumph. https://www.aspistrategist.org.au/indias-space-triumph/

15 https://isolaralliance.org/work/scaling-solar-application-agricultural-use

16 A seat for India at the world's most powerful table: What Biden's backing means. https://economictimes.indiatimes.com/news/india/a-seat-for-india-at-the-worlds-most-powerful-table-what-bidens-backing-means/articleshow/103530389.cms?from=mdr

17 Connect Central Asia Policy. https://www.drishtiias.com/Paper2/connect-central-asia-policy

18 India's Export Opportunities Along the International North South Transport Corridor. https://www.india-briefing.com/news/indias-export-opportunities-along-the-international-north-south-transport-corridor-22412.html/

19 The Constitution of India: Symbol of Unity in Diversity. Mahendra P Singh and Surya Deva. (2005) 53 Jahrbuch des Offentlichen Rechts der Gegenwart [Yearbook of Public Law, Germany] 649-686 file:///C:/Users/Asus%20VivoBook/Downloads/SSRN-id897021.pdf

20 Secularism and the Law. National Foundation for Communal Harmony New Delhi August 2010. https://nfch.nic.in/Home/PDF?filename=E-Books%2FSecularism.pdf

11

Uzbekistan and India: A New Stage of Historical and Friendly Relations

Amb Dilshod Akhatov and Sadriddin Suyarov

This year Uzbekistan celebrates the 33rd anniversary of its independence. There is no doubt that during these years Uzbekistan has made historic efforts to build a new state and society, and achieved high milestones thanks to the resolute will of the Uzbek people and the country's enormous potential.

Uzbekistan is now a full-fledged member of the international community, takes an active part in the activities of the United Nations and other leading international organisations, and maintains multifaceted partnerships with foreign countries.

The country's international co-operation has become even more dynamic since Shavkat Mirziyoyev was elected President of Uzbekistan in 2016. In the Action Strategy of Uzbekistan for 2017-2021, he identified the implementation of a balanced, mutually beneficial and constructive foreign policy as one of the most important tasks, and in the Development Strategy "Uzbekistan 2030" – the pursuit of an open, pragmatic and active foreign policy.

On this basis, today the key indicators of the new Uzbekistan are its openness to the world, the breadth of its foreign relations and giving them proper depth. In this regard, an important direction of Tashkent's foreign policy and foreign economic course is to build up interaction with the states of South Asia, especially India.

It should be emphasised that today India has a powerful economic, scientific, technological and military potential and is in the process of transition to the status of a global power. Given India's position and role in the global economy and politics, building sustainable strategic, diplomatic and economic ties with it is in Uzbekistan's national interests, giving a practical shape of the Uzbek-Indian strategic partnership.

Historical roots of interconnectedness, diplomatic relations and strategic partnerships

The friendly relations between the Uzbek and Indian peoples go back centuries. Uzbekistan, like India, is the cradle of ancient civilisations. Back in the eleventh century, the great Uzbek thinker and encyclopaedic scholar Abu Rayhon Beruni, whose 1,050th birthday anniversary was widely celebrated internationally last year, visited and lived in India, studied the history, culture and science of the Indian people and dedicated to it one of his famous works, "India" (Kitab ul-Hind), which contains information on Indian philosophy, history, science, geography, ethnic composition of the population, their customs, castes and religious beliefs.

The great poet and statesman Zahiriddin Muhammad Babur in the 16th century in his book "Babur-name" rediscovered the mysterious India to the whole world, and for the Indian people – the beauty of the Uzbek land. Babur also quoted poetic lines of Khusrav Dehlavi in his work "Mukhtasar or Risolai Aruz" ("Treatise on Aruz").

There is another remarkable page in the history of the interconnectedness of the Uzbek and Indian peoples. According to historical records, in 1433, the sovereign of the empire created by Amir Temur, his son Shokhrukh Mirzo sent ambassadors under the leadership of Khoja Abulmakoim to the Delhi Sultanate to establish good neighbourly relations with it. In response, Muhammad Shah IV sent his ambassadors to Samarkand in 1437. These and other sources state that both countries have always sought regional stability, as they do today. The dynasty that founded a great empire in India for more than 300 years has gone down in history as the Baburids. Thanks to the peace established here, material and cultural life developed and unique monuments and values were created. Political, economic, cultural ties and co-operation between the Uzbek and Indian peoples were widely developed.

Thus, Uzbekistan-India relations can be described as a natural partnership between two ancient civilisations linked by ancient trade and cultural ties.

Since Uzbekistan's independence, the comprehensive exchange between the two countries has been filled with new content, and their interrelationship has embarked on a path of consistent and dynamic development. It is important to note that on 26 December 1991, India was among the first countries to recognise Uzbekistan's independence. Diplomatic relations between the two States were established on 18 March 1992, when a Protocol on the Establishment of Diplomatic Relations was signed in Tashkent.

In September 1992, the Consulate of Uzbekistan started functioning in New Delhi, which was transformed into an Embassy in 1994. The Consulate General of India had been operating in Tashkent since August 1988, which was also transformed into an Embassy in 1992. In 2022, Uzbekistan and India widely celebrated the 30th anniversary of the establishment of diplomatic relations.

It should be noted that from the very beginning after the establishment of diplomatic relations, co-operation between the two countries has been stable, consistent and mutually beneficial. In May 2011, Tashkent and New Delhi signed a Joint Declaration on Strategic Partnership. This has expanded the opportunities for enhancing co-operation in a wide range of areas, including all aspects of political, economic, cultural and humanitarian spheres.

Today, the development of long-term and mutually beneficial co-operation with India is one of the priorities of Uzbekistan's foreign policy. The two countries do not have any systemic problems and conflicts of interest. In general, their interests and approaches on regional and global issues coincide or are close.

New Delhi is building relations with Tashkent on the premise that Uzbekistan is the most dynamically developing and stable country not only in Central Asia but also in the entire post-Soviet space, consistently and confidently implementing reforms and having clear priorities in its foreign policy.

Rashmini Koparkar, associate professor at the Centre for Russian and Central Asian Studies at Jawaharlal Nehru University, notes that "reforms aimed at improving the system of state and social construction are contributing to the wide recognition and image of New Uzbekistan in the international arena."[1] Uzbekistan, being the most densely populated state in the region, has a fairly developed economic potential and infrastructure, skilled labour resources and huge reserves of natural resources. This has been noticed by New Delhi Bilateral ties were given a qualitatively new direction by the state visit of President of the Republic of Uzbekistan Shavkat Mirziyoyev to India from 30 September to 1 October 2018, during which 20 documents on cooperation in various spheres were signed. The participation of the leader of Uzbekistan in January 2019 in the global investment summit "Dynamic Gujarat" as the chief guest reaffirmed Tashkent's aspiration to comprehensively promote a broad and long-term strategic partnership with New Delhi.

The virtual summit between the President of Uzbekistan and the Prime Minister of India in December 2020 was another important milestone on this path. Following the summit, the leaders of the two countries adopted a Joint Statement on Close Friendship and Strong Partnership. Nine documents were also signed during the summit to expand cooperation in a number of priority areas.

It should be noted that President Shavkat Mirziyoyev and Prime Minister Narendra Modi also meet regularly at various international and regional events. In particular, the two leaders held talks during Prime Minister Narendra Modi's visit to Samarkand in September 2022 to attend the SCO summit. The two sides discussed issues of further deepening mutually beneficial co-operation and expanding the scope of strategic partnership relations. The leaders noted the growth in bilateral trade. Investment projects in information technologies, healthcare, pharmaceuticals, agriculture and tourism are being successfully implemented. They noted the necessity of early adoption and implementation of cooperation programmes in trade and economic, investment, scientific and educational spheres, as well as the agreement on promotion and mutual protection of investments. The leaders paid special attention to strengthening partnership relations between the regions of the two countries.[2]

An important platform for active interaction between Uzbekistan and India is the India-Central Asia dialogue platform. This mechanism in the format of regular meetings at the level of foreign ministers was launched in

2019 at the joint initiative of Tashkent and New Delhi. As part of this dialogue, the India-Central Asia Business Council was established in February 2020.

India considers Central Asia to be in its *"extended neighbourhood"*,[3] sees it as a strategically significant region, rich in energy resources and an important transport and transit hub for access to the vast Eurasian space, as well as a promising political, trade and economic partner.

In this regard, to further advance engagement with our region, New Delhi has initiated raising this dialogue mechanism to the level of a leaders' summit in 2021. The first India-Central Asia online Summit held in January 2022 which opened another important page in the relations between our two countries.

In his speech at this summit, the President of Uzbekistan noted important areas of cooperation as development of human capital through active interaction in education and health care on the basis of broad introduction of India's best practices, knowledge and technologies; deepening economic partnership; cooperation in cultural and humanitarian sphere.[4]

In this context, Indian expert Meena Singh Roy, praising Uzbekistan's consistent reforms, notes that for the country, advanced education and knowledge are the basis for the development of society and the prevention of modern threats, which is also important for Central Asian partners interested in the sustainable development of the region.[5]

Uzbekistan has actively supported India's accession to the SCO, interaction within the framework of which is becoming an important part of bilateral political dialogue. Both countries are also using this platform to expand their cooperation in trade, investment, transport, security and cultural exchanges. As Dr Pravesh Kumar Gupta, a leading researcher at the Vivekananda International Foundation think tank, states, "for India and Uzbekistan, the SCO is the most important forum for strengthening bilateral relations, regional stability and economic cooperation."[6]

Uzbekistan has consistently supported India's candidature for permanent membership of the UN Security Council. In this regard, it is worth noting the parties' principled position in countering such threats and challenges as terrorism and extremism, drug trafficking and other cross-border crimes that directly affect regional and international security and sustainable development.

"India and Uzbekistan support multilateralism in addressing global and regional challenges and promote mutually beneficial cooperation based on dialogue, mutual trust and respect. India supports President Shavkat Mirziyoyev's initiative adopted by the UN General Assembly to strengthen international cooperation in tourism, regional interaction, interfaith harmony and sustainable development," Sanjay Kumar Pandey, Professor at the Centre for Russian and Central Asian Studies, Jawaharlal Nehru University, stresses.[7]

Since 2020, cooperation between think tanks of Uzbekistan and India has become institutionalised. The 3rd Forum of Think Tanks was held in January 2022.

Economic Co-operation

Uzbekistan and India have a huge untapped potential to further strengthen bilateral cooperation in trade, investment, technology.

In recent years, we have witnessed a significant intensification of bilateral economic cooperation. The establishment of the Uzbek-Indian Centre for Entrepreneurship Development in 2018 on the basis of the Chamber of Commerce and Industry of Uzbekistan, which also opened an "IT laboratory" in 2021, and the Uzbek-Indian Business Council together with the Confederation of Indian Industry – all this is aimed at ensuring intensive trade exchange and industrial cooperation between the business communities of both countries.

In 2023, trade turnover between Uzbekistan and India reached about $760 million. But this does not reflect the existing potential of mutual trade. Therefore, the leaders of the two countries have set a goal to raise the level of bilateral trade to $1 billion over the next few years.

It should be noted that over the past 6-7 years, the parties have achieved tangible results in expanding investment cooperation. The interest of Indian investors in Uzbekistan is growing. In particular, close co-operation has been established in such areas as pharmaceuticals, healthcare, higher education, development of tourism infrastructure, construction of modern residential and business complexes, production of automotive components, etc. The two sides have also established close co-operation. There are more than 420 enterprises with Indian capital in Uzbekistan, including 280 enterprises with 100 per cent Indian capital.

The Government of Uzbekistan creates favourable conditions and welcomes investments and modern technologies of Indian companies in the creation of production facilities in pharmaceuticals, textile, light, leather and jewellery industries, agriculture and many other sectors. Special attention is paid to the implementation of joint projects with Indian companies in Uzbekistan's free economic zones (FEZs), including the pharmaceutical cluster and pharmaceutical FEZs.

There are good prospects for co-operation in the energy transition, in particular on renewable energy, especially solar energy, energy efficiency systems and green hydrogen technologies.

Uzbekistan is interested in further deepening cooperation with India in the sphere of high technologies, which is one of the world leaders in IT technologies, occupying a dominant position in the global programming and IT outsourcing market. Promising areas of interaction include artificial intelligence, big data analytics, machine learning, photonics, blockchain, fintech, smart logistics.

In recent years, Indian technocrats have made a significant contribution to the development of Uzbekistan's IT sector. In 2019, the Joint Committee on Cooperation in Science and Technology was established. In the same year, the Tashkent IT Park was established with the assistance of the Software Technology Park of India.

Since 2018, Uzbek-Indian cooperation has been enriched with a new direction – direct interaction between regions and cities of the two countries. In particular, partnerships have already been established between Andijan and Gujarat, Ferghana and Haryana, as well as the historic cities of Samarkand and Agra.

Transport interconnectivity is an important area of strategic partnership between Uzbekistan and India. Cooperation in transport and logistics plays a significant role in promoting Uzbek-Indian relations. A radical improvement in transport and other infrastructure interconnectivity between the two countries, as well as between the regions of Central and South Asia, is necessary to ensure an increase in mutual trade, investment cooperation, tourism and cultural exchanges.

In this context, the leadership of Uzbekistan supported India's accession to the Ashgabat agreement (Uzbekistan-Turkmenistan-Iran-Oman transport corridor). Uzbekistan also supports New Delhi's efforts to develop Iran's Chabahar port, which is to become a key transit hub for India's trade with Afghanistan and other Central Asian states. The President of Uzbekistan approved the decision to join the North-South transport corridor.

There is significant potential for co-operation in civil aviation and air cargo transport. IndiGo Airlines has launched regular flights on the Delhi-Tashkent-Delhi route from September 2023. The airline's aircraft now fly between the two capitals four times a week. This has increased the mutual accessibility of the two countries for passengers and consequently promotes tourism and business contacts. Uzbekistan Airways aircraft traditionally fly on this route with a frequency of six times a week. On 2 April 2024, flights on the Tashkent-Mumbai-Tashkent route resumed twice a week. New Uzbek carriers are also expected to launch flights between Tashkent and various Indian cities in the near future.

Once upon a time, a caravan route called the Spice Route connected Indian lands with Central Asia. Today, there is an urgent need to create new reliable trade and transport links between the markets of Central and South Asia. In this sense, the participation of the two countries in promoting the interconnectivity of the Central and South Asian regions can become an important component of regional interaction between the two countries and a pledge to intensify bilateral and interregional trade and economic cooperation.

The high-level international conference "Central and South Asia: Regional Connectivity. Challenges and Opportunities", which was organized at the initiative of the President of Uzbekistan in Tashkent on 15-16 July 2021, demonstrated tremendous opportunities for deepening political dialogue, economic cooperation and people-to-people contacts between the two countries as well as neighbouring regions. The conference was attended by heads of state, foreign ministers and high representatives of Central and South Asia, other foreign countries, heads of international and regional organisations, global financial institutions and companies. India was represented by a high-level delegation led by Foreign Minister Dr Subrahmanyam Jaishankar.

The main objective of the conference was to strengthen the historically close and friendly ties, trust and good neighbourliness relations between the countries of Central and South Asia. At the inaugural session, President of the Republic of Uzbekistan Shavkat Mirziyoyev outlined 10 proposals aimed at opening up new opportunities for a fuller realisation of the trade, economic, cultural and civilizational potential of the countries of Central and South Asia.[8] All these proposals and initiatives aroused interest not only among the states of these regions, but also among the international community. In particular, the creation of new transport corridors linking Central Asia with the Indian Ocean was discussed.

Stanley Joni, an international columnist writes in Indian newspapers 'The Hindu', that President Shavkat Mirziyoyev is an advocate of consistent implementation of major projects of interconnectivity between Central and South Asia.[9]

Cultural and Humanitarian aspects of Bilateral Relations

A traditionally significant area of Uzbek-Indian relations is co-operation in culture, education, science and innovation, and healthcare. Cooperation in the cultural sphere is carried out within the framework of relevant intergovernmental cultural exchange programmes for the medium term. The current programme is for 2021-2025, which was signed during the visit of the Minister of State for Foreign Affairs and Culture, Ms. Meenakshi Lekhi, to Uzbekistan in September 2021. Possibilities of boosting cooperation in the cultural sphere were discussed during the visit of Dr Vinay Sahasrabuddhe, President of the Indian Council for Cultural Relations, to Uzbekistan in March 2021.

The Indian Cultural Centre in Tashkent celebrated its 25th anniversary in 2022. The India-Uzbekistan Friendship Society operates in New Delhi.

In 2023, popular Indian singer and music industry celebrity Shibani Kashyap toured concerts in a number of cities in Uzbekistan. "I believe that music creates a huge bond between two countries. When a representative of one country performs in front of music lovers of another country, it creates a favourable opportunity to strengthen mutual love. And when we receive such recognition, it serves to bring the two countries closer together. The situation becomes almost family-like. Moreover, there were several concerts where only local music lovers were sitting in the hall. They danced and sang my songs by heart. Not all of them understand Hindi, but they sang word for word. It was amazing," Shibani Kashyap shared her impressions after her creative trip to Uzbekistan.[10]

There are many such examples of the exchange of cultural traditions and wealth. In particular, every year the Tashkent International Film Festival "Pearl of the Silk Road" is attended by a representative Indian delegation, which includes well-known film-makers from the country. In December 2023, a delegation from Uzbekistan also took part in the 55th International Film Festival in Goa.

Uzbekistan participates on a permanent basis as a partner country in the world's largest crafts festival, the Surajkund Crafts Mela, which takes place in Haryana. Representatives of Uzbekistan showcase the rich and colourful handicrafts and cultural heritage and tourism potential of our country. Representatives of India are active participants in the International Folk and Applied Arts Festival in Kokand.

Cooperation in the field of higher education is very consistent. Uzbekistan's higher education institutions currently cooperate with more than 10 Indian universities, research institutes and centres. In 2018, branches of Indian universities Amity in Tashkent and Sharda in Andijan were opened. In December 2021, a branch of Sambhram Institute of Technology (Bangalore) started its activities in Jizzakh. In 2023, the "Acharya University of Uzbekistan", established jointly with the "Group of Acharya Institutes", opened in Bukhara province, which will train specialists in artificial intelligence, machine learning, data science, cybersecurity, etc. The university will also train specialists in artificial intelligence, machine learning, data science, and cyber security. At the same time, the number of Indian students studying in higher education institutions in Uzbekistan, especially in medical institutions, is increasing.

Uzbek language courses are currently being offered at Delhi's Jamia Millia Islamia and Jawaharlal Nehru Universities. The Centre for Uzbek Language, Literature and Culture was opened at Delhi University in November 2022.

The two sides are stepping up co-operation on the implementation of projects to set up multidisciplinary hospitals in Uzbekistan jointly with leading Indian clinics. Such projects have already been implemented with a number of Indian clinics, and work in this area continues.

Cooperation between Uzbekistan and India in the tourism sector is one of the priority areas, which is reaching a new level in the post-pandemic era. The majestic architectural monuments of Samarkand, Bukhara, Khiva and Shakhrisabz, inscribed on the UNESCO Cultural Heritage list, the picturesque nature and climate, and the hospitality of the Uzbek people are an integral part of the interests of Indians in modern Uzbekistan. There is an e-visa regime for tourists between the two countries. The year 2023 saw the highest number of travellers from India to Uzbekistan since the last three decades of cooperation.

Undoubtedly, cooperation between Uzbekistan and India has a huge potential and high opportunities due to the strong and solid foundations of bilateral relations – centuries-old friendship, mutual trust and understanding.

End Notes

1. Business Central Asia Magazine, September 2021, pp. 30-31, New Delhi, India.
2. Official website of the President of the Republic of Uzbekistan, 16 September 2022 (https://president.uz/ru/lists/view/5546).
3. Keynote address of Anil Wadhwa, Secretary (East), MEA, at the 6th IISS-MEA Dialogue on 'India's extended neighbourhood: Prospects and Challenges', March 04, 2014 (https://idsa.in/keyspeeches/6thIISSMEADialogue_secretaryeast).
   Distinguished Lecture by Ambassador Ashok Sajjanhar on "India-Central Asia Relations – The Emerging Partnership" at Central University of Punjab, Bathinda on 24th May, 2017 (https://mea.gov.in/distinguished-lectures-detail.htm?684).
4. Speech by the President of the Republic of Uzbekistan Sh. M. Mirziyoyev at the First India-Central Asia Summit, Official Website of the President of the Republic of Uzbekistan, 27 January 2022 (https://president.uz/ru/lists/view/4944).
5. Business Central Asia Magazine, September 2021, pp. 28-29, New Delhi, India.
6. Political events magazine, No. 26, 29 June 2023, pp. 38-39, New Delhi, India.
7. The Indian Express newspaper, 31 March 2022, p. 5, New Delhi, India.
8. Speech by President of the Republic of Uzbekistan Shavkat Mirziyoyev at the international conference "Central and South Asia: Regional Interconnectedness. Challenges and Opportunities", 16 July 2021 (https://president.uz/ru/lists/view/4484).
9. The Hindu newspaper, 11 May 2023, New Delhi, India (https://www.thehindu.com/news/international/uzbekistan-which-once-backed-anti-taliban-forces-is-now-betting-on-engagement/article66838019.ece).
10. Exclusive interview by Shibani Kashyap to The Sunday Guardian newspaper, 1 April 2023, New Delhi, India. (https://sundayguardianlive.com/culture/uzbekis-love-indian-culture-bollywood-shibani-kashyap).

12

India's Geopolitical and Geo-Economic Interests in the Central Asia and the SCO

Amb Ibrahim R. Mavlanov

ABSTRACT

The significant geopolitical changes taking place in Central Asia since the early 2000s, especially after 2016, and subsequently in the Shanghai Cooperation Organization (SCO) space, force us to take a fresh look at these regions, which are in the process of integration into the system of international relations and world economic relations in the conditions of modern transformation unpredictable processes of the beginning of the third decade of the present century. However, these processes did not always proceed smoothly; they were negatively affected by various factors. Under these conditions, the foreign policy interests of many countries in these regions quickly changed. In this regard, it was of great interest for us to explore issues concerning the trends in the development of India's foreign policy and foreign economic orientations and interests in the regions of Central Asia and the SCO. The work is based on the study of actual historical material, chronicles of the events of recent decades and personal observations of the author during the work on the materials of the region in the noted period. In the article, the author makes an attempt to analyze the process of formation of India's geopolitical and geo-economic interests in the Central Asia and the SCO. The author bases his research on the analysis of specific events in the international arena in recent years, related to the speeches and initiatives of the President of the Republic of Uzbekistan. The article analyzes the proposals of Prime Minister of India Narendra Modi at meetings of the Council of Heads of State of the SCO Member-States. The author builds his assessments on the basis of studies of official documents of the SCO and materials of the consultative meetings of the heads of states of Central Asia. Through the prism of analyzing the speeches of Indian officials, statesmen, experts, journalists of this country, the author tries to explore and understand the main aspirations of India in the region of Central Asia and the SCO. The article proves that modern developing India has geopolitical and geo-economic interests in the Central Asia region and the SCO.

Keywords: *Central Asia, Shanghai Cooperation Organization, Shavkat Mirziyoyev, Narendra Modi, Afghanistan, China, Kazakhstan, Kyrgyzstan, Tajikistan, Turkmenistan, Uzbekistan, Transport Corridors, International Trade.*

Introduction

The modern interconnected and interdependent world of the twenty-first century is undoubtedly full of all economic opportunities. But, at the same time, it also faces geopolitical difficulties and economic security problems. The political picture of the world, especially at the beginning of the third decade of the present century, in conditions of increasing confrontation, increasing conflicts, challenges to stability and security, leads to the transformation of the geopolitical and geo-economic interests of actors in world politics in various regions of the world. As a result, today we can see this on the example of the countries of Central Asia, the SCO and some of its member-states, including India. The rapid economic growth and political weight of India in the world is now becoming an obvious reality. We can see this reality through the prism of India's geopolitical and geo-economic interests in Central Asia and the SCO. The question arises, what is the reason for such interest?

Firstly. India has become a full member of the SCO in 2017, based on its geostrategic interests, security and the importance of expanding its regional economic cooperation and space. These considerations, in our opinion, are connected with India's vision of increasing the political and economic potential of the Central Asian region, the progressive development of relations between Central Asia and the Eurasian region, as well as with the hope of intensifying cooperation in the field of energy.

Secondly. The foreign policy activity and foreign economic afforts of the Central Asian countries is progressing rapidly in the international arena. Thanks to their joint efforts, they have created a fundamentally new political atmosphere in the Central Asian region and, where Uzbekistan is making great efforts to consolidate the region through the mechanism of Consultative Meetings of heads of State of Central Asia.

Third. In 2019 a dialogue was launched between India and Central Asian countries at the level of foreign ministers. On January 27, 2022, the first India Central Asia Summit was held (in an online format), which was attended by Prime Minister of India Narendra Modi and the Presidents of the Republic of Kazakhstan, the Kyrgyz Republic, the Republic of Tajikistan, Turkmenistan and the Republic of Uzbekistan. At this Summit, all countries agreed to hold regular meetings of Ministers of Foreign Affairs, Trade, Culture, secretaries of National Security Councils and the India-Central Asia Parliamentary Forum.

Fourth. The SCO is becoming an increasingly attractive global international structure for many States every year, who see it as a reliable international body working on the principles of mutual trust, justice, solidarity, open and constructive dialogue to solve international and regional problems of sustainable development, as well as the fight against terrorism and drugs to ensure security. In almost two decades, the SCO has become a key regional organization in the Eurasian space. It accounts for more than 60 per cent of the territory of Eurasia, more than 40 per cent of the world's population and almost a quarter of the world's GDP. To date, the SCO's priorities include regional development. And in this matter, the SCO platform can increase the level of trust and cooperation between India and other members of the organization in resolving the unstable situation in Afghanistan.

Fifth. President of Uzbekistan Sh. Mirziyoyev, in his speech at the meeting of the Council of Heads of SCO member-states in 2021, noted that "over the past period, the SCO has become an important subject of world politics, and has taken its rightful place among influential international structures."[1] In continuation of this thought, speaking at a meeting of the Council of Heads of State of the Shanghai Cooperation Organization in Samarkand on September 16, 2022, the President of Uzbekistan expressed his conviction that "Central Asia should retain its status as the 'geographical core' of the SCO."[2] According to the conviction of the President of Uzbekistan, the SCO "is a unique interstate structure that has managed to unite countries with various cultural and civilizational codes, its own foreign policy guidelines and models of national development."[3] It should also be noted that at the first "India–Central Asia" summit, held in a videoconference format on January 27, 2022, President of Uzbekistan Sh. Mirziyoyev identified strategic priorities and put forward concrete proposals to promote practical cooperation in the "India–Central Asia" format.[4]

These guidelines of the President of Uzbekistan Sh. Mirziyoyev determine the necessity and relevance of further expansion of systematic scientific research and analysis of India's geopolitical and geo-economic interests in the SCO and the Central Asia region. In continuation of our previous research in this direction, which we started about 15 years ago,[5] here we attempted to analyze the dynamics of the positions of Indian officials and experts in order to understand how India's foreign policy and foreign economic interests in the Central Asia region and the SCO have changed, especially after India became a member of the SCO.

I. India's interests in Central Asia and the SCO through the prism of the views of Indian officials

Indeed, it is possible to understand India's interests in Central Asia and the SCO only by deeply analyzing the positions of senior Indian officials in recent years. Let's turn to some of them.

Thus, former Indian Foreign Minister S.M. Krishna, speaking in the lower house of his country's parliament (Lok Sabha) on July 28, 2010, noted that "the importance of the SCO has grown rapidly and it plays an important role in promoting stability, economic development and the fight against terrorism in the Central Asian region, as well as in Afghanistan."[6] At the Summit of the Heads of state of the SCO member-states in 2011, S.M. Krishna underlines his position on the SCO, emphasizing the following: "We are impressed that the SCO has taken several important initiatives in recent years, especially in two main areas: in the fight against terrorism; and in promoting economic cooperation in the region."[7]

Prime Minister of India Narendra Modi at the Summit of the Heads of State of the SCO member-States in Ufa in 2015 in his speech highlighted the main areas of cooperation between India and the SCO: "We will work with the SCO in the fight against terrorism and extremism; India will deepen its cooperation with the SCO in such areas as human resource development, information and communication technologies, pharmaceuticals and healthcare, banking and capital markets, small and medium-sized microenterprises, microfinance, food security and agriculture; We will support efforts to create an environment that eases barriers and facilitates trade and investment in the region; Our ties with Central Asia are very long-standing," etc.[8] Prime Minister of India broadly outlined and expanded the range of interests of his country to the SCO and Central Asia.

At the Summit of the SCO member-states in 2016 in Tashkent, Prime Minister Narendra Modi made concrete proposals, "India will undoubtedly benefit from the strengths of the SCO in the field of energy, natural resources and industry; In turn, India's strong economy and its vast market can contribute to economic growth in the SCO region; India's opportunities in trade, investment, information and communication technologies, space, science and technology, agriculture, healthcare, small and medium-sized industries can bring large-scale economic benefits to the SCO countries; Within the SCO, India will be a productive partner in establishing strong trade, transport, energy, digital and interpersonal ties."[9] As we can see from the speech of Prime Minister Narendra Modi, the Indian side proposed to significantly deepen the spheres of cooperation in the SCO region, thereby showing a wider field of its geostrategic interests. After this, India made great efforts to practically implement the statements of its leader in bilateral and multilateral relations in the SCO region and Central Asia.

A year before the Samarkand Summit, on September 17, 2021, the 21st meeting of the Council of Heads of SCO member-states was held in Dushanbe. This was the fourth summit in which India participated as a full member of the

In his address to the plenary session of the Summit, Prime Minister Narendra Modi stressed that "the problems caused by the growth of radicalization and extremism in the SCO region contradict the history of the region as a bastion of modern and progressive culture and values."[10] In his speech, the Prime Minister "also spoke about India's experience in using digital technologies and offered to share these achievements with other SCO member-states."

The first virtual India–Central Asia summit was held on January 27, 2022. Commenting on it, Rezaul Laskar (editor of the Foreign Affairs Department of the Hindustan Times newspaper) noted that this summit "between Prime Minister Narendra Modi and the Presidents of Kazakhstan, Kyrgyzstan, Tajikistan, Turkmenistan and Uzbekistan reflected the growing interaction with Central Asia, which India accepts as part of its expanded neighbourhood."[11] At the same time, R. Laskar quoted the following words of Narendra Modi: "On behalf of India, I would like to clarify that Central Asia occupies a central place in the Indian vision of an integrated and stable expanded neighbourhood." According to the correspondent, Narendra Modi "listed three main goals of the summit: to clarify that mutual cooperation between India and Central Asia is important for regional security and prosperity, to create an effective cooperation structure and to create an ambitious roadmap for future cooperation." As noted in the article, the Prime Minister of India also stressed that "an effective cooperation structure will facilitate regular interaction at different levels and between different stakeholders, and the roadmap will allow the six countries to adopt an "integrated approach to regional communication and cooperation in the next 30 years."

The cited materials of the 'Hindustan Times' newspaper, sources of the Indian Foreign Ministry[12] and other Indian media show that following important results of the India–Central Asia summit were achieved:

- as part of the steps to institutionalize the cooperation framework between India and Central Asia, the leaders agreed to hold a summit every two years;
- in addition to the mechanism of dialogue between India and Central Asia at the level of foreign ministers, they agreed that the Ministers of Trade and Culture will meet regularly to develop cooperation in these areas;
- the leaders of the Central Asian and Indian countries agreed to continue regular meetings of the secretaries of the National Security Councils to discuss security developments in the region;
- India has made several proposals to develop cooperation with Central Asia, including the creation of a joint working group on the use of the Iranian port of Chabahar to solve the problem of free movement of

goods and services, the creation of an "Indian-Central Asian Center" in New Delhi to serve as the secretariat of the summit and the creation of an "IT/ITES task force" to work on digitalization and electronic control; and

- The leaders of Central Asia and India have adopted a comprehensive joint declaration outlining their shared vision of a strong and comprehensive partnership between India and Central Asia.

After the virtual India-Central Asia summit in January 2022, Secretary of the Ministry of Foreign Affairs, Reenat Sandhu, said at a briefing that the proposals of the Indian side at this summit "were welcomed by the leaders of the Central Asian countries."[13] She also added that "India is ready to plan, build, invest and participate in connectivity projects based on the priorities of transparency, broad participation, local priorities, financial sustainability and respect for the sovereignty and territorial integrity of all countries."

The January virtual summit was notable for two reasons: firstly, in 2022 India and the Central Asian countries celebrated the thirtieth anniversary of the establishment of diplomatic relations, and secondly, the rapidly changing geopolitical situation in South and Central Asia required discussion of the most important issues at the level of heads of State.

At the Samarkand Summit of the SCO Council of Heads of State in 2022, Indian Prime Minister Narendra Modi elaborated the role of the SCO and at the beginning of his speech he noted that "today, when the world is facing the challenges of economic recovery after the pandemic, the role of the SCO is becoming very important."[14] Drawing attention to the fact that "the whole world is facing an unprecedented energy and food crisis," as well as many "obstacles in global supply chains," Narendra Modi stressed that "the SCO should make efforts to develop reliable, sustainable and diversified supply chains in our region." From the speech of the Prime Minister of India, it can also be discerned that, focusing on the progressive achievements of his country's economy, Narendra Modi seeks to offer his country's experience to all SCO countries. At the same time, the Prime Minister of India noted the following: "our experience can be useful to many other SCO members, and for this we are ready to share our experience with the SCO member-states by creating a new Special Working Group on Startups and innovations." It is discerned from the speech of Prime Minister Narendra Modi, India's geostrategic interests are strengthening, especially after the country's accession to the SCO.

Thus, referring to the visit of Prime Minister Narendra Modi to Samarkand for the SCO Summit, the representative of the Indian Foreign Ministry stressed that this visit "symbolizes the importance that India attaches to cooperation with the countries of Central Asia, which are considered the "core" of the SCO."[15]

After Samarkand SCO Summit the researcher Gupta Pravesh Kumar in his article noted the following: "India urged Shanghai Cooperation Organisation member-states to give each other full right to transit, as it would enhance connectivity and help establish reliable and resilient supply chains in the region. India highlighted the initiative to promote millet to solve concerns linked to food security when the world is experiencing an unparalleled energy and food crisis."[16]

India hosted the SCO Summit in virtual format on 4 July 2023. At the Summit Indian Prime Minister Narendra Modi stressed the following: "Strong connectivity is crucial for the progress of any region. Better connectivity not only enhances mutual trade but also fosters mutual trust. However, in these efforts, it is essential to uphold the basic principles of the SCO charter, particularly respecting the sovereignty and territorial integrity of the Member-States. Following Iran's membership in the SCO, we can work towards maximizing the utilization of the Chabahar Port. The International North-South Transport Corridor can serve as a secure and efficient route for landlocked countries in Central Asia to access the Indian Ocean. We should strive to realize its full potential."[17] In his speech, the Prime Minister of India specifically emphasized the following: "it is essential for SCO to maintain its primary focus on the interests and aspirations of the Central Asian countries". In his speech, Narendra Modi did not ignore the situation in Afghanistan. He stressed that "We must come together to strive for the well-being of the people of Afghanistan" and suggested: "Humanitarian assistance to Afghan citizens; the formation of an inclusive government; the fight against terrorism and drug trafficking; and ensuring the rights of women, children, and minorities are our shared priorities".

It should be particularly noted here that almost all recent official reports of the Indian Foreign Ministry pay considerable attention to India's cooperation within the SCO.

II. Views and studies of Indian experts on the development of India's strategic interests in the Central Asia region and the SCO

After India's accession to the SCO, the academic community of India have significantly increased analytical publications on India's strategic interests in the Central Asia region and the SCO. Indian scholars emphasize that "Indian policy with Central Asia was strengthened in 2015, when Indian Prime Minister Narendra Modi became the first Indian head of state to visit all five countries in the period from July 6 to 13. significant progress has been made in cooperation, especially in the field of defense, the energy sector and mutual relations since then."[18] In their opinion, "this new attention to the region can be explained by the changing geopolitics of the region, in particular the formation of the Chinese initiative "One Belt, One Road" and external threats to security in the region." Focusing on the latter, they also note that "during the visit of the President of Uzbekistan Sh. Mirziyoyev to India in 2018, both sides agreed to expand cooperation in the field of combating terrorism, conducting joint military exercises, military education and military medicine."

P. Stobdan's opinion, "the visit of Prime Minister Narendra Modi to Kazakhstan, Uzbekistan, Tajikistan, Turkmenistan and Kyrgyzstan was not only symbolic, but also important in terms of activating Indian diplomacy in a strategically important region."[19] According to him, "Prime Minister Narendra Modi has already taken several initiatives to overcome India's geographical isolation from Central Asia and increase India's share in the Shanghai Cooperation Organization." At the same time, he emphasizes that "Uzbekistan is the center of the nervous system of Central Asia." Speaking about this, he notes that "the new government of Uzbekistan, headed by President Shavkat Mirziyoyev, seems to be more open to the development of relations between the country inside and outside the region. We see many positive trends in this regard," drawing attention to the fact that "the nature of the regional worldview is changing in favour of intraregional cooperation."

Special attention should also be paid to the article by Professor Debasis Bhattacharya (Amity Business School, Amity University), who gives a thorough overview of factual developments in India's relations with Central Asian countries, emphasizing that "over the past few years, India and Central Asian countries have rapidly consolidated strategic cooperation in solving emerging problems based on mutual trust understanding and a common vision of the security and progress of the peoples of both sides."[20]

At the conclusion of the Third Dialogue between India and Central Asia, held in New Delhi on December 19, 2021, Professor D. Bhattacharya, after conducting an analysis, notes that "both sides once again reaffirmed their commitment to establishing lasting cooperation in solving emerging global problems, while emphasizing the urgent need to strengthen security, stability and long-term joint economic cooperation for prosperity in the geopolitical architecture of India-Central Asia." [21] According to him, "India's proximity and growing rapprochement on issues of mutual interest with five Central Asian countries, including Kazakhstan, Kyrgyzstan, Tajikistan, Turkmenistan and Uzbekistan, are reflected in the expansion of cooperation in solving emerging geostrategic problems after the COVID-19 pandemic and the changing world order." According to the professor, "both sides have expanded discussions and cooperation in such areas as trade and communications, economic development, partnership for development, energy security, regional issues of mutual interest, as well as mutual geo-political concerns of each side about emerging problems in Afghanistan." According to D. Bhattacharya, "the third Dialogue between India and Central Asia had a catalytic effect due to the consolidation of the two sides, especially in the context of rapidly changing geopolitical fractures in the regional and trans-global dimensions." He further notes "increased activity, clearly visible in recent years on the India-Central Asia line," as well as "rejuvenation of strategic rapprochement between the two sides," which increases the effectiveness of the reformed multilateralism and transparency of global governance." We believe that these are very interesting observations of an Indian professor.

It should be remembered here that even earlier Indian scientists paid special attention to the Central Asian region, as we noted in our previous studies.[22] Thus, Professor of History S. Gopal (Patna University) wrote that "the Indian side was able to have access to the most important shopping centers in Central Asia,"[23] and Professor D. Kaushik (Institute of Asian Studies in Calcutta) stated that "economic relations between India and Central Asia continued to exist despite multiple obstacles."[24]

Referring also to the Central Asia region, expert Niranjan Marjani emphasizes the following: "This region is important for India from a strategic point of view and from the point of view of energy supply. In order to give impetus to relations with the countries of Central Asia, India has a mechanism in the form of an India-Central Asia dialogue."[25] In his article, N. Marjani particularly draws attention to the following: "India is also working to expand the coverage of Central Asia and Eurasia through various communication projects. India is currently involved in three communication projects in the region. These projects are the Chabahar port in Iran, the International North-South Transit Corridor (INST) and the Ashgabat Agreement. All these communication projects will strengthen India's trade and commerce with Central Asia and Eurasia. In addition, these projects will help India gain access to the rich energy resources that both regions offer. This allows India to diversify its energy needs."

In the recently published monograph, where leading scientists and experts from India and Central Asian countries reflected the results of their fundamental research on mutual strategic interests and cooperation between India and Central Asian countries.[26] In the monograph, most of the authors explore the geopolitical and geo-economic interests of India in the Central Asian region from a systemic perspective. They distinguish the SCO region as a special region of India's great future hopes for the development of trade, economic, energy cooperation and the promotion of its innovative technological goods and services.

As for India's strategic interests in the SCO, Roy Meena Singh, talked about India's strategic interests even before this country joined the SCO.[27]

Professor Nirmala Joshi (Director, India-Central Asia Foundation). In her article, she notes the following: "India's membership in the SCO has given a great impetus to its regional policy. Indian politics is rooted in the region and has a regional perspective. Membership in the SCO has given a regional presence and an opportunity to observe trends in the region, especially in the energy market."[28] According to her, "its (SCO) geopolitical position, bordering on two potential leading powers of Asia and rich in natural resources, attracted the attention of the whole world from the very beginning. As a result, there has been a fundamental shift in the international outlook from Europe to

Asia, including Eurasia." She further adds, "this is a growing need for cooperation between the leaders of Central Asia." At the same time, she emphasizes that "in this regard, the role of the President of Uzbekistan Shavkat Mirziyoyev is commendable. In her opinion, the main goal of Sh. Mirziyoyeva is "The Region first of all," and to achieve this goal, he began active diplomatic negotiations. These initiatives have elicited a positive response from other members." She has no doubt that "India's active role will strengthen their (Central Asia's) multi-vector foreign policy, and these countries perceive India's role as a soft balancer in the region where geopolitical competition has begun. It would be in India's interest to step up its participation, especially to work on their desire for a connection in the southern direction."

Rhea Menon (a senior communications coordinator and research assistant at Carnegie India) and Sharanya Rajiv (a senior program coordinator and research assistant at Carnegie India), summarizing the results of their research on India's strategic interests in Central Asia, they note that, "Stemming from its historic cultural and economic bonds, India is now well placed to take a more active role in the development of the region. India's growing global visibility and key contributions to multilateral forums – like the SCO – have catapulted India from an observer into a critical stakeholder in the region. As India looks beyond its borders, Central Asia provides India with the right platform to leverage its political, economic and cultural connections to play a leading role in Eurasia."[29]

As we can see, the academic and expert community of India pays great and close attention to the issues of fundamental and applied research on India's relations with the countries of Central Asia and the SCO, as well as monitoring the political and economic situation in these regions.

III. India's economic interests in the Central Asian region and the SCO through the prism of some state and non-state structures of India, Indian journalists and researchers

Today, being the fifth largest economy in the world, India has even more reasons to further deepen trade and economic cooperation with the countries of Central Asia and within the SCO in order to ensure the long-term development and cope up with the growing global geopolitical uncertainties and economic challenges in the world.

According to the Confederation of Indian Industry (CII), "Indian exports to the Central Asian region in 2020-2021 amounted to $ 658 million, the total volume of India's trade with Central Asian countries in 2020 amounted to $ 3 billion." According to CII CEO Chandrajit Banerjee, the India-Central Asia Summit gives an additional impetus to exploring new areas of cooperation for the development of trade and investment and finding new ways to overcome communication problems so that economic complementarity can be fully realized."[30]

After the Samarkand Summit, an international seminar "India and Central Asia: Challenges and Opportunities", organized by the Political Perspectives Foundation, was held in New Delhi from September 27 to 29, 2022. At the seminar, Sanjay Verma, Secretary of the Ministry of Foreign Affairs of India, said that "India will remain a loyal and reliable partner of the Central Asian countries in their development."[31] In his speech, Sanjay Verma presented information about the prospects and current situation in Indian-Central Asian relations. At the same time, he paid special attention to the development of trade and economic cooperation.

He further adds, "Kazakhstan is India's largest trading partner in Central Asia, the bilateral trade turnover is about 2 billion US dollars. Indian oil companies are interested in investing in oil projects in Kazakhstan. Kazakhstan has been a major supplier of natural uranium to meet India's energy needs. Indian companies are open to exploring trade and investment opportunities in Kazakhstan in sectors such as pharmaceuticals, textiles, automobiles, fertilizers and information technology."

He says, "the trade turnover between India and Kyrgyzstan is about 34 million US dollars. Sectors such as education, information technology, pharmaceuticals, agricultural processing and textiles are promising for increasing India's trade with the Kyrgyz Republic. The Memorandum of Understanding on the provision of a $200 million credit line to the Kyrgyz Republic is at an advanced stage of completion."

As for India's relations with Tajikistan, Sanjay Verma noted that the trade turnover between the two countries "is less than 75 million US dollars. Indian companies have invested in the construction of power plants and power lines, as well as a large hotel in Dushanbe. Pharmaceuticals are our largest export commodity. Tajikistan also has good potential in the production of hydroelectric power, solar energy, tourism, mining and processing of cotton and fruit, which can provide opportunities for Indian business."

According to him, "India's trade with Turkmenistan amounts to about 114 million US dollars per year. India could share with Turkmenistan its experience in the field of renewable energy sources, especially in solar energy. It is necessary to solve the geopolitical difficulties of the Turkmenistan-Afghanistan-Pakistan-India (TAPI) gas pipeline, and the companies participating in the TAPI consortium should work on business solutions to reduce various risks."

Speaking about relations with Uzbekistan, S. Verma said that "India has announced the opening of credit lines and a consumer loan for Uzbekistan for 1 billion US dollars. Projects including highways and other urban water-related infrastructure are under consideration. A bilateral trade target of US$ 1 billion (currently US$ 342 million) has been set. Indian companies are strongly interested in exporting pharmaceuticals, mechanical equipment, auto parts and services. Uzbekistan could export fruits and vegetables, fertilizers, juice products, extracts and lubricants to India."

If we compare the data on bilateral trade of India with the countries of Central Asia, which S. Verma announced, with the data of our research on bilateral trade in the first decade of the XXI century (see Table 1), then we can see a huge progress in the growth of bilateral trade of India with the countries of Central Asia in recent years, with the exception of with Kyrgyzstan, with which India's trade turnover remained at the level of the first decade of this century.

S. Verma also stressed that "the biggest barrier between India and Central Asia is the lack of land communication." According to him, "the international North-South transport corridor and support for the Chabahar port, the Ashgabat Agreement and the Convention on International Transport are among the key efforts to improve communications." He noted "ample opportunities for expanding cooperation between India and Central Asia," highlighting especially the energy sector. According to him, "Turkmenistan is among the top 5 countries in the world in terms of proven natural gas reserves. Kazakhstan has significant reserves of crude oil, and natural gas reserves have been discovered

Table 1: India's Trade Turnover with the SCO Member-states for 2000-2008

(*USD million**)

Indicators	*Years*							
	2000/01	*2001/02*	*2002/03*	*2003/04*	*2004/05*	*2005/06*	*2006/07*	*2007/08*
Kazakhstan								
Export to Kazakhstan	50,08	45,70	46,88	74,81	79,40	90,86	83,27	111,91
Import from Kazakhstan	14,04	7,39	12,73	9,26	15,35	26,30	88,13	76,83
Trade turnover with Kazakhstan	64,12	53,09	59,61	84,07	94,75	117,16	171,40	188,74
China								
Export to China	831,30	951,95	1975,48	2955,10	5344,88	6759,10	8287,48	10834,08
Import from China	1502,20	2036,39	2792,04	4053,23	6768,92	10868,05	17447,01	27115,64
Trade turnover with China	2333,50	2988,34	4767,52	7008,33	12113,80	17627,15	25734,49	37949,72
Kyrgyzstan								
Export to Kyrgyzstan	17,59	10,97	14,67	38,20	49,10	28,09	37,21	31,58
Import from Kyrgyzstan	4,43	0,56	0,47	0,54	0,62	1,47	0,77	0,91
Trade turnover with Kyrgyzstan	22,02	11,53	15,14	38,74	49,72	29,56	37,98	32,49
Russia								
Export to Russia	889,01	798,18	704,00	713,76	605,39	733,15	902,17	940,20
Import from Russia	517,66	535,51	592,61	959,63	1280,89	2022,19	2407,61	2469,70
Trade turnover with Russia	1406,67	1333,69	1296,61	1673,39	1886,28	2755,34	3309,78	3409,90
Tadjikistan								
Export to Tadjikistan	3,55	1,22	8,65	4,47	6,25	6,24	7,45	12,42
Import from Tadjikistan	0,54	1,34	0,08	3,95	3,98	5,89	8,05	9,69
Trade turnover with Tadjikistan	4,09	2,56	8,73	8,42	10,23	12,13	15,50	22,11
Uzbekistan								
Export to Uzbekistan	9,39	6,53	5,08	15,14	19,66	24,44	29,66	40,32
Import from Uzbekistan	10,58	17,27	20,54	27,70	29,43	26,13	33,85	16,08
Trade turnover with Uzbekistan	19,97	23,80	25,62	42,84	49,09	50,57	63,51	56,40
Total								
Export to the SCO countries	1800,92	1814,55	2754,76	3801,48	6104,68	7641,88	9347,24	11970,51
Imports from the SCO countries	2049,45	2598,46	3418,47	5054,31	8099,19	12950,03	19985,42	29688,85
Trade turnover with the SCO countries	3850,37	4413,01	6173,23	8855,79	14203,87	20591,91	29332,66	41659,36
India's total trade turnover	95096,75	95240,02	114131,56	141991,66	195053,39	252256,27	311866,77	414546,16

* *Compiled by the author.*

Source: Calculations are based on statistics from the Department of Commerce, Ministry of Commerce and Industry, Government of India. Export Import Data Bank. Country–wise. http://commerce.nic.in/eidb/iecnt.asp

in Uzbekistan." Having said this, S. Verma stressed that "India, being the third largest consumer of energy in the world, can become a major buyer of energy carriers from Central Asia." He also added that "India, which ranks 4th in the world in terms of installed capacity of renewable energy sources, is ready to share its experience in using renewable energy sources with the countries of Central Asia."

According to other experts, "the lack of direct transport links with the landlocked countries of Central Asia was a serious obstacle to the expansion of trade. But India hopes to use the Iranian port of Chabahar to promote the trade route, since Iran has a long border with both Turkmenistan and Afghanistan.[32]

Revealing the issues of intensifying India's trade and economic cooperation with the SCO region in recent years, *Global Times* correspondent Wang Yi notes that "since India joined the SCO five years ago, its economic and trade cooperation with Russia, China and other SCO members has significantly expanded."[33] The article also notes the following: (1) "on the eve of the Samarkand SCO Summit," the Kremlin announced that the volume of Russian-Indian trade increased by almost 120 percent this year (in 2022); (2) Last year (in 2021), bilateral trade between China and India broke the 100 billions of dollars mark and this year (in 2022) has maintained high growth rates; (3) India's trade with Central Asian countries has almost doubled and reached $2.7 billion in 2019-2020." Correspondent Wang Yi also emphasizes that "active participation in economic cooperation within the SCO clearly contributed to the economic growth of India. The further deepening of such mutually beneficial economic cooperation with other SCO member-states undoubtedly contributes to the further development of India's economy." Wang Yi justifies his conclusions by saying that "the SCO, consisting of developing countries, has a great demand for economic development and a huge development potential. As a major Asian economy, India is inseparable from the Asian supply chain and production chain. Strengthening economic cooperation with the countries of the region is necessary for the development of India, especially given its goals to improve the economic structure and revitalize production." At the same time, he referring to the issues of global economic governance, draws attention to the fact that "the SCO member-states proposed to continue to support and strengthen an open, transparent, fair, inclusive and non-discriminatory multilateral trading system based on the WTO, which is certainly beneficial for India's economic development." Wang Yi argues "in many respects, the SCO mechanism represents the potential of India's future development. India's participation will also help the SCO to further expand cooperation in a wide range of areas."

In this regard, it is interesting to see information published on one of the websites of the Parliament of India about the prospects and opportunities of this country in the SCO.[34] At the very beginning of this publication, it is emphasized that "in the Eurasian region and beyond, the SCO plays a very important role and India will probably benefit more in the long term by joining the organization. The SCO also provides an opportunity for India to realize its national interests." Considering the issues of economic, trade and investment cooperation, it is noted that "today the growing economy of India and its scientific and technological progress is perceived as a profitable direction for the region." At the same time, the article also emphasizes the importance of "cooperation in three important areas: energy, trade and transport links, and the fight against traditional and non-traditional security threats that can be implemented through the SCO mechanism." Focusing on energy cooperation, the article states that "India will receive mutual benefits from cooperation in the energy sector, including the widespread use of renewable and alternative energy sources, supporting the use of various economical and environmentally friendly technologies that reduce the negative impact on the environment and contribute to energy security and the transition to cleaner and more environmentally friendly sources energy in an energy-efficient economy".

Dante Schulz, a junior fellow, South Asia program, Stimson Center in Washington, D.C., in his research, concerning the interests of India in the Central Asian region, made the following conclusions: "Security is the foundation of India's relationships with Central Asian countries, and it continues to be the most compelling factor in bridging New Delhi with the region. Nevertheless, India and the Central Asian states must diversify their relationships to include other sectors and means of cooperation to bolster the relationships' resiliencies and forge multi-pronged partnerships moving forward."[35]

Conclusion

In conclusions, it should be emphasized that today India is an active member of the SCO, whose diplomatic relations with the SCO member-states receive their active and comprehensive development both at the bilateral and multilateral levels. India's active and fruitful cooperation with the SCO member-states in recent years has manifested itself in the form of mutual visits of Presidents, Prime Ministers, Foreign Ministers and parliamentary delegations.[36]

1. Today, India notes the strengthening of mutual understanding, political dialogue and economic bilateral, regional and multilateral cooperation between the Central Asian States and the SCO member-states, recognizing this as not only a decisive positive step, but also a strategically important and promising direction for the development of the regions of Eurasia, Central Asia and South Asia.
2. The countries of Central Asia and the SCO undoubtedly consider India a reliable, trustworthy and predictable partner, which is increasingly involved in resolving issues of a global political and economic nature. The role and importance of India in resolving regional security issues and the fight against terrorism is significantly increasing.
3. The countries of Central Asia and the SCO see India not only as a promising market for exporting their products, but also as a country with a powerfully developing scientific and technological potential, especially in the field of information technology, pharmaceuticals, biotechnology and other areas.
4. In turn, India sees the Central Asian states and the SCO member-states not only as a huge economic and natural resource potential, but also sees them as natural partners in political dialogue and trade and economic cooperation, as well as in ensuring regional security.
5. For India, the geostrategic and geo-economic potential of the SCO member-states with the "core" of Central Asia consists in: the presence of impressive reserves of energy resources (oil, gas, raw materials for nuclear power plants); a developed system of transport communications and the implementation of new transport and

communication projects in the SCO and Central Asia to access adjacent regions with the purpose of effective trade, economic and investment cooperation where the creation of joint ventures in the field of small and medium-sized businesses represents a key sector and gives the industry and the economy of India as a whole advantages in the long term.

We believe that India's chairmanship in the SCO, which passed to it after the Samarkand SCO Summit in 2022, allowed India to promote the SCO's role on the world stage, make a significant contribution to strengthening strategic partnership within the SCO, significantly develop India's relations with Central Asian countries and Uzbekistan, as well as contribute its role and significance to the development of the interconnectedness of the countries of Central and South Asia.

It can be said that during the period of New Delhi presidency in the SCO, India has made every effort to give this organization an advanced position on the world stage.

Above mentioned analysis confirms the significance of the words of the President of Uzbekistan Sh. Mirziyoyev in the implementation of the priorities of our country's foreign policy in relation to the Central Asian countries, the SCO and India, which advocate active long-term and multifaceted cooperation with Uzbekistan in all promising and priority areas reflected in the Strategy "Uzbekistan-2030".

References

1. Address by the President of the Republic of Uzbekistan Shavkat Mirziyoyev at a Meeting of the Council of Heads of States of the Shanghai Cooperation Organization. 18.09.2021. https://president.uz/en/lists/view/4622
2. Speech of the President of the Republic of Uzbekistan Shavkat Mirziyoyev at the meeting of the Council of Heads of the Member-States of the Shanghai Cooperation Organization. 16.09.2022. https://president.uz/en/lists/view/5542
3. Shavkat Mirziyoyev's article "The Samarkand SCO Summit: Dialogue and Cooperation in an Interconnected World" has been published. (Opublikovana stat'ya SHavkata Mirziyoeva «Samarkandskij sammit SHOS: dialog i sotrudnichestvo vo vzaimosvyazannom mire».) https://nuz.uz/politika/1254943-opublikovana-statyashavkata-mirziyoeva-samarkandskij-sammit-shos-dialog-i-sotrudnichestvo-vovzaimosvyazannom-mire.html
4. Shavkat Mirziyoyev took part in the India-Central Asia Summit. January 27, 2022. (Shavkat Mirziyoev prinyal uchastie v sammite «Indiya - Central'naya Aziya». 27 yanvarya 2022 goda.) https://www.uzreport.news/politics/shavkatmirziyoev-prinyal-uchastie-v-sammite-indiya-tsentralnaya-aziya

5 Mavlanov I.R. Economic diplomacy of India in the SCO region // World and National economy. MGIMO (U) of the Ministry of Foreign Affairs of Russia. – Moscow, 2009. – ¹ 3-4 (10-11). (Mavlanov I.R. Ekonomicheskaya diplomatiya Indii v regione SHOS // Mirovoe i nacional'noe hozyajstvo. MGIMO (U) MID Rossii. – Moskva, 2009. – ¹ 3-4 (10-11)).

6 Unstarred Question' Q.675 Shanghai Cooperation Organisation, Lok Sabha, Ministry of External Affairs, Government of India, July 28, 2010, at http://www.mea.gov.in/loksabha.htm?dtl/16486/Q675+Shanghai+Cooperation+Organisation.

7 "Statement by EAM at the SCO Heads of States Summit" 15 June 2011, Ministry of External Affairs, Government of India at http://mea.gov.in/SpeechesStatements.htm?dtl/373/Statement+by+EAM+at+the+SCO+Heads+of+States+Summit. 8 PM Narendra Modi's speech at SCO Summit: As it happened... Written by Kamna Arora. https://zeenews.india.com/news/india/pm-narendra-modis-speech-at-scosummit-as-it-happened_1627857.html

9 Speech by Prime Minister at SCO Summit (June 24, 2016). https://mea.gov.in/Speeches Statements.htm?dtl/26948/Speech_by_Prime_Minister_at_SCO_ Summit_June_ 24_2016

10 Prime Minister virtually participates in 21st Meeting of the Council of Heads of State of the Shanghai Cooperation Organisation. Ministry of External Affairs, Government of India. September 17, 2021. https://www.mea.gov.in/pressreleases.htm?dtl/34281/prime+minister+virtually+participates+in+21st+meeting+of+the +council+of+heads+of+ state+ of+the+shanghai+cooperation+organization

11 India-Central Asia cooperation key to regional stability: PM Modi. By Rezaul H Laskar. India News. Published on Jan 28, 2022 01:00 AM IST. https://www.hindustantimes.com/india-news/indiacentral-asia-cooperation-key-toregional-stability-pm-modi-101643311801073.html

12 India-Central Asia Virtual Summit. January 27, 2022. Ministry of External Affairs, Government of India. New Delhi. https://www.mea.gov.in/pressreleases.htm?dtl/34774/IndiaCentral_Asia_Virtual_Summit

13 India-Central Asia cooperation key to regional stability. Op.cit.

14 PMModi's remarks at SCO Summit in Samarkand, Uzbekistan. https://www.narendramodi.in/prime-minister-narendra-modi-s-remarks-at-scosummit-in-samarkand-uzbekistan-564434

15 Remarks by Secretary (West) at the Plenary Session of the International Seminar on "India and Central Asia: Challenges and Opportunities" (September 29, 2022). https://www.mea.gov.in/SpeechesStatements.htm?dtl/35776/Remarks_by_Secretary_West_at_ the_Plenary_Session_of_the_International_Seminar_on_India_and_Central_ Asia_Challenges_and_Opportuni ties_September_29_2022

16 Gupta Pravesh Kumar. Central Asia: A Look Back at 2022 and Projections for 2023. https://www.vifindia.org/article/2023/january/04/central-asia-a-look-back-at2022-and-projections-for-2023

17 English Translation of Prime Minister Shri Narendra Modi's Remarks at the 23rd SCO Summit. July 04, 2023. https://www.mea.gov.in/Speeches-Statements.htm?dtl/36750/English_Translation_of_Prime_Minister_Shri_Narendra_Mo dis_Remarks_at_the_ 23rd_SCO_Summit

18 Menon Rhea, Rajiv Sharanya. Realizing India's Strategic Interests in Central Asia. December 01, 2019. Seminar. https://carnegieindia.org/2019/12/01/realizing-india-s-strategic-interests-in-centralasia-pub-80576

19 India's presence in Central Asia: Professor Stobdan assesses. CAA Network. https://www.caa-network.org/archives/9775

20 India-Central Asia Summit: Shaping geopolitics in the extended neighbourhood. https://www.orfonline.org/expert-speak/india-central-asia-summit/

21 India-Central Asia relations: Growing convergence brings relations to strategic heights. By Debasis Bhattacharya. Jan 11, 2022. https://www.orfonline.org/expert-speak/india-central-asia-relations/

22 Мавланов И.Р. Экономическая дипломатия Индии в регионе ШОС. Там же; Мавланов И.Р. Научные подходы к исследованиям тенденций развития региона Южной Азии и его интересов к Центральной Азии // Международные отношения. – Ташкент, УМЭД, 2021. – № 1-2. – С.25-38.

23 Gopal Surendra. India and Central Asia: Cultural, Economic and Political Links. Shipra Publications. New Delhi, 2001. p. 25.

24 Kaushik Davendra. The Economic Relation between India and Central Asia in 19th Century //India and Central Asia . . ., op. cit. p.71.

25 Niranjan Marjani. Is Shanghai Cooperation Organisation relevant for India? https://timesofindia.indiatimes.com/blogs/nolimits/is-shanghai-cooperationorganisation-relevant-for-india/

26 India-Central Asia Relations: The Road Ahead / Edited by Athar Zafar / Indian Council of World Affairs, New Delhi (India), KW Publishers Pvt. Limited, Published by Kalpana Shukla, ISBN: 978-93-83445-49-3, 2021.

27 Roy Meena Singh. The Shanghai Cooperation Organisation. India Seeking New Role in the Eurasian Regional Mechanism. / IDSA Monograph Series No. 34 February 2014. Institute for Defence Studies and Analyses, New Delhi.

28 Joshi Nirmala. India's Role in the Shanghai Cooperation Organisation. / Journal of the United Service Institution of India, Vol. CXLIX, No. 615, January-March 2019. https://usiofindia.org/publication/usi-journal/indias-role-in-the-shanghaicooperation-organisation/

29 Rhea Menon, Sharanya Rajiv. Realizing India's Strategic Interests in Central Asia. December 01, 2019. https://carnegieindia.org/2019/12/01/realizing-indias-strategic-interests-in-central-asia-pub-80576

30 India-Central Asia cooperation key to regional stability: PM Modi. By Rezaul H Laskar. India News. Published on Jan 28, 2022 01:00 AM IST. https://www.hindustantimes.com/india-news/indiacentral-asia-cooperation-key-toregional-stability-pm-modi-101643311801073.html

31 India and Central Asia: Challenges and Opportunities for Cooperation. 03/10/2022. http://www.newscentralasia.net/2022/10/03/india-and-central-asiachallenges-and-opportunities-for-cooperation/

32 Modi Holds First-Ever Summit With Central Asian Leaders. By Anjana Pasricha. January 27, 2022 11:20 AM. https://www.voanews.com/a/modi-holdsfirst-ever-summit-with-central-asian-leaders/6415129.html

33 India's economic opportunity lies in SCO, not IPEF. By Wang Yi. *Global Times*. Sep 15, 2022 11:16 PM. https://www.globaltimes.cn/page/202209/1275371.shtml

34 India and the Shanghai Cooperation Organisation (SCO). Reference Note. No.06/RN/Ref/February/2022. Reference Division. Parliament library and reference, research, documentation and information service (LARRDIS). https://www.orfonline.org/expert-speak/sco-2019-opportunities-and-challengesfor-india-51614/

35 Schulz Dante. How India Can Broaden its Relationships with Central Asia. December 10, 2022 https://thediplomat.com/2022/12/how-india-can-broaden-itsrelationships-with-central-asia/

36 Annual Report 2019-2020. Ministry of External Affairs, Government of India. New Delhi, 2020, P. 92-103; Annual Report 2020-2021. Op.cit. P. 66-73; Annual Report 2021-2022. op. cit. pp. 79-83.

13

Central and South Asia: Strategic Priorities for Regional Cooperation

Prof Rustam Djumayev

ABSTRACT

Modern transformational geopolitical processes and challenges faced by the world community in the first quarter of the XXI century, cause the need to find new ways to strengthen peace, international cooperation, expanding trade turnover, ensuring sustainable development and progress. The article analyses the strategic priorities of Central Asian states, including Uzbekistan, in strengthening mutually beneficial cooperation with both neighbouring countries and the South Asian region.

The paper considers the main directions of political, economic, socio-cultural cooperation with Afghanistan, India, Pakistan, problems and prospects in the development of transport and logistics corridors, related infrastructure, optimisation of export-import relations. The work pays much attention to the problems of combating threats of terrorism, issues of strengthening global and regional security. The author explores these and other issues based on the provisions and norms of the new Constitution of the Republic of Uzbekistan, the Concept of Foreign Policy and "Strategy Uzbekistan 2030", as well as the ideas and initiatives of the President of Uzbekistan Sh. M. Mirziyoyev, voiced from the rostrums of the UN, SCO, international forums and conferences.

Keywords. *Transformational geopolitical processes, international and regional cooperation, global and regional security, strategic priorities, transport and logistics corridors, volume of trade turnover*

It is generally recognised that the Republic of Uzbekistan pursues an open, mutually beneficial and constructive foreign policy based on the national interests. The current foreign policy course of the Republic is based on the dynamically changing situation in the world and the region, as well as large-scale internal transformations in the country. Commenting on the results of President Shavkat Mirziyoyev's participation in the first summit of leaders of Central Asian countries and the United States in the "C5+1" format and the speech of the head of our state at the 78th session of the UN General Assembly, Glen Howard, Senior Advisor to the Jamestown Foundation, said: "President Shavkat Mirziyoyev's speech at the UN General Assembly at such a crucial moment touched upon critically complex problems and challenges in the region, including the Aral Sea, climate change, transport and logistics. The transformational processes affecting the region today are observed around the world, mainly when it comes to climate change and challenges. The President of Uzbekistan also focused on the processes taking place in Afghanistan, on which the prospect of access to the Indian Ocean depends, which is a strategically significant aspect for the region."[1]

The main goal of Uzbekistan's foreign policy is to consolidate the country's independence and sovereignty, strengthen its place and role in the international arena, create a belt of security and stability around the country, and actively promote the country's foreign economic interests. The principal position of the Republic's foreign policy is adherence to the policy of non-alignment with any military-political blocs, non-positioning of foreign military bases and facilities on its territory, non-participation of the country's military personnel in peacekeeping operations abroad, and resolution of all contradictions and conflicts only through peaceful political means.

In order to achieve this goal, the following objectives are set:

- forming the most favourable foreign policy conditions for the effective implementation of the democratic reforms being carried out in the country and dynamic processes of modernization of society and economy;
- preserving and strengthening peace and stability in Central Asia, transforming the region into a zone of security and sustainable development;
- forming a balanced multidimensional system of strategic partnership

with the world's leading states and international organisations;

- promotion of Uzbekistan's international initiatives in the most important areas of regional and international policy;
- assisting in increasing the volume of exports of domestic products and expanding their geography;
- active promotion of foreign direct investment and advanced technologies in priority sectors of the national economy;
- facilitating the attraction of foreign tourists and the development of tourism infrastructure of the republic;
- assisting in the expansion and deepening of co-operation in the field of transport and transit, development of international transport communications and logistics infrastructure;
- ensuring the comprehensive protection of the rights and interests of Uzbek citizens and legal entities outside Uzbekistan; and
- strengthening ties with compatriots living abroad.

Uzbekistan's policy in Central Asia is aimed at ensuring peace and stability in the region and addressing key regional security issues, including facilitating the settlement of the situation in Afghanistan. The Uzbek side is making every effort to strengthen regional trade and economic cooperation, develop regional transport and transit infrastructure, ensure rational and integrated use of water and energy resources of transboundary rivers of Central Asia and environmental sustainability of the region and complete the processes of delimitation and demarcation of borders.

Uzbekistan is interested in strengthening friendly and good-neighbourly ties with the countries of the region, developing scientific, technical, cultural and humanitarian cooperation with them, and strengthening contacts between parliaments, border regions, public organisations and ordinary citizens. The interests of the Central Asian (CA) countries are also served by the joint creation of international transport corridors and international transport infrastructure in the region, which will help reduce transport costs when supplying CA exports to world markets. It should be noted that all countries in the CA region are interested in increasing export volumes and diversifying their foreign trade, entering new foreign markets, as well as creating and using new transport routes.

In his speech at the international conference "Central and South Asia: Regional Interconnectedness. Challenges and Opportunities" on 16.07.2021.[2] The President of the Republic of Uzbekistan Shavkat Mirziyoyev noted that Central and South Asia, located at the crossroads of the Great Silk Road, have for many centuries facilitated an active dialogue between peoples and civilizations. Thanks to the close interaction between the two regions, new knowledge and philosophical ideas, achievements in medicine and astronomy, geography and mathematics, and architecture, the art of diplomacy and state administration, high cultural and spiritual and moral values have been disseminated. The peoples of our regions have repeatedly found themselves within the framework of common state formations, as well as common political, economic and humanitarian space. The Harappan civilization, the Greco-Bactrian and Kushan kingdoms, the Turkic Khaganate, Khorasan and Maverannahr, the states of the Ghaznavids, Temurids, Baburids and others, which left a deep trace in the history of mankind, appeared here.

Central and South Asia have always been connected by reliable trade arteries, being a bridge for the countries of the West Asia, Europe and China. This is also mentioned in the writings of the ancient Greek historian Strabo, who wrote that the Ox River, now the Amu Darya, "delivered goods across the Caspian and Black Seas to Europe". As far back as the third or second millennia B.C., a network of trade routes connecting us passed through the Khyber and Bolan passes. In Central and South Asia, thanks to the spread of Islam, Buddhism and Hinduism and unique folk traditions, distinctive ethno-cultural communities were formed and a diverse and rich Eastern culture was formed.

Close ties between our peoples have fuelled rapid intellectual and spiritual progress. This gave the world such outstanding scientists and thinkers as Charaka and Sushruta, Brahmagupta and Al-Khwarizmi, Al-Ferghani and Farabi, Beruni, Ibn Sino, and many others. The works of great scientists Abu Rayhan Beruni and Zahiriddin Muhammad Babur are considered real encyclopaedias on history, science and culture of the regions of Central and South Asia. In particular, Babur wrote in his seminal work "Baburname" that in the sixteenth century, a regular caravan route was laid between India and Central Asia through the territory of Afghanistan, along which thousands of camels transported various goods every year. By his decree, caravanserais were improved and wells were built along the trade routes. Babur's grandson – Great Akbar, continuing his work, also left a bright trace in the history of India as a tolerant and far-sighted ruler. According to historical data, the ruler of India Aurangzeb in 1695 issued a permit to Russian merchant Semyon Small to trade in the country. It is noteworthy that this decree was written in the old Uzbek language. It should be noted that trade relations of Central and South Asia in those times were also carried out with Iran, Arabia, the Ottoman State, China, Russia and other countries.

The works of the classics of literatures are well known all over the world. First of all, they are Khusrav Dehlevi, Alisher Navoi, Abdurahman Jami, Muhammad Haidar, Makhtumkuli, Mirzo Golib, Abay, Rabindranath Tagore, Sadriddin Aini, Chingiz Aitmatov. They made a great contribution to the development of the ideas of peace, freedom and humanism, friendship and mutual understanding between different peoples. Unfortunately, President Mirziyoyev noted, in the nineteenth century, due to historical circumstances, the interconnectedness of the two neighbouring regions was broken.

Various obstacles emerged between Central and South Asia, borders were closed, and contradictions escalated, which increasingly turned into conflicts. The era of co-operation and mutual understanding was replaced by a period of confrontation and mistrust. The negative consequences of this are still being felt in the regions today – there are no effective cross-border routes, trade and economic ties are underdeveloped, and the potential of cultural and humanitarian relations has not been fully utilised.

President of Uzbekistan Shavkat Mirziyoyev at the 78th session of the United Nations General Assembly (20.09.2023), describing the fundamental changes in the system of international relations, stressed that now "*...there is a crisis of confidence, increasing problems in the activities of global security institutions and departure from the norms of international law. All this causes growing tension in the world. Geopolitical contradictions are creating new obstacles to the free flow of trade, investment and innovation. Even dialogue on issues that concern the fate of humanity as a whole, such as climate change, hunger and inequality, has been markedly undermined*" [3].

Under the current circumstances, the President stressed, "*...it is more* *necessary than ever to preserve the spirit of harmony and practical cooperation, to unite countries on the basis that common interests are higher than existing contradictions*" [3.1].

President Mirziyoyev once again voiced the main goal of the New Uzbekistan formulated in the "Samarkand Solidarity Initiative for Common Security and Prosperity" (2022). This is "*a deep awareness of responsibility for. the present and future of our countries and peoples, involvement in global dialogue of all parties ready for open and constructive cooperation*" [3.2].

The strategic goals and tasks indicated by the President affect, first of all, Central Asian region, which is intensively developing today along the path of good-neighbourliness, cooperation and increasing openness.

The interest of the international community in the transformation processes in Central Asia, and in particular in Uzbekistan, is not accidental. After all, thanks to the efforts of the leadership of New Uzbekistan and cooperation with the leaders of neighbouring countries, it has been possible to solve long-standing problems related to water use, transport corridors, and state borders.

The policy of increasing openness of Uzbekistan and the countries of the region to the world is becoming the main condition for ensuring the security and sustainable and peaceful development of Central Asia and the consolidation and prosperity of the peoples in the region.

President Mirziyoyev has repeatedly stressed the importance of strengthening the sense and awareness of regional identity, common past and common future, coincidence of vital interests, which act as real ways to expand regional cooperation. "Turning Central Asia into a peaceful and prosperous region will remain a priority goal of Uzbekistan's foreign policy," the leader stressed [3.3].

The President emphasised: "*Only through common aspirations and joint efforts can lasting peace and prosperity be achieved. More than ever, we need mutual trust, solidarity and co-operation*" [3.4]. In these conditions, the revival of mutual ties between Central and South Asia, which today is home to about two billion people, is becoming an even more necessary and objective process.

Based on the enormous historical, scientific, spiritual and cultural heritage the complementarity of economies, and the availability of intellectual potential, the consolidation of joint efforts will undoubtedly have a powerful effect in co-operation between the countries of Central and South Asia.

According to President Shavkat Mirziyoyev, interconnectivity, cooperation, dialogue and, most importantly, trust are the driving force for ensuring stability and sustainable development, raising the living standards and well-being of the peoples of our regions. This approach is the need of the times. All this creates the necessary prerequisites for the formation, on the one hand, of a space of interregional cooperation and partnership, free from conflict and socio-economic turmoil, and, on the other hand, of a vast market for goods and services, investment and innovation.

The expansion and strengthening of ties between Uzbekistan and the countries of South Asia is caused by the following:

First, strengthening peace and friendship, trust and good-neighbourliness, expanding mutually beneficial cooperation between our countries, building an open and constructive policy are in the common interests of all Central and South Asian States.

Secondly, Uzbekistan favours the formation of sustainable trade and economic, transport and communication ties, which should become the main driver of further development of our countries in the long term.

Thirdly, security and stability are the main prerequisites for the sustainable development between the two regions and the strengthening of partnership. The security of Central and South Asia is indivisible and can be ensured only through constructive dialogue and joint efforts.

President Mirziyoyev stressed that an active and constructive dialogue between the countries of Central and South Asia would open new opportunities for a fuller realization of their trade and economic, cultural and civilizational potential.

The leadership of Uzbekistan has formulated strategic priorities in expanding and strengthening co-operation between the two regions. One of the main tasks is to create favourable conditions for the development of trade and economic ties and the growth of mutual investments.

A practical contribution to resolving these issues would be the development and implementation of effective measures for the free movement of investments, goods and services, the formation of a developed system of transport communications and energy infrastructure.

Just as our common ancestors did by convening mejlis and kurultais, loya jirga, wasi mushavarat and sabha, an annual interregional forum is proposed to discuss topical issues of expanding the economic agenda of cooperation, deepening cooperation and investments between the countries.

Recommendations and proposals developed within the framework of such dialogue can be transformed into concrete programmes and projects aimed at creating new jobs, developing potential and ensuring sustainable growth of the economies. In addition, Uzbekistan has initiated a joint expert study of the conclusion of a multilateral agreement on economic cooperation between the countries of our regions, as well as the creation of a modern, efficient and safe transport and logistics infrastructure in Central and South Asia.

It is necessary to develop specific measures to implement digital interconnectivity – in trade, transit and border crossing – and to adopt a Joint Action Strategy. It is important to involve leading experts from our countries and UN specialised agencies in this work. It is necessary to develop collaborative approaches for ensuring food security in India and Central Asia. Recently, there has been a rapid rise in the prices of basic foodstuffs, and in some regions of the world the population is experiencing acute shortages.

The President of Uzbekistan suggested that under the auspices of the Food and Agriculture Organization of the United Nations (FAO) a meeting of the Ministers of Agriculture should be held to develop a programme to overcome these challenges. This document should provide for joint development and research, introduction of advanced technologies, and implementation of production cooperation projects.

Consolidation of efforts to combat common challenges and threats to stability and security is of no small importance. Joint efforts can be combat terrorism, extremism and transnational crime, including in cyberspace, more effectively. As a first step, it was proposed to develop a Joint Anti-Drug Action Plan, with the participation of the UN Office on Drugs and Crime.

Combating the threat of terrorism is an important area in which efforts need to be coordinated. Tashkent in 2022 organised a special expert meeting on these issues with the participation of representatives of the two regions. This meeting took place on the margins of the international conference held in Tashkent in November 2022 to mark the tenth anniversary of the adoption of the Joint Plan of Action for the Implementation of the UN Global Counter-Terrorism Strategy in Central Asia.

Environmental issues and the promotion of green development require the utmost attention. Countries of Central and South Asia are experiencing rapid industrial and demographic growth against the backdrop of global climate change. Water scarcity, atmospheric and environmental pollution, soil degradation and desertification are common problems. A sad consequences of the negative impact of environmental challenges is the problem of the drying up of the Aral Sea, which is increasingly taking on a planetary character. It is necessary to take all possible measures to mitigate its consequences, as well as to prevent similar disasters in the future, relying on the experience of our ancestors, who strived to live in harmony with nature.

In order to better unlock the unique tourism potential of Central and South Asia, recognisable tourism brands, new, accessible products and itineraries are needed, especially given the growing interest in pilgrimage tourism, the widespread introduction of the concept of "Tourism in a New Environment", with mutual recognition of vaccination certificates. In this context, it is proposed todevelop within the framework of the World Tourism Organisation a Programme for Central and South Asia, which will be aimed at promoting the historical and cultural heritage of our peoples.

Expansion of scientific, cultural and humanitarian exchanges is one of the important conditions for strengthening friendship and trust. The implementation of joint programmes in education and science, culture and sport, with the wide involvement of young people, who make up the majority of the population of our countries, is a priority.

High achievements in science, technology and innovation are an important factor in the accelerated development of the countries. It is necessary to encourage joint research and innovation work, the organisation of scientific and educational internships and experience exchange programmes. In this regard, the leadership of our country proposes the introduction of an easier visa regime for scientists and researchers, as well as the creation of an online platform for cooperation between universities and research centres in Central and South Asia.

Today it is more important than ever to develop thoughtful solutions based on a systematic study and analysis of development trends and the interconnectedness of our regions. In 2021, the International Institute of Central Asia was opened. On the basis of this think tank, a permanent expert pool of prominent scientists and researchers from the countries of the two regions has been created to promote scientific cooperation.

Taking into account that at present the main trade routes of Central Asian countries laid in the northern direction meet certain difficulties, in order to diversify foreign trade, a promising direction of economic cooperation is the southern direction, including with the countries of South Asia, which geographically include Afghanistan, Bangladesh, Bhutan, Maldives, Nepal, Pakistan, India and Sri Lanka.

Uzbekistan will continue to expand ties with Afghanistan and actively participate in international efforts to peacefully resolve the situation in that country. The Uzbek side will continue to promote the economic recovery of Afghanistan and the development of its transport, production, energy and social infrastructure. A stable and prosperous Afghanistan is a guarantee of regional security in Central Asia. Promoting peace and stability in Afghanistan and combating transnational threats and challenges are important areas of bilateral cooperation between the countries of Central and South Asia.

Uzbekistan's exports account for the major share (99.7%) of trade turnover with Afghanistan, which makes Afghanistan a favourable trade and economic partner. The main share of Uzbekistan's exports to Afghanistan is electricity (30 per cent of exports), wheat flour and pulses (24.1 per cent), and metallurgical products [4].

In Afghanistan, it is also planned to implement an investment project for the construction of the Surhan-Puli-Khumri 500 kW power transmission line, 260 kilometres long and costing about $150 million, using Asian Development Bank loans, of which Uzbekistan will finance $45 million. This transmission line will connect Afghanistan's power system to the unified power system of Uzbekistan and Central Asia [4.1].

Co-operation is also underway on the implementation of the project

"Financing, design and construction of the railway line Mazar-e-Sharif - Herat", which will be a continuation of the railway line "Hairaton - Mazar-e-Sharif" and will form a new trans-Afghan transport corridor.

In November 2020, the President signed two important documents concerning Afghanistan – the Decree on measures to further expand and strengthen economic co-operation with the Islamic Republic of Afghanistan and the Decree on measures to further develop the activities of special economic and small industrial zones in Surkhandarya province and the city of Tashkent [5]- which create new legal conditions for strengthening economic co-operation with Afghanistan.

The documents envisage the signing of a preferential trade agreement between Uzbekistan and Afghanistan and bringing the annual volume of bilateral trade to $2 billion by 2024.

To this end, a free trade zone "International Trade Centre Termez" is being established in the territory of the city of Termez bordering Afghanistan, with appropriate logistics infrastructure and a special visa-free regime for Afghans and foreign nationals entering this zone from Afghanistan.

In addition, the Decree provides for the elaboration of all aspects of the Mazare-Sharif-Kabul railway project with the interested countries and international financial institutions. In this regard, on 2 February 2021, a meeting of the trilateral working group was held in Tashkent between Uzbekistan, Pakistan and Afghanistan on the implementation of this project. As a result of the meeting, a joint "Road Map" on the implementation of the Mazare-Sharif-Kabul-Peshawar railway project was signed.

The construction of this railway will significantly reduce the time and cost of transporting cargo between South Asia and Europe via Central Asia.

The railway will provide access to the Pakistani seaports of Karachi, Qasem and Gwadar and will link the South Asian railway system with the Central Asian and Eurasian railway systems and significantly increase the transit potential of Central Asia.

Afghanistan plays a geographically important role in promoting the interconnectedness of Central and South Asia. However, Tashkent understands that without long-term stabilisation of the situation in the areas directly bordering Uzbekistan, it is extremely difficult to talk about sustainable economic development of the country and the entire Central Asian (CA) region, diversification of transport corridors, and connectivity with South Asia.

Failures in attempts to resolve the situation in Afghanistan by military means over the past more than 40 years make it clear that new methods for solving the Afghan conflict must be found. It is socio-economic projects that closely connect Afghan territories with neighbouring countries and regions that can give an initial impetus to the search for compromises between the various Afghan political forces.

As international forces become involved in stabilising the situation in Afghanistan, the country has become a key site for renewing historical contacts between Central and South Asia, which are vitally interested in the stability of the neighbouring country. In this regard, a stable Afghanistan, which previously served as a buffer territory separating Eurasian regions, could become the centre of a new macro region connecting Central and South Asia.

It is likely that a kind of border between Central and South Asia runs through the central provinces of Afghanistan, with the northern and northwestern provinces of the country geographically closer to Central Asia and the southern and eastern provinces closer to South Asia. The natural divide between Northern Afghanistan and the rest of the country is the Hindikush mountain system, which stretches across almost the entire central part of Afghanistan.

The implementation of infrastructure projects uniting the divided provinces of Afghanistan will also result in increased interaction between the regions of Central Asia and South Asia. The construction of roads and railways crossing Afghanistan as the shortest route to connect the regions can spur not only the growth of socio-economic cooperation, but also an increase in political, cultural and humanitarian contacts.

On the other hand, implementation of large-scale economic projects can stimulate job creation, generation of state budget revenues and service chains to ensure efficient operation of roads and railways.

It is expected that with the full implementation of the Mazar-e-Sharif-Kabul-Peshawar railway project, it will take only 3-5 days to transport goods from Pakistan to Uzbekistan instead of 35 days. According to projected estimates, the cost of transporting a container from Tashkent to Karachi will tentatively amount to US$1,400-1,600, compared to US$2,600-3,000 for the already operational Tashkent-Bandar Abbas route [6]. The construction of the railway from Mazar-e-Sharif to Peshawar involves the creation of systemic infrastructure in the form of 264 bridges [7]. Seven tunnels and 641 culverts, which could give a new impetus to the development of the crossing areas in Afghanistan and Pakistan. At the same time, projects for the construction of Central Asia South Asia (CASA)-1000 power transmission lines from Central Asia to South Asia, as well as the trans-Afghan gas pipeline TAPI (Turkmenistan-Afghanistan-Pakistan-India) have been discussed for a long time, which could also deepen the level of cooperation between the neighbouring regions and create a full-fledged connection between the north and south of Eurasia, having a stimulating effect on the economic development of different parts of the continent[6.1].

The potential for economic co-operation between the countries of Central and South Asia, in particular Uzbekistan, is as follows. The total volume of Uzbekistan's foreign trade with South Asian countries in 2022 was about $1.5 billion, or about 4 per cent of the total foreign trade volume. In Uzbekistan's trade turnover with South Asian countries, the largest volume is accounted for Afghanistan – 56.2 per cent, India – 32 per cent and Pakistan – 8.9 per cent. Trade turnover with Sri Lanka, Maldives and Nepal is insignificant, and there is virtually no trade with Bhutan [8].

India ranks second in terms of Uzbekistan's trade turnover with South Asian countries. At the same time, in mutual trade with India, Uzbekistan's exports lag far behind imports, which are mainly represented by pharmaceutical products in demand in Uzbekistan. Uzbekistan's exports to India consist mainly of textile products (13.6 per cent share), non-precious metals (8.4 per cent), food products (5.8 per cent) and others. Uzbekistan's imports from India are growing mainly due to the increase in purchases of "pharmaceutical products", whose share in imports is 47 per cent, while the second position with a share of 28.6 per cent is occupied by "mechanical equipment". At the same time, investment co-operation in the pharmaceutical sector is successfully developing with India, and joint ventures have been set up in the Andijan-Pharm FEZ. Branches of Indian universities Amity in Tashkent and Sharda in Andijan have been opened to train IT specialists. The feasibility of concluding a "Preferential Trade Agreement" between Uzbekistan and India is currently being studied.

The volume of mutual trade turnover now reaches $300mn a year [9]. Uzbekistan's trade and economic co-operation with Pakistan has been actively developing in recent years, and exports of finished, mainly agricultural products to the Pakistani market have increased. In the structure of Uzbekistan's exports to Pakistan: food products account for 81 per cent; textile products – 10.5 per cent; services – 3.5 per cent. In the structure of imports from Pakistan: pharmaceutical products account for 37 per cent; food products (potatoes, citrus fruits, rice, etc.) – 36 per cent; transport services; – 10 per cent; chemical products – 4.5 per cent.

In addition, Uzbekistan is interested in expanding cooperation with Pakistan in the transport sector and joint implementation of the above-mentioned project of construction of the railway line "Mazar-Sharif-Kabul-Peshawar". The volume of mutual trade turnover is about 100 million dollars a year. The volumes of mutual trade turnover and economic co-operation with other South Asian countries are insignificant (for example, the volume of mutual trade with Sri Lanka does not exceed $55 million).

Conclusion

The Republic of Uzbekistan favours the development of comprehensive and mutually beneficial relations with the countries of South Asia in trade and economic, transport and communications, tourism and other areas.

Given the export-oriented models of economic development, Central Asian countries are in urgent need of new markets for goods and services produced in the region. In the last century, the current post-Soviet space served as the main distribution markets for Central Asia. Along with positive results, this lopsided development of export directions has narrowed the region's opportunities to choose the most optimal markets. The situation was aggravated by the Russian-Ukrainian conflict and numerous international sanctions imposed on Russia and Belarus.

Moreover, the population of the post-Soviet countries grew by only 4.2 per cent between 1989 and 2019, from 285.7 million to 297.8 million. At the same time, the main contribution to this growth was made by Central Asian countries and Azerbaijan, while the rest of the post-Soviet republics are experiencing a steady decline in population, which by 2050 could drop to 284 million and be smaller than the population of a country like Nigeria.

In this light, South Asia's population of 1.95 billion, high rates of economic development and the presence in this part of the world of such leading regional powers as India and Pakistan make the region an attractive partner for Central Asia. The intensification and strengthening of Uzbekistan's co-operation with the countries of the South Asian region is the need of the times.

End Notes

1. "Address by the President of the Republic of Uzbekistan Shavkat Mirziyoyev at the 78th session of the United Nations General Assembly" (20.09.2023) /https//prezident./en/lists/view/6677
2. Speech by President of the Republic of Uzbekistan Shavkat Mirziyoyev at the International Conference "Central and South Asia: Regional Interconnectedness: Challenges and Opportunities", Narodnoe slovo- 16.07.2021
3. J. Gordon Melton, Martin Baumann. A Comprehensive Encyclopedia of Beliefs and Practices.- Oxford, England: ABC CLIO, 2010.
4. National Geografiphic Atlas of the Word. 7th Washington, DC: National Geografiphic, 1999.
5. "Asia" (pp. 90-110): Olivier Roy, The Central Asia: the creation of nations, I.B. Tauris, 2000.
6. Laziz Rakhmatov. Dunyo mamlakatlari: Australiadan [2]indistonngacha. T.: "Yangi Kitob", 2020.
7. Potapov M.A., Salitsky A.I., Shakhmatov A.V. The Economy of Modern Asia. International Relations, 2008
8. Khakimov F. South Asia-strategically important region in the foreign policy of Uzbekistan/ Strategy of Uzbekistan, 1 (2021)/ISSN 2181
9. Ibragimova U.N., Ibragimov D.T. Ways to increase the transport potential of Central Asia: Deepening interregional cooperation// Collection of scientific works of the IY International Scientific and Practical Conference "Transport and Logistics", Rostov-on-Don, 2020-S.94-101.

14

Current Status and Trajectories of Regional Cooperation in Central Asia

Dr Sherzod Arapov and Raxmatullayev Abdulaziz

ABSTRACT

The article analyzes the current state of regional cooperation in Central Asia. An overview of the main areas of regional cooperation, their progress, as well as key problems of intra-regional cooperation is being carried out. The article focuses on two areas. Firstly, Regional security is the most important area, which includes cooperation on issues such as the demarcation of borders and the fight against international threats such as terrorism. Secondly, Economic cooperation – includes trade, investment, energy cooperation. Both directions are closely related and the processes in each of them strongly influence each other.

Introduction

The importance of the Central Asian region is growing in the world. The logistical potential of the region is enormous, allowing Central Asian States to participate and be important participants in global infrastructure projects as the Silk Road Economic Belt or the North-South Trade and Economic Corridor. Security issues become important after the withdrawal of US troops and their allies from Afghanistan. Against this background, the development of relations between the Central Asian countries themselves is of key importance.

After gaining independence, the Central Asian countries faced with several unsolved problems of regional character: the demarcation of borders between the countries of the region, problems of sharing transboundary water resources, weak economic ties, as well as the issues of regional security. The solution of these problems is essential for promoting regional cooperation. The development of economic cooperation to develop productive potential, expand the market and provide access to it, and in general to improve the welfare of the population, is important against the backdrop of a systemic conflict between the two powerful neighbours of the region, China and Russia, with Western countries.

Uzbekistan is the only country neighbouring with all other countries of the region, has the largest demographic and economic resources. Uzbekistan often acts as one of the initiators in strengthening regional cooperation in various areas. For example, Uzbekistan was one of the initiators of securing the non-nuclear status of the region. Since 2018, Uzbekistan has been accelerating border negotiations with its neighbours: a demarcation agreement has already been signed with Kazakhstan, in the final stage with Kyrgyzstan, and significant progress has been made with Tajikistan. Uzbekistan is also one of the important stakeholders in resolving the situation in Afghanistan. Uzbekistan is consistently liberalizing its economy and economic ties with its neighbours, which has a positive effect on regional cooperation.

This paper aims to find out the main directions (trajectories) of regional cooperation in Central Asia and identify their status. It focuses on the Central Asian States regional cooperation and its prospective as a research problem.

The countries of Central Asia became separate subjects of international relations only in the 1990s. A lot has changed since then. The difficult international political situation forces medium and small countries to interact more actively, especially on a regional basis. On this basis, one can notice the desire for regionalism in Europe (EU), Southeast Asia (ASEAN), etc. The process (or model) of regional cooperation in Central Asia is unlike any of the above examples.

The main pillars of regional cooperation in Central Asia are made up of security and economic domains. The security primarily deals with the issues of determining the boundaries between the countries of the region, such international threats as terrorism and drug trafficking. The economic direction consists of such issues as trade, energy cooperation, investment, as well as water diplomacy. The two directions are very strongly intertwined with each other. For example, the deterioration of the economic (socio-economic) situation in the region can increase the followers of radical movements. Conversely, an increase in socio-economic well-being significantly reduces the level of radicalization of society.

Security and Borders

Solving security problems is always at the top of the agenda of meetings at all levels between the Central Asian countries. The economic situation of the countries of the region, the investment climate, and the security of logistics routes depends on the stable military-political situation in Central Asia. Security problems can be divided into traditional and non-traditional. Among the traditional problems, the most prominent is the problem of border demarcation; it was inherited from the Soviet past and often exacerbates other security threats. In addition to the risk of conflicts between States, demarcation problems contribute to drug trafficking. The second group of threats includes international terrorism and drug trafficking. The last two problems are closely related to the internal political situation in Afghanistan, which often acts as a source of threats. This makes Afghanistan a separate area of regional cooperation.[1]

The problem of defining borders became one of the most acute after the independence of most of the Central Asian countries. The problem of demarcation even served as a pretext for the formation of the Shanghai Five, which was later transformed into the Shanghai Cooperation Organization (SCO). Problems of demarcation, although slowly, are being resolved between States. By the end of the 2010s, only a few of the most difficult border issues remained.

In addition to the problem of drug trafficking, the problem of demarcation also exacerbates many other threats. As clashes on the Tajik-Kyrgyz border have shown, full-scale conflicts between states can become the most dangerous consequences. If the problem of drug trafficking or terrorism is aggravated in dynamics, an inter-ethnic conflict, or even more so a local war, can flare up spontaneously, which will cause much more damage to the structure of regional security.

The topic of demarcation in Central Asia became the most relevant in the early 2020s, two processes were running in parallel during this period. During this period, bilateral negotiations were completed on the definition of borders between Uzbekistan-Kazakhstan, Uzbekistan-Kyrgyzstan, Uzbekistan-Tajikistan, and Tajikistan-Kyrgyzstan. At the same time, in 2020-2021 the confrontation on the Tajik-Kyrgyz border sharply escalated.

One of the biggest achievements was the resolution of the issue of the Uzbek-Kazakh border in 2022. The parties spent almost 20 years on the solution of this issue. The demarcation agreement was signed between the countries in December 2022.[2]

Uzbekistan and Kyrgyzstan also reached an agreement on the delimitation of borders in 2022. This is also a major achievement, given the complex ethnic composition of the border areas, which created the risk of ethnic conflicts. The parties are actively continuing the negotiation process on the demarcation of borders, which will completely close the issue of the Uzbek-Kyrgyz border. This will significantly stabilize the situation in the Ferghana Valley.

An active negotiation process is underway on the demarcation of the Tajik-Uzbek border. In 2019, the parties agreed on the delimitation of the border. The most difficult was the solution of the problem of ownership of the Farkhad Hydroelectric Power Plant (HPP). The parties agreed that the HPP will remain under the control of Uzbekistan, and the territory on which the HPP is located will go to Tajikistan.[3]

The most acute issue remains the Tajik-Kyrgyz border. The parties have not yet reached an agreement on delimitation. The problem is exacerbated by the complex ethnic composition in the border areas, with growing populations on both sides, tensions are rising. This is the most difficult border issue in the region, and both sides need to make great efforts to prevent conflict as in 2021 and resolve the issue as soon as possible. Full resolution of border issues between Uzbekistan, Kyrgyzstan and Tajikistan will lead to stabilization in the Ferghana Valley.

Solution of border issues in Central Asia depends on bilateral relations, the fight against international terrorism more often acquires a multilateral character. In this direction, it is difficult to build an exclusively regional structure since the participation of external actors here is often critical. This is not only about large neighbouring states, but rather about institutions, primarily the SCO and the Collective Security Treaty Organization (CSTO) for some members. In the Treaty of Friendship, Good Neighbourliness and Cooperation the Central Asian countries agreed on regional cooperation to combat terrorism.

A unique situation has developed in Afghanistan after the withdrawal of US troops from there. All countries in the region recognize a common interest in defense against potential threats from the southern borders. From the outset, however, countries have had different approaches. Uzbekistan has maintained ties with Afghanistan from the very beginning despite the Taliban coup and is the most active donor of humanitarian aid to the population of Afghanistan. Tajikistan had a different approach, it behaved with the new "government" more distantly.[4]

Economics and Trade

The economic picture of the region is too uneven to speak of any regional trade and economic system. only three of the five countries in the region are members of the WTO, Uzbekistan is in the process to become member of WTO. Kazakhstan and Kyrgyzstan are members of the EAEU. But at the same time, the countries of the region also have different resource bases. For example, Kyrgyzstan and Tajikistan are rich in freshwater reserves. Uzbekistan, Kazakhstan, and Turkmenistan have gas reserves. This creates opportunities for regional cooperation.[5]

In 2018, the Tajik energy system was reconnected to Central Asian Power System (CAPS). From the same year, Tajikistan began to supply electricity to Uzbekistan. The system includes all (except Turkmenistan) countries of Central Asia, it contributes to the development of energy cooperation. However, the modernization of infrastructure appears to be difficult without external financial assistance.[6]

Another important achievement is the increase in the volume of intra-regional trade by more than 73 per cent from 2018 to 2022. It currently stands at more than $10 billion.[7] Such impressive figures do not prevent the region from continuing to actively integrate into the world economy.

Now there are also significant changes in the transport and logistics infrastructure. The mass opening or expansion of border checkpoints is taking place not only at the borders of the region. In 2018, the opening of 10 new border crossing points between Uzbekistan and Tajikistan was announced. Kazakhstan and Kyrgyzstan have agreed to build a logistics complex at the Ak-Tilek and Karasu checkpoints. Both of the above processes will take place in parallel with the process of digitalization of border control.

An important factor in the development of the economy is digitalization. In this regard, the region is not very developed and does not show convincing growth dynamics. However, Kazakhstan and Uzbekistan still stand out strongly in this direction. Both regional leaders, with a difference of several years, announced their large-scale digitalization programs. Uzbekistan is actively developing its Digital Uzbekistan 2030 program proposed by President Mirziyoyev. It involves a multiple increase in the level of digitalization of public and social services (education and health system), the banking sector, and the entire economy, as well as ensuring the transition to 5G by 2030.[8] Digitalization is an essential element of the transition to a post-industrial economy, which will give an impressive impetus to the development of the entire region.

Problems of the Regional Cooperation

Several problems stand in the way of regional cooperation. The most obvious of these is geography. Central Asia is the most geographically closed region in the world without access to the sea. This automatically makes the countries of the region dependent on external trade routes. Secondly, the volume of the market is clearly not enough to maintain competitiveness. Thirdly, the weak institutionalization of the regional structure. This does not mean that a new institution needs to be created. In the case of Central Asia, it shows that the regional structure is largely based on bilateral agreements.

The problem of trade logistics comes from the geographical location. Of course, on the one hand, the situation is very advantageous. But on the other hand, any international infrastructure projects like the Belt and Road Initiative or the North-South Corridor will always be a priority over the development of intra-regional infrastructure. Of course, these projects also contribute to the development of intra-regional infrastructure, but when planning and implementing them, external factors will be considered first.

The small size of the domestic market is a very strong constraint on regional cooperation. For countries of Central Asia, a neighbour in the region is not the main trading partner. In trade and economic terms, large neighbours will remain priority partners for the countries of the region. It was the size of the market that became one of the determining factors for the success of regional cooperation in Europe, North America, Southeast Asia. However, the countries of the region are still on the path of their economic development.

The absence of a unified regional institutions can be explained by many factors. The states of Central Asia are not ready to transfer part of their sovereignty to supranational institutions, which is typical for almost all states in Eurasia. Therefore, most regional organizations like the SCO, the Commonwealth of Independent States (CIS) do not have such signs of integration. It should also be noted that if the countries of Central Asia rarely use the platforms of the Eurasian regional organizations to solve intra-regional problems. The countries of Central Asia will continue to emphasize bilateral ties within the framework of regional cooperation. However, according to Sodiq Safoev "today there is a need to create a legal, and in the future, an institutional framework for interaction" through formulating common principles and concept on the basis of mutual trust.[9]

Conclusion

The level of regional cooperation of Central Asia is increasingly growing. In the given process bilateral ties are the basis that shapes the process of regional cooperation. Regional cooperation develops in parallel with cooperation with non-regional powers that continue to play a critical role in regional processes.

Central Asian countries are jointly addressing regional development problems and countering traditional and non-traditional challenges and threats to security. It's of paramount importance for Central Asian countries to ensure peace and security, advocating the settlement of regional conflicts by exclusively peaceful political and diplomatic means in order to strengthen relations between them so that the friendship of their peoples is passed on from generation to generation.

Most importantly, leadership of the region has a strong political will to further develop cooperation in the fields of politics and security, trade, economy, finance and investment and other domains with the aim of building a peaceful, secure and prosperous region.

END NOTES

1 Modern Central Asia: Resilience and Capacity Building Tashkent, 2021, 158-307

2 Dogovor mejdu Respublikoy Kazaxstan i Respublikoy Uzbekistan o demarkasii kazaxstansko-uzbekskoy gosudarstvennoy granisi (Tashkent, 22 dekabrya 2022 goda), https://online.zakon.kz/Document/?doc_id=37544108

3 Tadjikistan i Uzbekistan zavershili etap peregovorov po demarkasii granis, https://www.asiaplustj.info/ru/news/tajikistan/politics/20220718/tadzhikistan-i-uzbekistan-zavershili-etap-peregovorov-po-demarkatsii-granits

4 Tajikistan and Uzbekistan Take Different Approaches to Afghanistan, https://thediplomat.com/2021/09/tajikistan-and-uzbekistan-take-different-approaches-to-afghanistan/

5 International Affairs. Interdisciplinary Scientific and Theoretic Journal Tashkent, 2021, 21-199

6 ADB Grant to Help Tajikistan Reconnect to the Central Asian Power System, https://www.adb.org/news/adb-grant-help-tajikistan-reconnect-central-asian-power-system

7 Five Trade Trends in Central Asian Connectivity https://astanatimes.com/2023/06/five-trade-trends-in-central-asian-connectivity/

8 Kak Uzbekistan i Kazaxstan prevrashayutsya v sifrovoy xab, 2023, https://kz.kursiv.media/wp-content/uploads/2023/03/bg_kz.pdf

9 Sentralnaya Aziya: ot regionalnogo vzaimodeystviya k sovmestnomu ustoychivomu rostu // Yuksalish, 2021, https://yumh.uz/ru/news_detail/315

15

Economic Integration as a Factor in the Development of International Transport Corridors: Prospects for the Development of the North-South Transport Corridor from the Perspective of International Law

Dr Umidkhon Azamxodjayev

ABSTRACT

In order for international transport corridors to function as effectively as possible, it is important that the states through which the corridor passes have legal relations not only in the field of transport, but on all issues to a greater or lesser extent related to the transportation of goods and passengers. In this article, the author considers the issue of legal regulation and functioning of international transport corridors within the framework of economic integration of the EU and ASEAN in order to identify the necessary legal framework for the successful functioning of corridors. The author concludes that international transport corridors cannot function effectively in the absence of multilateral treaties aimed at economic integration and cites the North-South ITC as an example. It is this corridor, legally founded back in 2000, that due to the lack of international treaties adopted for the purpose of economic integration between the participating countries, is still not functioning at the proper level.

Keywords: *International transport corridors, economic integration, free transit, North-South ITC.*

Introduction

Trade relations of states, foreign trade turnover of the country, and foreign economic relations of any state in general are closely connected with international transport corridors, which provide the most efficient cross-border movement of goods and passengers, thus accelerating the growth of the economy. In fact, these corridors arise as a result of the connection of transport arteries of several states that agree on the creation of a single corridor.

International transport corridors (hereinafter referred to as ITC) are primarily designed to ensure cross-border movement and transit of goods and passengers across the territory of two or more states. Consequently, the legal regulation of ITC touches upon the issues related to these tasks, which include a wide range of legal relations of both international-public character and international-private legal relations. International-public legal relations between the states through which the ITC passes, or, if I may put it this way, the countries-participants of the ITC, require special attention. It is the agreements of states on public issues such as tariff regulation, border crossing, transit, customs procedures, etc., that predetermine the effectiveness of ITC functioning. All these issues in a comprehensive approach can be regulated in the process of economic integration, both regionally and globally.

A Brief Historical Sketch of the Legal Basis of Economic Integration

Perhaps one of the first to put forward a modern theory of economic integration is the eminent economist Professor Balassa, who presented it in The Theory of Economic Integration. According to Balassa, the theory of economic integration can be seen as part of international economics, but it also extends the field of international trade theory by examining the impact of merging national markets on growth and exploring the need to coordinate the economic policies of countries. The classical theory proposed, utilizes five stages of economic integration: Free Trade Area; Customs Union; Common Market; Economic Union; Full Economic Integration. (Balassa 1961).[1]

According to Marsha Echols, a professor at Harvard Law School, regional economic integration is primarily ensured by tariff and non-tariff agreements. In addition, to date, integration has also been achieved through agreements in the areas of services, intellectual property, investment, labour and competition. Economic integration is usually expressed in regional and bilateral agreements between states, the purpose of which is primarily to achieve mutually beneficial access to the markets of the contracting parties by regulating tariffs.[2]

Economic integration is manifested in multiple cases in the form of free trade zones and customs unions. The basis is trade agreements, mostly in the form of free trade agreements in a regional format, one of the goals of which is to bring tariffs to the lowest levels, down to zero. States have entered into various types of trade agreements for many hundreds of years. However, it can be believed that the Anglo-French trade treaty of 1860 has a very clear beginning of modern trade agreements, as this treaty was based on the idea of mutual binding tariff reductions. The concept of tariff reduction commitments formed the basis of international trade agreements over a hundred years later and even today is arguably the most important part of these agreements.

The League of Nations economic conferences in the 1920s and 1930s resulted in various bilateral trade agreements that provided for a broader trade regime. The new agreements they developed, first as bilateral agreements in the 1930s and 1940s and later as the General Agreement on Tariffs and Trade (GATT), went beyond the earlier tariff reduction agreements by establishing a set of more general rules.[3]

After World War II, the focus shifted from bilateral agreements to a multilateral approach. Regional economic integration became one of the most important international phenomena after the end of the war.[4]

In economic integration on a global scale, the World Trade Organization (WTO) Agreements occupy a special place. This agreement expanded traditional trade commitments to include a number of new requirements more indirectly related to trade. At the same time, the WTO system itself has traditionally allowed for agreements that provide more favourable market access in the form of lower tariffs or related border measures for States in free trade zones or customs unions.[5]

Ensuring free trade within the framework of economic integration is primarily conditioned by free transit between the states involved in integration, which in turn gives rise to the need for detailed international legal regulation of ITCs through which transportation is carried out. Legal regulations of ITC include all legal relations related to the functioning of the ITC itself and directly affecting the viability of the ITC. All successful economic integrations pay special attention to the legal regulation of the ITC, enshrining the relevant norms in fundamental multilateral agreements, as well as developing separate international treaties regulating legal relations in the field of transport.

Impact of Economic Integration on the Development of Transport Corridors in the EU

Undoubtedly, the most successful integration scheme of our times is the European Union, which originated in 1957 in the form of the European Economic Community in accordance with the Treaty establishing the European Economic Community (Treaty of Rome) concluded between the Federal Republic of Germany, the Kingdom of Belgium, the French Republic, the Italian Republic, the Republic of Luxembourg, and the Kingdom of the Netherlands. It was with the establishment of this Community that the creation of free trade areas and common markets became a reality.

The Treaty of Rome, in terms of economic integration, set the goal of creating a common market and economic union, for the achievement of which specific actions are defined. Among the main objectives for achieving economic integration, it is easy to see preferential measures in the form of the elimination of duties in trade between countries, as well as free transit of goods and a common transport policy between countries. Trade arrangements go hand in hand with transport arrangements, supported by the approximation, or in modern terminology "harmonization" of national legislations, which additionally contributes to law enforcement.

At the same time, special attention is paid to transport policy, according to article 70 of the Treaty of Rome, the general transport policy implies the establishment of general rules applicable to international traffic to and from the territory of a member-State or through the territory of one or more member-States.

ITC, which are referred to in the document as "transport routes", are also addressed separately. According to Article 75 of the Treaty of Rome, in the case of intra-Community transport, all discrimination consisting in the application by transport agencies of different tariffs and different conditions for the transport of the same goods and along the same transport routes, depending on the country of origin or destination of the goods transported, must be abolished.

Article 154 of the Treaty of Rome, which defines international transport corridors by the term "trans-European networks in the field of transport", defines that the Community shall promote the establishment and development of trans-European networks in the field of transport.

The Treaty of Rome was further amended by the 1992 Maastricht Treaty, which formed the EU and gave the Treaty the name, Treaty, establishing the European Community, and later by the 2007 Lisbon Treaty, which was renamed the Treaty on the Functioning of the European Union and also renumbered the articles.

At all stages of the Treaty's evolution, the norms relevant to the functioning of the ITC have remained constant. In addition to those mentioned above, the Treaties pay much attention to one of the most important factors – free movement of goods. Article 26 of the Treaty on the Functioning of the European Union defines that the EU is a territory without internal borders in which the free movement of goods, persons, services and capital is ensured.

Protection of the free movement of goods is realized, among other things, by removing national barriers of EU members, through harmonization of laws at the EU level, which can be seen as deepening the process of integration through law. The result of harmonization at the EU level is a common set of business rules. These principles, on which the development of the EU internal market is built, challenge national trade barriers.[6] It is the free movement of goods that contributes to the realization of the most basic task of ITC – ensuring the most efficient transportation of goods.

It should be noted that the adoption of international agreements regulating from the point of view of international-public legal relations, can be attributed to the following agreements: European Agreement on International Motorways 1975, European Agreement on International Main Railway Lines 1985, European Agreement on Main International Combined Transport Lines and Related Facilities 1991, European Agreement on Main Inland Waterways of International Importance 1996.

In addition, a considerable number of conventions of international private law nature have been adopted that regulate transportation issues, which can undoubtedly be attributed to international sources of ITC regulation. The Customs Convention on the International Transportation of Goods under Cover of TIR Carnets (TIR Convention, 1975) is a prime example.

The course taken by the European Union for the development of transport corridors within the framework of economic integration established by the Treaty of Rome, has led not only to the creation of a legal framework, but also to the emergence of large-scale projects for the development of transport corridors, creating a common policy and a common legal framework (supranational) for the regulation and development of corridors at the level of the European Union.

First of all, it is worth mentioning the Trans-European Transport Network (TEN-T), which is a planned network of roads, railways, airports and water infrastructure in the European Union. The current Regulation on Union guidelines for the development of the TEN-T was adopted by Decision No. 1315/2013 of the European Parliament and of the Council of December 11, 2013.

One of the main objectives of the Regulation is to ensure that the international passenger and freight mobility capacity of the trans-European transport network and the use of this capacity should be optimized and, where necessary, expanded by removing infrastructure bottlenecks and providing missing infrastructure links within and between Member-States and, where necessary, neighbouring countries.[7]

We would like to pay special attention to the administrative regulation of ITC in the European Union. EU legislation provides for ITC management, which allows for effective implementation of corridor development plans. The 2010 European Rail Network Regulation for Freight Transport, an initiative to create seamless rail freight transport corridors in Europe, provides for the management of these transport corridors.[8]

At the same time, it is necessary to mention the role of pan-European transport conferences held on the initiative of the European Parliament and the Commission. During the second Pan-European Transport Conference held in 1994 on the island of Crete (Greece), which was a great success, large-scale issues were discussed. It resulted in the adoption of the Cretan Declaration on Principles, Objectives and Measures for a Pan-European Transport Policy. The Declaration is non-binding, but as it is largely self-binding, it forms the basis for pan-European cooperation in the field of transport.

The Declaration stipulates that the transport sector should be organized according to the principles of a social market economy and free competition. Transport markets should be gradually opened up on a reciprocal basis as progress is made in harmonizing competitive conditions.

It is also prescribed that legal and administrative provisions should be harmonized, especially with regard to the compatibility of technical systems and fiscal measures, as well as the establishment of minimum standards in social, environmental, energy and transport safety policies.

These principles are followed by a number of individual measures that are intended to define the overall approach for the coming years, such as: liberalizing cross-border transport; improving border crossings; setting priorities for infrastructure corridors and coordinating planning and implementation; financing infrastructure with private capital, and improving border crossings. The Cretan Declaration identifies nine priority transport corridors that are intended to operate as extensions of the Trans-European Networks (TENs).[9]

Impact of Economic Integration on the Development of Transportation Corridors in ASEAN

Another successful example of regional economic integration within the framework of which ITCs are dynamically developing is the Association of Southeast Asian Nations (ASEAN). ASEAN, originally established by Indonesia, Malaysia, Singapore, Thailand and the Philippines in 1967 on the basis of the ASEAN Declaration, had the objectives of accelerating economic growth, social progress and cultural development in the region by working together to promote regional peace and stability, without any specific objectives or measures necessary for their realization.

Only 10 years later, the first agreements aimed at economic integration were adopted, such as the Treaty of Amity and Cooperation in Southeast Asia (The Treaty of Amity and Cooperation in Southeast Asia 1976) and the Agreement on ASEAN Preferential Trading Arrangements 1977 (Agreement on ASEAN Preferential Trading Arrangements 1977).

This agreement did not have any significant effect and the reason for this was political. Like all newly independent states in the Third World Movement, ASEAN members strenuously defended their independence and sovereignty. ASEAN countries decided to integrate their economies into the world economy.

ASEAN ideology emphasized national sustainability accompanied by regional sustainability. The concept of sustainability included strong national sovereignty. thus, even economic cooperation, which requires national economies to adapt to some extent to regional changes, has been difficult for ASEAN countries.[10]

Fear of becoming an outsider in a world increasingly divided into trading blocs, as well as the economic power of rising powers such as India and China in the region, with whom they became strong competitors for foreign direct investment inflows, led ASEAN to establish the ASEAN Free Trade Area (AFTA) in 1992 to support high growth by creating a single market and international production base; attracting foreign direct investment; and expanding intra-ASEAN trade and investment.[11]

The legal basis for the implementation of AFTA was the Agreement on the Common Effective Preferential Tariff (CEPT) Scheme for the AFTA 1992. The agreement provided for a sectoral approach and fifteen product groups were selected for immediate liberalization through tariff reductions. These groups covered all industrial products, including agricultural products.[12]

It was with the establishment of the 1992 AFTA covering trade in goods, supplemented by the 1995 ASEAN Framework Agreement on Services (AFAS) and the 1998 ASEAN Investment Area (AIA) agreement, that serious economic integration efforts among ASEAN members began. In 2003, it was decided to deepen economic integration with the formation of the ASEAN Economic Community (AEC) to create a single market and production base through the free flow of goods, services, foreign direct investment, skilled labour and freer flow of capital.[13]

Deepening economic processes have prompted ASEAN countries to pay special attention to ITC development. Thus, according to Article 2 of the 1992 Agreement on a Single Effective Preferential Tariff Scheme for the AFTA, Member-States agree to further strengthen regional cooperation to ensure a safe, efficient and innovative transportation infrastructure network. This provision has given rise to a number of important legal instruments within ASEAN in the area of ITC regulation.

In accordance with the ASEAN Framework Agreement on the Facilitation of Goods in Transit 1998, where ITCs are defined as "transit transport routes", the list of ASEAN road ITCs was approved. The Agreement allows unimpeded access and movement of vehicles, including people and goods, along transport routes, establishes the adoption of standards and requirements for the technical design of the ASEAN road network, defines measures to harmonize border control of goods, harmonize traffic regulations and road signs in force on the territory of each state, unifies the requirements for permits for road transport, and more. In addition, the Agreement regulates issues related to the designation of border posts, railroads, including border and interchange stations, customs transit system, sanitary and phytosanitary measures.

Article 7 of the Agreement stipulates that the Parties agree to establish border posts at the border points specified in Protocol 2 to the Agreement to facilitate transit transportation. However, in practice, these measures have not been implemented, which in turn leads to difficulties in cross-border transportation and sometimes requires unloading and reloading of goods at state borders. Land transport sometimes requires passing through the territory of third countries and, in the absence of a transit transport agreement, carriers need to go through customs procedures twice, when entering a third country; and when entering the country of destination from a third country.[14]

The ASEAN Framework Agreement on Multimodal Transport was signed in 2005, defining the legal responsibilities of multimodal transport operators and shippers, as well as the standard format of their transport contracts. The Agreement applies to international multimodal transport services provided by registered transport operators of ASEAN members. All ASEAN members are required to adopt domestic legislation on multimodal transportation.

In order to simplify and harmonize transport, trade and customs regulations and requirements, as well as to facilitate inter-state transport of goods, the ASEAN framework agreement on the facilitation of inter-state transport was adopted in 2009, which also addresses ITC-related issues.

Measures taken by ASEAN Member-States to develop transport across all directions are leading to the creation of new ITC projects, such as the flagship project to connect Singapore to Kunming, China, the so-called Singapore-Kunming Rail Link (SKRL). SKRL will connect major cities in seven ASEAN member-states, namely, Singapore, Malaysia, Thailand, Cambodia, Vietnam, Lao People's Democratic Republic and Myanmar. SKRL currently links Singapore-Malaysia, Malaysia-Thailand and Thailand-Laos PDR.[15]

Consequences of the Lack of Economic Integration between the Countries through which the North-South ITC Passes

Based on the history of development of successful ITCs, it is obvious that ITCs cannot function effectively without economic integration of the states through which the transport corridors pass. One such example is the North-South ITC established by Russia, India and Iran in accordance with the Agreement on the North-South International Transport Corridor of 2000. The agreement was later joined by Armenia, Kazakhstan, Azerbaijan, Belarus, Kyrgyzstan, Oman, Syria, Tajikistan, Turkey and Ukraine. The document does not fix a detailed route, does not specify unified technical requirements for transportation routes, and specifies an approximate route from India by sea through Iran, the Caspian region to Russia and back. It was planned to provide a shorter route from Southeast Asia to Europe and compete with the transit of goods through the Suez Canal.[16]

The North-South ITC in the southern direction envisages three routes for freight transportation by rail: However, the parties lack the most basic arrangements necessary for the functioning of the ITC, in particular, there are no free trade agreements between all participants, no effective interstate body to coordinate ITC activities, no defined plan for the development of the transport infrastructure network along the entire route, no legal mechanisms to simplify goods transportation procedures, no harmonization of customs transit and border control, no liberalization of cross-border transport, and no common transport policy.

Barriers can also include administrative barriers (*consisting the access of suppliers to provide services that are restricted at the legislative level*). This is seen for international road transport of goods by ITC: permit system, transportation quotas, differences in procedures for issuing permits to carriers, licensing criteria, various charges, etc. Intergovernmental bilateral agreements on road transport lay down different legal regimes for the transportation of goods between individual states.

The lack of legal mechanisms to simplify procedures for the transportation of goods and harmonization of customs transit leads to lengthy customs clearance at border crossing points, which leads to significant downtime of vehicles and rolling stock.

In addition, there is no harmonized policy on visas for drivers. The length of stay of truck drivers varies from country to country, and there are differences in costs and procedures for obtaining entry and transit visas. In some countries there is no practice of issuing long-term multiple-entry visas for drivers, resulting in truck drivers having to apply for a new visa for each trip. There is also no practice of issuing visas at border crossing points, forcing drivers to apply for visas at embassies in their country of residence, which in turn forces them to interrupt travel while their visa application is being processed.

Administrative barriers also include non-harmonized customs procedures in transit countries. There are differences in customs regulation in transit countries in terms of requirements and procedures despite the fact that all ITC countries are parties to the Kyoto Customs Convention, updated in 1999, as well as most transit countries of the International Convention on Harmonization of Frontier Controls of Goods, 1982. Customs authorities of transit countries use different information systems that are not integrated with each other, which does not allow receiving information on cargo and vehicles in advance along the entire route.

Border crossing for cargo transportation is double (except for Russia, Kazakhstan and Belarus). Customs, border, sanitary and other procedures are carried out twice at road border crossing points, by the services of one country at exit and by the services of the other country at entry. Joint control, which provides for close cooperation between customs, border and other authorities of neighbouring countries, is practically not used.

However, physical inspections of vehicles, cargo and containers are conducted at rail and road crossing points because Customs authorities often do not trust documents issued in neighbouring countries and therefore physically inspect the cargo to ensure that the data contained in the documents match.

It should also be noted that there is no agreement among ITC participants on the development of rail and road links along ITC routes. Many of the rail and road crossing points were designed and built for much smaller cargo flows and now do not meet the growing trade volumes and demand for border crossing. Insufficient capacity at BCPs is related to the length of receiving tracks and platforms for customs and other controls, as well as the lack of container relocation equipment at those BCPs where the rail gauge (1520/1435) is changed. Limitations in road capacity are due to insufficient number of lanes for trucks to pass border, customs, and other controls, resulting in queues.[17]

In general, there is a great deal of ambiguity regarding the ITC itself, in particular, many studies[18] indicate the above-mentioned lines (or branches) of routes, while there are no approved routes. The eastern (railroad) route through Turkmenistan and Uzbekistan raises many questions, as these states are not parties to the North-South ITC agreement. In addition, the studies mention a road route running through the territory of Georgia and passing through the Russian-Georgian road crossing point Daryali/Upper Lars, although Georgia is also not a party to the ITC.

Meetings of the ITC North-South Coordination Council, headquartered in Tehran, are held infrequently and irregularly, making it impossible to address operational issues to create a favourable environment for transport and simplify border crossing procedures.

The lack of a contractual and legal framework between the ITC participants on the above issues leads to non-functioning of the ITC itself, which is expressed in higher costs and longer delivery times of cargoes; falling efficiency of transportation, lower competitiveness of export goods and national carriers in foreign markets; increased trade costs for countries that are landlocked; rising costs of transported goods and transportation services.

As a consequence, all this leads to the rejection of the use of cargo delivery routes via the North-South ITC in favour of traditional routes, including via the Suez Canal.

Legal problems and gaps in the regulation of the North-South ITC lead to the fact that each country separately undertakes efforts to implement the project independently. For example, India is a de jure participant of the North-South ITC, but does not carry out transportation along this ITC. India, having great needs in Central Asian resources, is actively promoting projects to build another ITC through Iran to Central Asia. Thus, in 2016, India, Afghanistan and Iran signed the Agreement on Establishment of International Transport and Transit Corridor (Chabahar Agreement). The agreement provides for the establishment of a transit and transport corridor between the three countries using Chabahar Port as one of the regional hubs for maritime transportation in Iran, in addition to multimodal transportation of cargo and passengers. Chabahar Port is considered as a gateway to more trade opportunities for India, Iran and Afghanistan with Central Asian countries, besides expanding trade between the three countries due to Pakistan's denial of transit access to India.[19]

Conclusion

It can be assumed that economic integration processes and ITC have a certain (backward/bilateral) relationship, in which integration processes contribute to the functioning of ITC, and ITC contributes to the development of economic integration processes. It is obvious that ITCs cannot function effectively without economic integration of the states through whose territories the transport corridors pass. For the effective functioning of the ITC, it is necessary to have economic integration between the states through which the ITC passes, by concluding multilateral agreements on simplification of procedures for the transport of goods, harmonization of customs transit and border control of goods, liberalization of cross-border transport, improvement of border crossings, adoption of a common transport policy, harmonization of national legislation in the field of transport.

End Notes

1 Balassa (1961).

2 Marsha A. Echols. Regional Economic Integration. The International Lawyer Vol. 31, No. 2, International Legal Developments in Review: 1996 (SUMMER 1997), pp. 453-462. Published By: American Bar Association. https://www.jstor.org/stable/40707325

3 Simon Lester. The role of the international trade regime in global governance. UCLA Journal of International Law and Foreign Affairs. Vol. 16, No. 2 (Fall 2011), pp. 209-277.

4 Stefan A. Riesenfeld. Legal Systems of Regional Economic Integration. The American Journal of Comparative Law. Vol. 22, No. 3 (Summer, 1974), pp. 415-443.

5 Robert Howse. Regulatory cooperation, regional trade agreements, and world trade law: conflict or complementarity? Law and Contemporary Problems. Vol. 78, No. 4, New Approaches to International Regulatory Cooperation (2015), pp. 137-151 (15 pages) Published by: Duke University School of Law. https://www.jstor.org/stable/43920634?read-now=1&seq=1#page_scan_tab_contents

6 Stephen Weatherill. Free movement of goods. The International and Comparative Law Quarterly. Vol. 61, No. 2 (APRIL 2012), pp. 541-550 (10 pages). Published by: Cambridge University Press. https://www.jstor.org/stable/23279904?read-now=1&seq= 7#page_scan_tab_contents

7 Official Journal of the European Union. L 348/1. 20.12.2013. https://eur-lex.europa.eu/legal-content/EN/TXT/?uri=CELEX%3A32013R1315

8 Maria Öberg. Governance Structure for Transport Corridors. Luleå University of Technology. 2014. pp. 83-84. https://www.diva-portal.org/smash/get/diva2:991753/FULLTEXT01.pdf

9 Official Journal of the European Communities. 15.7.1996. No C 204/99. https://eur-lex.europa.eu/legal-content/EN/TXT/PDF/?uri=CELEX:51996IE0547&from=ES

10 Lay Hong Tan. Will Asean Economic Integration Progress beyond a Free Trade Area? The International and Comparative Law Quarterly. Vol. 53, No. 4 (Oct., 2004), pp. 935-967.

11 Daniel Seah. The ASEAN Charter. The International and Comparative Law Quarterly, Vol. 58, No. 1 (Jan., 2009), pp. 197-212.

12 Lay Hong Tan. Will Asean Economic Integration Progress beyond a Free Trade Area? The International and Comparative Law Quarterly. Vol. 53, No. 4 (Oct., 2004), pp. 935-967.

13 Chia, S.Y. 2013. The ASEAN Economic Community: Progress, Challenges, and Prospects. ADBI Working Paper 440. Tokyo: Asian Development Bank Institute. Available: https://www.adb.org/publications/asean-economic-community-progress-challenges-andprospects juda qiziq ma'lumotlar bor!

14 So Umezaki. Transport Facilitation in the Era of the ASEAN Economic Community. Chapter 2 of Research report: Cross-border Transport Facilitation in Inland ASEAN and the ASEAN Economic Community. Economic Research Institute for ASEAN and East Asia and Institute of Developing Economies, Japan External Trade Organization (IDE-JETRO), 2019, pp. 28-29. https://www.ide.go.jp/library/English/Publish/Reports/Ec/pdf/201902_01_cover.pdf

15 ASEAN Transport Development. The ASEAN Secretariat, Jakarta, 2017, p. 31.

16 Sanchita Chatterjee. International North South Transport Corridor (INSTC) connecting India Central - Asia. International Journal of Research in Social Sciences. Vol. 8, Issue 4, April 2018. pp. 601-616.

17 North-South International Transport Corridor: Investment Solutions and Soft Infrastructure. Reports and working papers. Eurasian Development Bank, 2022. https://eabr.org/upload/iblock/a2b/EDB_2022_Report-2_INSTC_rus.pdf

18 The North-South International Transport Corridor and Transregional Integration Scenarios. Report of the Valdai International Discussion Club. June 2019. https://ru.valdaiclub.com/files/27685/

19 Harsh V. Pant and Ketan Mehta. India in Chabahar: A Regional Imperative. Asian Survey Vol. 58, No. 4 (July/August 2018), pp. 660-678. Published by: University of California Press

16

Current Trends in the Development of Scientific and Technical Cooperation between Uzbekistan and India

Dr Rustam Mahmudov

ABSTRACT

The article is devoted to the state and prospects of development of cooperation between Uzbekistan and India in the scientific and technological sphere, which can give an additional impetus to the expansion of bilateral trade, economic and investment ties. The paper analyzes the measures taken by Uzbekistan towards the development of high-tech industry after the start of socio-political reforms in 2016, including legislative acts and implemented IT projects. It also analyzes India's performance in digital technology development, startup ecosystem, IT services, software products, ER&D and specialized education. The prospects of technological cooperation between Uzbekistan and India are considered through the prism of the Fourth Industrial Revolution.

In particular, cooperation in the field of industrial robotics has great potential, as India demonstrates quite high growth rates of robotization of the manufacturing industry and a number of large national companies specializing in the development of new solutions in this area operate in its market. Also promising is cooperation in the field of artificial intelligence, where Uzbekistan is just starting its way, and India is one of the world leaders in terms of the pace of development of IT startups and the investments they attract. There is great potential for cooperation in the production of electric vehicles, as well as in the market segments of raw materials related to new generation technologies, such as copper, rare earth metals and lithium. In addition, the importance of establishing an Uzbek-Indian expert dialogue to study possible threats and challenges posed by the Fourth Industrial Revolution to the internal stability of states and international security has been noted. First of all, we are talking about further robotization of industrial production and introduction of artificial intelligence, which will endanger many jobs created on the basis of technologies of the Second and Third Industrial Revolutions.

Keywords: *Uzbekistan, India, information technology, robotics, artificial intelligence, industrial revolution, electric car, startups, rare earth metals, lithium*

Introduction

Science and technology in the modern world are becoming one of the key sources of national wealth, military and geopolitical power of countries. It was the scientific and technological breakthrough that allowed the West, starting from the 18th and 19th centuries, to become the leading military, political and economic power, determining the key intellectual trends of the last centuries. The East's rethinking of its priorities in the direction of balancing the spiritual and material aspects of its existence led to the emergence, at the first stage, of new scientific and technological centres represented by Japan and the four "Asian tigers" – South Korea, Singapore, Hong Kong and Taiwan.

However, the biggest step towards transforming Asia into a global centre of modern technology and knowledge has been made thanks to the unprecedented development of India and China, two of the world's oldest civilizations and the most populous countries on the planet. At the same time, India has already firmly taken a leading position in the production of many high-tech products and services, and forecasts show that its status as a high-tech power will only continue to strengthen. This makes it a priority partner for Uzbekistan, which sets the development of knowledge-intensive industries and increasing the share of innovative products in its exports as one of the goals of its reforms.

Scientific and Technical Cooperation can become a Source of Strengthening Trade and Economic Ties between Uzbekistan and India

It should be recognized that the current state of trade and economic cooperation between Uzbekistan and India appears to be insufficient. Despite the fact that India ranks 10th in the list of Uzbekistan's leading trade partners, the volume of trade leaves much to be desired, although it has been growing in recent years. While bilateral trade volume stood at $444 million in 2020 and $490 million in 2021, it has increased to $690 million by the end of 2022. By comparison, trade with Russia totaled nearly $9.3 billion, with China $8.9 billion, and with Germany $1.159 billion.[1]

The structure of trade in terms of the share of high-tech products also leaves much to be desired. In 2021, machinery and equipment accounted for only 16 per cent of the value of bilateral trade. The leader was chemical products (71%).[2] This, in turn, poses a challenge for the countries to find additional sources of growth in economic cooperation, and one of them may be interaction in the field of high technology.

This issue is being discussed at the interstate level. Cooperation in the field of high technologies was on the agenda of the 13th meeting of the Uzbek-Indian Intergovernmental Commission (IGC) on trade-economic and scientific-technical cooperation held in New Delhi on July 28, 2022. The participants of the meeting noted that more than 85 joint projects worth over $3 billion are currently being implemented in Uzbekistan together with Indian partners in the fields of education, IT-technologies, healthcare and pharmaceuticals, production of construction materials, textiles and others. In order to intensify investment cooperation, including in the sphere of information technologies, the two sides agreed to work out in the near future all necessary issues for signing an agreement on encouragement and mutual protection of investments.

Delhi plans to open branches of three Indian universities in Uzbekistan: Glocal, LNCT and Integral. In addition, New Delhi and Tashkent plan to develop and adopt an Uzbek-Indian road map, which envisages opening new joint general, professional and higher educational institutions, expanding cooperation in scientific research and technology, including commercialization of innovations and startups. Uzbekistan and India also agreed to accelerate negotiations on a draft preferential trade agreement. All these projects and agreements are expected to increase bilateral trade to $1 billion.[3]

It should be noted that the parties not only demonstrate intention, but are also able to achieve a breakthrough in accelerating cooperation in the scientific and high-tech sphere. Uzbekistan, after the start of fundamental socio-political and economic reforms in 2016, began to pay great attention to education, science and technology.

Uzbekistan's Five-Directional Development Strategy for 2017-2021 sets the task of stimulating research and innovation activities, creating effective mechanisms for introducing scientific and innovative achievements into practice, creating scientific and experimental specialized laboratories, high-tech centres, and technoparks.[4] In the same year, the Ministry of Innovative Development of Uzbekistan and the Fund for Support of Innovative Development and Innovative Ideas were established.

In 2018, the Strategy for Innovative Development of the Republic of Uzbekistan for 2019-2021 and the corresponding Roadmap for its implementation were approved. The goals of innovative development of the Republic of Uzbekistan until 2030 were also defined, among which is Uzbekistan's entry into the top 50 advanced countries of the world according to the Global Innovation Index by 2030. In addition, the Strategy "Digital Uzbekistan-2030" was adopted, aimed at active development of digital economy, widespread introduction of modern information and communication technologies in public administration, education, health care and agriculture.

In particular, more than 220 priority projects have been launched. They are aimed at improving the e-government system, further developing the domestic market of software products and information technologies, organizing IT parks in all regions of the country and providing this sphere with qualified personnel.[5]

Two more key documents regulating relations in the field of science, scientific and innovative activity have been adopted. The law "On Science and Scientific Activity" was adopted in 2019 and the law "On Innovation Activity" was adopted in 2020. These laws should provide scientific solutions to problems related to achieving competitiveness and efficiency of the Uzbek economy, increasing labour productivity, creating new industries, improving the quality of life, science and education system.[6]

In the practical sphere, Uzbekistan has embarked on several major projects, of which two can be singled out.

The first project is One Million Uzbek Coders (OMUC), which is being implemented jointly with the United Arab Emirates. The project is a free online platform for teaching programming and digital skills to the population. The platform covers four areas: data analytics, android development, front-end development and full-stack development. As of June 2022, 2.5 million students and schoolchildren have registered on the platform, of which more than 1.5 million have received certificates of participation. It should be noted that 47 per cent of project participants are girls.[7]

The second most important project for the development of technological and digital culture in Uzbekistan is the Tashkent IT Park. It was opened on July 24, 2019. Notably, its opening was preceded by President Shavkat Mirziyoyev's visit to India in 2018. During the first visit, the Uzbek and Indian sides agreed to expand cooperation in IT. The Uzbek side expressed interest in establishing an IT park in Uzbekistan jointly with Indian high-tech companies.[8]

Tashkent IT Park develops cooperation with Indian science and technology centres and technology companies. On February 27, 2021, IT Park signed a memorandum of cooperation with the Jawaharlal Nehru Uzbek-Indian Centre for Information Technology at Tashkent University of Information Technology. The purpose of the memorandum was to establish cooperation for the development of a startup ecosystem among the youth of the Republic of Uzbekistan, as well as development in the field of education.[9] The Jawaharlal Nehru Uzbek-Indian Centre for Information Technology was established in 2006. The Centre became the first example of cooperation between our countries in the field of technology.

Uzbekistan's efforts to develop high-tech areas are already yielding the first financial dividends. In 2022, the volume of IT services increased by 125.5 per cent to 22.9 trillion Uzbek soums ($2 billion), according to Uzbek Minister of Digital Technologies Sherzod Shermatov. Exports of IT services reached 323 million dollars, exports of software products and services tripled compared to 2021 and reached 140 million dollars. Today, more than 100 thousand people work in the IT sector of Uzbekistan. At the same time, the need for human resources is growing. Uzbekistan is trying to meet this need by creating an ecosystem of digital education, including specialized schools and universities.[10]

A significant contribution to the development of the Uzbek IT sector is the so-called. "resettlement effect" caused by the relocation of a large number of Russian technically savvy specialists in connection with the Russian-Ukrainian war. Between February and September 2022, about 3,000 IT specialists were relocated to the country. They were attracted by full exemption from all corporate taxes, reduction of personal income tax from 12 per cent to 7.5 per cent, simplification of business registration procedures and hiring of foreign specialists. As part of the move, 68 foreign companies became residents of the IT park in Tashkent, and the total number of resident companies exceeded 850.[11]

In this regard, speaking about the significance of cooperation with India for the development of high-tech industry in Uzbekistan, we can say that it contains a huge potential, given that New Delhi is a leading player in the global scientific and technological market and the market of innovative products and services. Here are some of India's achievements that make it a strategically attractive partner.

India is among the seven space-faring nations along with the USA, Russia, China, France, Japan and South Korea. The country has also been ranked among the top 20 "Most Technologically Advanced Countries" by World Population Review in 2023.[12] US News magazine's "Best Global Universities for Computer Science" ranking includes 24 Indian technology universities, among which the highest ranked are Thapar Institute of Engineering & Technology (Patiala), Vellore Institute of Technology (Tamil Nadu), Indian Institute of Technology (IIT) – Kharagpur, Indian Institute of Science (IISC) – Bangalore, Indian Institute of Technology (IIT) – Bombay.[13]

The Indian IT industry currently employs about 4.5 million people. In recent years, Indian companies have increased their investments in the IT services sector and boosted exports. IT spending in India was expected to grow by an estimated 0.5 per cent to $110.3 billion in 2023 from $109.7 billion in 2022.[14] According to analysts at IDC, the Indian IT services market grew 7.2 per cent year-on-year to reach $14.15 billion in 2021.[15] According to the Reserve Bank of India, India's software services exports grew to 88.8 per cent in FY 2021-22 from 82.8 per cent five years ago. India's software services exports (excluding exports through commercial presence) are estimated to have increased by 17.2 per cent to $156.7 billion during this fiscal year.[16] In comparison, in 2000, India's IT industry exports were US$ 6.2 billion.[17]

According to Nasscom estimates, the Indian technology industry revenue was expected to grow by $245 billion in reported currency in FY 2023, with a 2 per cent cross currency impact. Growth is seen in segments such as IT services, BPM, software products, ER&D and domestic market. It was expected that services export revenue in India would be $194 billion in USD, up 9.4 per cent from FY 2022.[18] India has become the third largest startup ecosystem in the world. Since 2014, annual venture capital funding for Indian startups has grown eightfold, from $5 billion in 2014 to $42 billion in 2021. At the same time, the number of Indian "unicorns" has grown about 18 times, from 6 to 105.[19]

With over 1300 tech startups in India in 2022, there are currently around 25-27 thousand active tech startups in India.[20] The 6 Indian startups that made it to the list of top 100 unicorns in the world include BYJU's, Swiggy, OYO Rooms, Dream11, Razorpay and Ola Cabs. BYJU's, an education technology platform, is valued at $22 billion at the end of December 2022 and is the most valuable startup in India and 12th in the world, according to the list. Foodtech platform Swiggy is valued at $10.7 billion, OYO Rooms at $9 billion, online gaming portal Dream11 at $8 billion, payment gateways Razorpay and Ola at $7.5 billion each.[21]

Such "big tech giants" as Meta, Google, Amazon, Microsoft, IBM, Intel, as well as American and Arab investment funds are actively investing in the Indian high-tech industry. The centre of investment activity is the "Indian Silicon Valley" Bangalore, located in the state of Karnataka. In terms of the number of "unicorns" Bengaluru (23 companies) in 2022 was ranked 6th in the world after San Francisco (176), New York (120), Beijing (90), Shanghai (69), London (39) and Shenzhen (33).[22] Bengaluru and London are among the top 10 cities in the world in terms of highest venture capital investment in the last five years. In the first three quarters of this year, Bengaluru-based technology companies raised a record $7.5 billion in venture capital funding, up from $5.2 billion in 2021.

These data show that India is a very promising partner for Uzbekistan in the field of high technologies.

The Fourth Industrial Revolution and its Impact on Prospects for Uzbek-Indian Technological Cooperation

Meanwhile, speaking about the prospects of technological cooperation between Uzbekistan and India, it is necessary to take into account the current global context. We are living in the era of the fourth industrial revolution, which brings with it many completely new types of technologies. This era can be called the era of smart technologies. It brings with it a series of fundamental changes in manufacturing, services, transportation, energy, urbanism, medicine, man-machine relations, labour market and politics.

It is obvious that those countries that can succeed in the development, introduction and implementation of new technologies, as well as successfully address the socio-economic, moral and ethical challenges posed by them, will be able to take leading positions in their regions and the world, and improve the well-being of their peoples. For Uzbekistan and India, the introduction and development of technologies of the Fourth Industrial Revolution is a matter of strategic importance, which, in turn, opens up prospects for bilateral cooperation in several directions.

Industrial Robotics. Uzbekistan is just beginning its journey in the development of industrial robots, as well as robotics automation in the service and agricultural sectors. The ongoing economic reform process in the country will only increase the Uzbek economy's need for modern industrial robots, and Indian companies could become one of the promising partners.

In turn, India, although not yet a world leader in industrial robotics, being behind such countries as South Korea, Singapore, Japan, the USA and China, nevertheless demonstrates quite high growth rates of robotization. There are several large domestic companies operating in the Indian market. Some of them include the following: Gridbots (advanced robotics and artificial intelligence), Sastra Robotics (robotic solutions for automated human-centred testing of real physical devices), Grey Orange Robotics (design, manufacture and implementation of advanced robotic systems for warehousing, distribution and other industrial applications), Systematic Robotics (Bengaluru-based company, a market leader in automation and robotics in India), Navstik labs (robotics solutions for the Indian aerospace industry), Omnipresent Robot Tech (state-of-the-art unmanned aerial vehicles, river cleaning robots, and software for robot sensing, navigation and information perception).[23]

Artificial Intelligence. In 2022, Uzbekistan established an Advisory Council on Artificial Intelligence (AI) under the Ministry of Innovative Development. The new structure will develop proposals for the development of Uzbekistan's

National Strategy on Artificial Intelligence and its implementation in agriculture, banking and finance, public, road and rail transportation, healthcare and e-government.

India is an attractive partner for Uzbekistan in this case, especially in the development of AI startups. According to Stanford University's AI Index report, India ranks fifth in terms of investment received by startups offering AI-based products and services in 2022. The total investment in AI startups in India amounted to $3.24 billion, ahead of South Korea, Germany, Canada and Australia. However, India still lags behind the USA, China, UK and Israel in terms of AI investments received. According to the same report, between 2013 and 2022, AI startups in India received a cumulative funding of $7.73 billion, which puts the country in sixth place among the countries with the highest amount of AI investment during this period. Nearly 40 per cent of this funding was received in 2022 alone.[24]

Electric Vehicles. Uzbekistan is currently focusing on a gradual transition from internal combustion engine vehicles to electric vehicles (EVs). The government has set targets to create an EV industry and reach production of 25,000 electric vehicles per year.[25] On December 19, 2022, the President of Uzbekistan signed a decree on state support for the organization of electric vehicle production. The development of electric vehicle production should lay the foundations for a green economy in the country and contribute to the reduction of carbon dioxide emissions.[26]

Uzbekistan has already taken the first place in Central Asia in terms of imports of electric cars. In January-November 2022, the country imported 1,912 electric vehicles from abroad (+1,223 compared to 2021) worth $61.3 million. Of these, China accounted for 1,675 EVs, UAE – 111, Germany – 56, Hong Kong – 42, Lithuania – 10, South Korea – 7.[27]

India is known to be the third largest automotive market in the world, ahead of Germany and Japan. According to Economic Survey 2023, India's domestic electric vehicle market is projected to grow at a CAGR of 49 per cent between 2022 and 2030, with annual sales reaching 10 million units by 2030. Prominent Indian automakers such as Tata Motors and Mahindra & Mahindra have launched electric vehicles.[28]

It should be noted that such a factor as abundance of natural resources in Uzbekistan, which play an important role in the fourth industrial revolution, speaks in favour of the development of Uzbek-Indian technological cooperation. First of all, it is copper, the reserves of which are estimated at 45 million tons. The global demand for copper will only grow as the production of electric cars increases in the world. Global demand for copper is projected to increase by at least 40 per cent by 2030.[29]

The fourth industrial revolution is leading to a growing demand for rare earth metals and lithium, which are essential for the production of green technologies, electronic devices and gadgets. China is currently the world's leading producer and exporter of rare earth metals. In turn, the largest proven reserves of lithium are held by Chile, Australia, Argentina, China and the United States. Given the growing global demand for these metals, competition for them will only intensify, which can be seen as a challenge, for example, for Indian companies' plans to increase their own production of lithium-ion batteries.

In this regard, Uzbekistan and India could consider turning to the natural resources of Afghanistan, which is believed to have huge reserves of lithium and rare earth metals. According to Bloomberg, "Afghanistan is home to deposits estimated at $1 trillion or more, including possibly the world's largest lithium reserves."[30] Uzbekistan is already actively cooperating with the Interim Government of Afghanistan in organizing transit freight traffic from Central Asia to South Asia and back, as well as preparing conditions for the construction of the Termez-Mazar-e-Sharif-Kabul-Peshawar railroad.

In considering the fourth industrial revolution, we must also consider not only the prospects and dividends, but also possible threats and challenges to the internal stability of states and international security. Automation and artificial intelligence could jeopardize many of the jobs created by the technologies of the second and third industrial revolutions. This, in turn, could potentially leave a large number of people unemployed and vulnerable to various protest ideologies and external manipulations.

According to Carl Benedict Frey, an economic historian at Oxford University, the new industrial revolution will be based on "substitute technologies," i.e., technologies that will replace jobs that previously required human participation. Such technologies could leave large numbers of people unemployed and vulnerable to various protest ideologies and external manipulation.

With this in mind, governments implementing automation, artificial intelligence, autonomous transport, and robotization programs need to start simultaneously developing long-term programs to reform education systems to create new types of jobs. Lack of synchronization in this matter may lead to the fact that workers and employees displaced by new technologies may become sources of socio-political instability. The first technological revolution, which was also dominated by substitute technologies, gave rise to a rebellious working class and Marxism.[31]

The technologies of the fourth industrial revolution may also have a negative impact on traditional global value chains based on cheap labour. According to many economists, the increasing efficiency and cost-effectiveness of modern technologies underlying so-called "light-out manufacturing" and "dark factories" will reduce the importance of cheap labour, which was a key driver of economic growth in the nineteenth, twentieth and first decades of the twenty-first century. This, in turn, will hit developing economies hoping to make economic breakthroughs and attract investors by exploiting demographics.

The intensification of competition for world leadership in the context of the fourth industrial revolution is also a serious challenge to international relations and globalization. Today, we see an increasing use of non-market competition tools, such as financial, economic, personal, secondary and technological sanctions, as well as direct political and military pressure, to gain advantages over competitors. Apparently, we should not expect the tensions in international relations to ease in the coming years.

Technological progress can have a powerful impact on traditional values. Genetic engineering, nanotechnology, 3D printing in medicine, and the fusion of humans and technology can strengthen the position of proponents of the scientific immortalism and transhumanism movement in the public space. Obviously, their technological values will come into conflict with traditional value systems, which may consider new technologies as human interference in the design of higher powers.

All the above challenges and threats directly affect the long-term technological interests of Uzbekistan and India, and therefore can become the subject of joint discussion and research at the academic and analytical level.

Conclusion

Summarizing the results, I would like to note that scientific and technical cooperation between Uzbekistan and India has all chances to become a locomotive for further development of bilateral state, economic and trade relations. Taking into account the challenges of modern geopolitics, the rivalry of great powers for military-political and economic dominance, as well as the Fourth Industrial Revolution, cooperation between Uzbekistan and India can become the first step towards the creation of a "technological security community" in Central and South Asia. The emergence of such a community will make it possible not only to respond effectively to contemporary challenges, but also to use the historical chance to return our common cultural and historical space to the centre of the world's scientific and technological processes, which it occupied in the Middle Ages.

End Notes

1 Sblizheniye s Rossiyey. Kitay - glavnyy postavshchik. Kak izmenilas vneshnyaya torgovlya Uzbekistana v 2022 godu // Gazeta.uz. October 10. 2022. https://www.gazeta.uz/ru/2023/01/24/trade-partners/

2 Infografika: Obyem torgovli mezhdu Uzbekistan i Indiyey // Review.uz. January 27. 2022. https://review.uz/post/infografika-ozbekiston-va-hindiston-ortasidagi-savdo-hajmi

3 Uzbekistan i Indiya zaplanirovali dovesti tovarooborot do 1 mlrd dollarov // Darakchi.uz. July 29. 2022. https://darakchi.uz/ru/14938

4 Ukaz Prezidenta Respubliki Uzbekistan o Strategii deystviy po dalneyshemu razvitiyu Respubliki Uzbekistan// Lex.uz. July 29. 2022. https://lex.uz/ru/docs/3107042

5 Ukaz Prezidenta Respubliki Uzbekistan ob Utverzhdenii Strategii "Tsifrovoy Uzbekistan - 2030" i merakh po eye effektivnoy realizatsii // Lex.uz. February 07. 2017. https://lex.uz/ru/docs/5031048

6 Nodira Kurbanbayeva. Analiz probelov v sfere nauki. ,tekhnologiy i innovatsiy (NTI) v Uzbekistane // UNECE.org. November2020. https://unece.org/sites/default/files/2021-03/STI%20gap%20analysis_Uzbekistan_Report_Nodira%20Kurbanbaeva_RUS.pdf

7 "Odin million uzbekskikh programmistov": chestvovaniye pobediteley sovmestnogo proyekta // Xalq so'zi. June 11. 2022. https://xs.uz/ru/post/odin-million-uzbekskikh-programmistov-chestvovanie-pobeditelej-sovmestnogo-proekta

8 IT Park Today // IT-park.uz, June 11, 2022. https://it-park.uz/en/itpark/about

9 IT Park signed a memorandum with the Uzbek-Indian Centre for Information Technologies // IT-Park.uz, January 03, 2021. https://it-park.uz/en/itpark/news/it-park-signed-a-memorandum-with-the-uzbek-indian-center-for-information-technologies-named-after-

jawaharlal-nehru-at-the-tashkent-university-of-information-technologies-named-after-muhammad-al-khorazmiy

10 Pavel Nosachev. Pochemu Uzbekistan prevrashchayetsya v tsentr razvitiya IT-industrii // Kursiv.Media, March 31, 2023. https://kz.kursiv.media/2023-03-31/ministr-czifrovyh-tehnologij-uzbekistana-sherzod-shermatov-prakticheski-po-vsem-pokazatelyam-my-nablyudaem-rost-prevyshayushhij-ozhidaniya/

11 Rost konkurentsii i lokalnoy ekspertizy: chemu privela privela massovaya relokatsiya IT-spetsialistov v Uzbekistan // Spot.uz, September 23. 2022. https://www.spot.uz/ru/2022/09/23/relocation/

12 Most Technologically Advanced Countries 2023 // World Population Review, 2023. https://worldpopulationreview.com/country-rankings/most-technologically-advanced-countries

13 Best Global Universities for Computer Science in India // USNews.com, 2022-2023. https://www.usnews.com/education/best-global-universities/india/computer-science

14 India IT spending to reach $110.3 bn in 2023 amid global slowdown: Report // Business Standard, January 18, 2023. https://www.business-standard.com/article/companies/india-it-spending-to-reach-110-3-bn-in-2023-amid-global-slowdown-report-123011800664_1.html

15 Indian Domestic IT Services Market Grows by 7.9% in 2021 with Enterprises Continuing to Invest in Digital Transformation Initiatives // IDC Reports, April 28, 2022. https://www.idc.com/getdoc.jsp?containerId=prAP49061322&utm_medium=rss_feed&utm_source= alert&utm_ campaign=rss_syndication

16 Exports of Indian software services increased to 88.8% in FY22: RBI // The Economic Times, September 09, 2022. https://economictimes.indiatimes.com/tech/information-tech/exports-of-indian-software-services-increased-to-88-8-in-fy22-

17 India's AI roadmap in 2023: From CAGR 20% growth to creating endless job opportunities by Anand Mahurkar // The Times of India, February 8, 2023. https://timesofindia.indiatimes.com/blogs/voices/indias-ai-roadmap-in-2023-from-cagr-20-growth-to-creating-endless-job-opportunities/

18 ITech industry revenue set to reach $245 billion in FY2023E: Nasscom // The Economic Times, March 01, 2023. https://economictimes.indiatimes.com/tech/technology/indian-tech-sector-to-grow-8-4-in-fy23-to-245-billion-nasscom/articleshow/98329731.cms?from=mdr

19 The State Of Indian Startup Ecosystem Report, 2022 // INC42.com, 2022. https://inc42.com/reports/the-state-of-indian-startup-ecosystem-report-2022/?login=1

20 India Adds Over 1,300 Tech Startups In 2022, Nasscom Report Shows by Priyal Mahtta // VCCIRCLE, February 15, 2023. https://www.vccircle.com/indiaadds-over-1-300-tech-startups-in-2022-nasscom-report-shows

21 These 6 Indian startups are among world's top 100 unicorns // The Economic Times, March 21, 2023. https://economictimes.indiatimes.com/markets/stocks/news/these-6-indian-startups-are-among-worlds-top-100-unicorns/articleshow/98863726.cms?utm_source=contentofinterest &utm_medium=text&utm_campaign=cppst

22 Cities with the highest number of unicorns worldwide in 1st half 2022 // Statista. https://www.statista.com/statistics/1062457/cities-highest-number-of-unicorns/

23 Top 10 RoboTech Companies to Work for in India in 2023 by Shiva Ganesh // Analytic Insight, February 18, 2023 // https://www.analyticsinsight.net/top-10-robotech-companies-to-work-for-in-india-in-2023/

24 India ranks 5th in countries with most AI investments by Sumit Arora // Current Affairs, April 13, 2023. https://currentaffairs.adda247.com/india-ranks-5th-in-countries-with-most-ai-investment/

25 Importers and proizvoditeli elektromobiley poluchat ryad lgot. Gosudarstvo takzhe budet chastichno pogashat protsenty po kreditu pri pokupke takikh avto // Podrobno.uz. 24.11.2022. https://podrobno.uz/cat/economic/importery-i-proizvoditeli-elektromobiley-poluchat-ryad-lgot-gosudarstvo-takzhe-budet-chastichno-poga/?sphrase_id=5328695

26 Proizvodstvo elektromobiley v Uzbekistane poluchit gosudarstvennuyu podderzhku // Gazeta.uz. 22.12.2022. https://www.gazeta.uz/ru/2022/12/19/ecars/

27 Uzbekistantsy potratili 61.3 milliona dollarov na import elektromobiley v etom godu // Podrobno.uz. 19.12.2022. https://podrobno.uz/cat/obchestvo/uzbekistantsy-potratili-61-3-milliona-dollarov-na-import-elektromobiley-v-etom-godu/#:

28 India's EV Economy: The Future of Automotive Transportation by Aditi Singh // Invest India, February 07, 2023. https://www.investindia.gov.in/team-india-blogs/indias-ev-econo my-future-automotive-transportation

29 17th International Exhibition on Mining, Metallurgy and Metalworking - Mining Metals Uzbekistan 2023 // Mining Metals Uzbekistan. November 03, 2023. https://mining.uz/en/mediacentre/novosti.php?ELEMENT_ID=55045#:~:text=According%20to%20international%20assessment%20criteria,rhenium%20and%20other%20rare%20metals.

30 Chinese Miners in Talks to Access Vast Afghan Lithium Reserves by Eltaf Najafizada // Mining Metals Uzbekistan, November 24, 2021. https://www.bloomberg.com/news/articles/2021-11-24/chinese-firms-show-interest-in-afghanistan-s-mineral-reserves#xj4y7vzkg?lead Source= uverify%20wall

31 Rustam Makhmudov. New Technologies as a Challenge to Stability in Greater Eurasia // Valday Discussion Club, October 31, 2019. https://valdaiclub.com/a/highlights/new-technologies-as-a-challenge-to-stability/

17

Modern Foreign Policy of the N. Modi Government

Prof A.A. Sharapov

ABSTRACT

It is obvious that India's foreign policy is currently attracting more and more interest among representatives of academic and political circles of different countries of the world. Most likely it is caused first of all by the civilizational peculiarity of India, increasing importance of India in the process of formation of the new world order in the XXI century. As well as more pragmatic foreign policy pursued by N. Modi. India's relations with the Central Asian region are of no small importance.

Keywords. *India, Indian civilization, foreign policy, N. Modi, Central Asia.*

Among the states of the modern world, there are not many states that can draw on ancient civilization. One of them is India. As scientists G.M. Bongard-Levin and A.V. Gerasimov note, it is not by chance that ancient India is called the country of sages and thinkers. This characterization is undoubtedly connected with the high level of development of Indian science, philosophy and spiritual culture in general in the distant past. Here, already at the dawn of civilization, knowledge was treated with special respect, moreover, reverence; its achievement was declared the goal of human life. Having such rich experience, the country is able to be a leader in the modern world, where knowledge plays a major role in the development of mankind.

"Even the gods envy the wise," says one of the works of the Buddhist canon, "Dhammapada", "If someone speaks or does with true knowledge, then happiness follows him like an unstoppable shadow". Through the centuries Indians have carried the memory of the creators of original philosophical systems and scientific schools – mathematicians, astronomers, grammarians; they called their outstanding thinkers, scientists, writers and poets "great sages".[1]

The first surviving monument of Indian spiritual culture is the Vedas – collections of religious hymns containing a lot of information about mythology, cosmology, social relations and life of ancient Indians. Archaeological research in the Indus Valley revealed to the world a highly developed autochthonous civilization called the Indus or Harappan civilization (after the place of excavations in one of the settlements of the Western Punjab). Chronologically, Harappa turned out to be a contemporary of the most ancient states of Egypt and Maveranahr: the birth of the Indus culture dates back to the first half of the 3rd millennium B.C., and its blossoming continued for more than ten centuries.[2]

Nevertheless, the history of India has its own peculiarities in terms of political organization. As one of the authoritative scholars of India notes "India is the world's oldest civilization and largest democracy. It is the centre of connection between East and West Asia, as well as a confident guardian of the Indian Ocean.... Unlike the history of China, which can be clearly divided into periods of rule by dynasties such as Yuan, Ming or Qing, India's past is mottled with multiple centres of power, desperately fighting among themselves. Even at the height of the empire, none of the three great Indian empires – the Mauryas, the Guptas and the Mughals – controlled the entire subcontinent.[3]

Certainly, it is necessary to consider the importance of modern research on international relations, where recently special attention has been paid to non-Western theories of international relations, where the specificity of India's theory of international relations can be noted.

The main dividing line in the history of Theory of International Relations (TIR) development in India is considered to be the formation of the independent Indian state in 1947 and the coming to power of J. Nehru. The following stages can be distinguished:

Doneruvian interpretation of Indian nationhood (or nationalism), is based on a deep cultural context – the Vedic tradition, ancient Hindu epics such as the Ramayana and Mahabharata, and the understanding of nationhood, peace and war embedded in them. This interpretation is extremely difficult to fit within the framework of Western concepts. This is the first problem of Indian TIR – the incongruity between the "conventional" Western approach, where international relations theory exists as a separate discipline, and the highly contextualized Indian historical-political tradition, which undoubtedly has a broad base for the formation of unique theoretical positions, but which is not separable from the laws of the functioning of society and the place of the individual in it.

The Nehruvian period comes with the emergence of modern India in 1947 and the beginning of the formation of Indian statehood on the Western model.

For **Neo-Ruvianism**, the basic position is the ability of states and people to understand each other and achieve sustainable peace despite the inevitability of war and rivalry. At the same time, war is not considered a natural state of interstate relations, and one of the main reasons for the outbreak of wars is the misperception of the opponent. The anarchic nature of international relations can be overcome through agreement, adherence to international law and cooperation. The roots of these ideas can be found in one of the most important concepts (from the point of view of Indian philosophy) – "ahimsa" (the principle of non-violence).

All these provisions are also similar to the principle of **non-alignment**, of which J. Nehru was one of the main adherents and leaders.

From the perspective of **hyperrealism**, which has become the main paradigm for contemporary Indian TIR, states are doomed to an endless cycle of war, deterrence, and shifting balance of power, and no amount of international cooperation will change that.

Another important concept that has left its mark on the Indian view of international relations is the legacy of M. Gandhi, called **Gandhianism.** For Gandhi, the causes of any social processes originated at the level of the individual and were determined by the consciousness of each individual member of society, while the nation-state and any other kind of human community came second, as they were considered formal entities.

Concept – **political Hinduism** is not only the ideological basis of the Bharatiya Janata Party currently ruling India, but also a worldview concept that has a significant impact on the formation of various aspects of Indian foreign policy and national identity within the world community.

For political Hinduism, the main object is the relationship between civilizations and people as bearers of a particular culture. In the case of India, the civilizational aspect is key; the country is positioned as a unique civilization.

The strengthening of this approach in combination with hyperrealism can be observed in N. Modi's policy today. Modi's "personal philosophy of governance" and management style, including in foreign policy, are based on a combination of the principles of Hindu nationalism and hyperrealism, according to which in order to fulfil its "purpose", ensure security, achieve greatness and prosperity, the country must protect its cultural essence from threats from within and outside.

Under N. Modi, India's "special role" as a great power and the need to strengthen its "global authority" became more explicitly articulated. The main contribution of the Modi government to the modification of its approach to foreign policy lies, perhaps, in the explicit pursuit of the idea of India as a "world guru" inherent in Hindu nationalism, the need to ensure recognition and respect for its civilizational and historical heritage. India should become such a guru with respect to its immediate neighbours (the priority of developing relations with them is reflected in the principle of "*neighbourhood first*"), the global South, and the ITR.[4]

From the point of view of political thought, the masterpiece of Indian political thought is Kautilya's Arthashastra, which deals with the governance of the state: the interests of the state, which are centred on security, wealth and prestige, through three fundamental goals that flow one into the other: good governance (promoting the welfare of subjects) leads to good economy (acquiring wealth), which in turn allows for the expansion of territory.[5]

This can be observed in the contemporary policies of the N. Modi government. According to Dattesh Parulekar, Associate Professor at Goa University, Modi has made concerted efforts over the past five years to restore India's lost strategic status in South Asia and to recognize New Delhi as a regional leader in line with the country's de facto role in the region. To this end, he has strengthened India's partnership with neighbouring countries and has been engaged with them in the political arena through official visits to all South

Asian countries and revitalization of institutional mechanisms for bilateral dialogue. In addition, the well-thought-out coordinated efforts of the highest echelons of power to revive interstate infrastructure projects that had lost dynamism served this purpose in order to accelerate their completion and rehabilitate the shaken faith in their viability, to consolidate the imperative notion of the expediency of multi-vector ties, logistically compact commodity exchange, as well as civilizational similarity, which is the key basis for large-scale regional economic transformation and mobility. In the coming period, we can expect a significant intensification of efforts to promote the chosen course.

It is worth noting that it is an obvious fact that Beijing's economic efforts have a direct impact on New Delhi's behaviour. In this regard, Dattesh Parulekar notes that New Delhi cannot change the harsh reality of South Asian countries' trade dependence on China and is unable to counter Beijing's inevitable large-scale industrial and infrastructural offensive across the Himalayas and South Asian sea lanes, which are India's traditional sphere of influence, and must resort to a counterbalance strategy. Such a strategy combines elements of direct retaliation in certain contexts with the implementation of a sophisticated and carefully crafted differentiated paradigm to shape the region. It can be seen in the new and revived functional regional economic cooperation initiatives [Bay of Bengal Initiative for Multi-Sectoral Techno-Economic Cooperation (BIMTEC)] as well as sub-regional integration models [Four Countries Initiative: Bangladesh, Bhutan, India and Nepal (BBIN)] etc., aimed at gaining weight in the region.[6]

After becoming the Prime Minister of India in 2014, Narendra Modi has shown remarkable *strength* in formulating foreign policy. A hugely experienced administrator who has held key government positions as Chief Minister of an Indian state for over a decade and now as Prime Minister, he has always seen value in foreign policy and has emphasized it with his unique entrepreneurial flair and consistent approach. set of ideas. All areas of Indian foreign policy – commercial diplomacy, defence diplomacy, diaspora outreach, cultural diplomacy, geo-strategy and soft power – have been transformed by him with a sense of destiny not seen in recent times.[7]

Thanks to N. Modi's policy, the "Neighbourhood First" policy has become the most popular and effective. This approach, on the one hand, is a continuation of India's persistent efforts to streamline its regional environment, and on the other hand, the strategy proposed by N. Modi has a number of specific features that reflect both changes in the global environment of the country and its changing understanding of its place and role in the modern world.[8]

It should be noted that this was a response to the geopolitical situation in the world, which was caused by the collapse of the socialist system and the Soviet Union and the economic strengthening of China.

This further led to the formation of the "Look East" policy aimed at strengthening Delhi's relations with its neighbours. Moreover, Delhi's initiative took into account the low effectiveness of the South Asian Association for Regional Cooperation (SAARC) formed in 1985.

Another idea was embodied in the so-called **Gujral Doctrine**. The approach proposed by I.K. Gujral (1919-2012), India's Foreign Minister and, since April 1997, Prime Minister, significantly changed the format of the country's bilateral interactions with its closest neighbours.

According to them:

(1) India does not demand reciprocity from its neighbours, Bangladesh, Bhutan, Maldives, Nepal and Sri Lanka, but instead gives and accepts what it can on the basis of goodwill and trust;

(2) no country in South Asia should allow its territory to be used against the interests of another country in the region;

(3) no country should interfere in the internal affairs of another;

(4) all South Asian countries should respect each other's territorial integrity and sovereignty;

(5) all their differences should be resolved through peaceful bilateral dialogue.[9] Based on the existing theories on conflictology, it can be argued that the Gujral doctrine is a vivid example of a non-Western approach to conflict resolution, taking into account the interests of the parties.

This was evidenced by agreements on previously controversial issues, including the agreements:

(a) India with Nepal in the field of hydropower;

(b) with Bangladesh on water sharing, It was first mentioned in the annual report of the Ministry of Foreign Affairs (1995-1996), although no official statement defined the principles of this policy;

(c) Sri Lanka on enhancing development cooperation.

This doctrine formalized the first concepts of subregional cooperation in the form of the South Asia Growth Quadrangle (SAGQ), later endorsed by the Asian Development Bank (ADB) as the South Asia Subregional Economic Cooperation (SASEC). The idea of "collective prosperity", manifested in practice in a "bottom-up approach" or "cooperative sub-regionalism", became one of the fundamental principles of India's regional policy in the second half of the 1990s.[10]

Addressing the debate at the 69th session of the United Nations General Assembly (UNGA) in September 2014, N. Modi said, "The destiny of a nation is linked to its neighbourhood. That is why my government gives top priority to promoting friendship and cooperation with its neighbours." In this one can observe a certain continuity of ideas in India's foreign policy.

Three main drivers define the goals and content of the Neighbourhood First strategy. First is the imperative of economic growth. Until recently, India's woefully low level of economic development and growth rates remained. Strong economy, as N. Modi has repeatedly stated, is the driving force behind an effective foreign policy. Reflecting this idea, the Look East Policy (LEP), adopted by the Indian government in 1992, was updated and transformed into the Act East Policy (AEP) in 2014.[11]

Given the border and geopolitical situation, New Delhi is paying more attention to India's northeastern states, especially Arunachal Pradesh, which act as India's connectors to the ASEAN region. Initiatives such as the Kaladan Multi-Modal Transit Transport Project, the India-Myanmar-Thailand trilateral highway, the RiTiddim road, the India-Bangladesh Border Haats trading posts and a number of others are designed to facilitate this.[12]

In India's foreign policy, an important place is occupied not only by relations with its neighbours but also with Washington. As is known, the idea originally proposed (although it has a long history) by a naval officer from India became the theoretical basis for the U.S. Indo-Pacific Initiative.

According to researcher A.B. Volynchuk, the most popular and frequently used example of global transformation is the shift of the centre of world politics and economy from the Atlantic region to the Asia-Pacific Region (APR). The almost thirty-year practice of using the abbreviation "APR" has not brought scientists to a consensus on the reality of the existence of this region. At the same time, in geopolitical and geostrategic documents of many countries a new spatial and political construct has appeared, which in terms of its relevance can very quickly displace the Pacific Asia from the pages of scientific and specialized literature. This is the Indo-Pacific, or the Indo-Pacific Region (IPR).[13]

It cannot be said that the term "Indo-Pacifica" is something completely new for the science and practice of international relations. For the first time, the toponym very close to the localization of the ITR appeared in the middle of the XIX century in the monograph of English ethnologist J. Logan "Ethnology of the Indian Archipelago: a comprehensive study of the continental relations of the inhabitants of the Indo-Pacific Islands" (1850).[14]

The second attempt to introduce the term into scientific circulation was made by the German geographer and geopolitician C. Haushofer, whose publications in the mid-20-30s of the XX century unambiguously singled out the Indo-Pacific in the list of other political and geographical spaces.

Nevertheless, the most sustained scholarly interest in this region emerged in the early 21st century and was associated with the actualization of strategic and geopolitical discourse.

Since the autumn of 2017, the concept of "Indo-Pacific" has become an integral part of American foreign policy discourse and the subject of extensive international discussions. As we know, the term itself and the concept of this strategic megaregion are far from new. The concept of Indo-Pacific has different content depending on the context and purposes of use. Initially, this was the name of the most extensive biogeographic area of the World Ocean – a huge part of water space and land between 40°N and 40°S, which is bounded by the east coast of Africa and the Red Sea in the west, extends from Hawaii to French Polynesia in the east, reaches Taiwan Island in the north, and includes the territory of Australia in the south. At the centre of this space is the Strait of Malacca between Malaysia and Indonesia, the main sea route from the Indian Ocean to the South China Sea.[15]

The Free and Open IndoPacific (FOIP) strategy was first put forward in modern history by Shinzo Abe in August 2006, on the eve of his first term as leader of Japan. Abe envisioned the Indo-Pacific region as a single strategic entity led by a coalition of pro-free trade democracies, with the so-called "Quad" consisting of Australia, India, Japan and the United States at its core.

The USA and its allies in the form of maritime liberal regimes are rapidly seizing the initiative to frame the Indo-Pacific as part of their ITR vision. Their ultimate goal is to displace Beijing from its dominant position in the region's trade, economic and financial spheres. The US, Japan, Australia, and India form the core of the main participants in the construction of a "liberal" Indo-Pacific. The United Kingdom and France are extra-regional players, which have an exclusive interest in the "overseas" agenda and are mostly on the side of the anti-China alliance. Thus, the transoceanic structures that are currently being formed are being created with a built-in option of increased "protection" from China's influence. Thus, the creation of new (QUAD-2) and modernization of the "old" existing alliances (QUAD) allowed to adjust the allies' approaches to the ITR and bring the main goals of the participating countries to a common denominator, which, by common consent, is based on the growing threats to regional security due to China's strengthening in the region.

It is noted that the practical implementation of the IPS strategy is carried out through the creation of multilateral formats of cooperation. The main of them is considered to be the QUAD association, designed to "unite the four democracies" of the Indo-Pacific region – the United States, Japan, Australia and India. As some Chinese experts believe in this regard, "There are two main lines of geopolitics in Eurasia: the issue of control over the 'world island' from the position of land power and the connection of the Mediterranean Sea with the Indian Ocean and the Pacific Ocean from the position of sea power. In the context of the chaotic and turbulent Eurasian land power structure caused by the Ukrainian crisis, the EU will inevitably turn to the second main line, increase resource investments in the Indo-Pacific region, secure supplies of key raw materials and display its geopolitical influence."[16]

Tracing the current trends in world politics, regional cooperation has become more prominent in India's foreign policy. On this basis, the importance of Central Asia as part of the "extended neighbourhood" for India can be noted for the following reasons:

- The nations of the region and India have an ancient history of relations;
- India's energy security in Central Asia, which has the richest natural deposits, plays an important role;
- This requires stable development in Afghanistan;
- When advancing its interests in Central Asia, New Delhi takes into account the nature of its relations with the Russian Federation and competition with China.

The revitalization of India's foreign policy in Central Asia was conceptualized in 2012, when a new foreign policy strategy called *Connect Central* Asia was formulated. It focused on high-level engagement, including within multilateral organizations, security, energy and natural resources, cooperation in education and digital services, and increased cultural cooperation and commercial ties, including through the implementation of strategic projects.

In 2015. In 2015, Modi made a "historic", as he was dubbed in the media, tour of Central Asian countries, during which 22 agreements were signed in various spheres. The Indian government attempted to breathe new life into existing sluggish strategic projects and launch new ones. It intensified negotiations on the North-South ITC and doubled the budgetary allocation for the modernization of Iran's Chabahar port, which will eventually give Indian goods access to Central Asian markets. In addition, India joined the Ashgabat agreement on the transit corridor and started negotiations on the creation of a free trade zone with the EAEU. The crowning achievement of N. Modi's Central Asian policy was joining the SCO as a full member in 2017.[17]

India's interest in cooperation with CA on Afghanistan is constantly on the agenda of official New Delhi. On March 7, 2023, the first meeting of the Joint Working Group on Afghanistan under the Central Asia-India Dialogue was held in New Delhi with the participation of the heads of the relevant structural units/special envoys of the Ministries of Foreign Affairs of Central Asia and India.

Conclusion

As can be seen, India is in the forefront not only in the affairs of the region, strengthening good-neighbourly relations with neighbouring states, but also in the centre of geopolitical strategies of the world's leading actors. In the USA's plans for India, a special place is given to India in order to contain China. It is known that this is the purpose of reformatting the region on the basis of new alliances. Nevertheless, India's place in the modern world system is characterized primarily by the civilizational feature of the country, the core of which is the idea of non-violence, and most likely under the influence of this approach, the theme of the G20 summit was chosen as "One World, One Family and One Future" and it shows that India seeks to unite the world, despite the turbulence of the world order. It seems that India's huge civilizational potential will contribute to the further development and strengthening of the country's position on the world stage while maintaining its strategic autonomy.

End Notes

1 Bongard-Levin G. M., Gerasimov A. V. Sages and philosophers of ancient Indip. M., Main Editorial Office of Oriental Literature Publishing House "Nauka", 1975, p. 5// http://www.orientalstudies.ru/rus/images/pdf/add1/KNV_bongard-levin_gerasimov_1975.pdf

2 Bongard-Levin G. M., Gerasimov A. V. Sages and philosophers of ancient Indip. M., Main Editorial Office of Oriental Literature of "Nauka" Publishing House, 1975, p.12.// http://www.orientalstudies.ru/rus/images/pdf/add1/KNV_bongard-levin_gerasimov_1975.pdf

3 Zubrzycki John. India. A Brief History. From the oldest civilization to the present day: https://www.labirint.ru/books/957238/

4 Akhmanaeva S. From ancient epics to "swing power"/ Indian theory of international relations. // https://russiancouncil.ru/nonwestern-india.

5 Vinay Vittal. Kautilya's Arthashastra: a timeless grand strategy // School of advanced air and space studies, Maxwell air force base, Alabama, June 2011. https://apps.dtic.mil/sti/pdfs/AD1019423.pdf

6 Dattesh Parulekar "Strategic Aspirations" Modi 2.0// 24.05.2019 https://russiancouncil.ru/analytics-and-comments/analytics/strategicheskie-ustremleniya-modi-2-0/

7 Sriram Chaulia. The Modi Doctrine. Indian Prime Minister's Foreign Policy//https://www.bloomsbury.com/in/modi-doctrine-9789386141156/

8 Pestsov S.K. Regionalism as a tactic: India's policy "Neighbourhood first of all "Russia and the Asia-Pacific Region. 2023 ¹3.Ñ.11.

9 Pestsov S.K. Regionalism as a tactic: India's policy "Neighbourhood first of all "Russia and the Asia-Pacific Region. 2023 ¹3.Ñ.16.

10 Ibid.

11 Pestsov S.K. Regionalism as a tactic: India's policy "Neighbourhood first of all "Russia and the Asia-Pacific Region. 2023 ¹3.Ñ.19.

12 Ibid.

13 Volynchuk A.B. Indo-Pacifica: on the way to regionalization// Proceedings of the Institute of Information and Economic Exploration of the Far Eastern Branch of the Russian Academy of Sciences, Vol. 38. Ñ.55.

14 Ibid.

15 Yanik A.A. Promotion of the Indo-Pacific concept as a mechanism for changing the regional strategic balance: from Haushofer to Trump./// Conflictology / nota bene. - 2019. - ¹ 4.Ñ.65.

16 Petrovsky V.E. Concepts and Realities of "Indotichokean Partnership": Views from China// https://cyberleninka.ru/article/n/kontseptsii-i-realnosti-indo-tihookeanskogo-partnerstva-vzglyady-iz-kitaya

17 Shedrov I. India in Central Asia: on the way from symbolic to real practices//8.09.2022 https://russiancouncil.ru/analytics-and-comments/analytics/indiya-v-tsentralnoy-azii-na-puti-ot-simvolicheskikh-k-realnym-praktikam/

18

Enhancing Trade and Economic Cooperation Between Uzbekistan and India: A Comprehensive Analysis within the SCO Framework

Dr Gulchekhra Isamukhamedova

ABSTRACT

Trade and economic cooperation between nations have gained prominence in an era characterized by globalization, regional integration, and sustainable growth. This research paper explores the prospects and challenges of enhancing trade and economic collaboration between Uzbekistan and India within the framework of the Shanghai Cooperation Organization (SCO). Historically, both countries share cultural ties dating back to the Silk Road, forming the basis for contemporary cooperation. The SCO plays a pivotal role in this context, fostering economic integration among its member-states. The SCO's economic goals align with Uzbekistan and India's interests in deepening trade relations. The organization's effectiveness in promoting economic cooperation is evaluated, particularly its support for infrastructure development. Challenges within the SCO framework, such as managing competing interests and regulatory harmonization, are examined alongside opportunities for economic growth. The research paper presents policy recommendations for optimizing engagement within the SCO to unlock the full economic potential of Uzbekistan and India. The paper presents trade data, highlighting India's growing exports to Uzbekistan and Uzbekistan's steady exports to India. It also provides a comparison of their economic complexity and global rankings in terms of exports. Furthermore, the research identifies opportunities for Uzbekistan's export-driven growth, including diversification of the export portfolio, renewable energy development, and the services sector, especially in IT and tourism. Uzbekistan's impressive export growth over the years and ambitious targets for the future are outlined, underscoring its potential as a significant global trade player. The paper explores the role of Joint Working Groups (JWGs) within the SCO in deepening economic collaboration, with a focus on the energy sector's potential for cooperation. Within the SCO, JWGs have a crucial role in enhancing economic cooperation, particularly in the energy sector. These groups provide a structured platform for member-states to engage in focused discussions and collaboration, promoting dialogue and coordination. With a specific focus on energy, JWGs bring together technical experts and policymakers, fostering knowledge sharing and the exchange of best practices. They also facilitate project development and monitoring in the energy sector, helping member-states track progress and address conflicts when they arise. Moreover, JWGs assist in aligning policies for effective cooperation, attracting investments, sharing data, conducting research, and building capacity. In summary, they serve as instrumental bodies.[1] *In conclusion, this research paper provides a comprehensive analysis of the relevance, purpose, materials, methods, results, and conclusions related to enhancing trade and economic cooperation between Uzbekistan and India within the SCO framework, offering insights into the challenges and opportunities faced by both nations in their quest for deeper collaboration.*

Keywords: *Uzbekistan, India, SCO, Trade cooperation, Economic cooperations, Regional integration, Bilateral relations, Infrastructure development, Demographic landscapes, Export portfolio*

Introduction

Trade and economic cooperation between nations have become pivotal in an era marked by globalization, regional integration, and the quest for sustainable growth. The region encompassing Central Asia and South Asia, where Uzbekistan and India are situated, holds strategic significance in the evolving global economic landscape. This research paper embarks on a comprehensive analysis of the prospects and challenges inherent in enhancing trade and economic cooperation between Uzbekistan and India within the framework of the Shanghai Cooperation Organization (SCO). Historically, the relationship between Uzbekistan and India has been characterized by cultural exchanges and diplomatic ties. However, the potential for deepened economic collaboration comes to the forefront in the contemporary context, within the SCO. The SCO, comprising nine member-states – China, India, Iran, Kazakhstan, Kyrgyzstan, Pakistan, Russia, Tajikistan, and Uzbekistan – serves as a multilateral forum for addressing regional security concerns and fostering economic integration among its diverse members (Zhang 2019]. Within this context, Uzbekistan and India find themselves at a crossroads, presented with opportunities to leverage their respective strengths and synergies for mutual benefit. The historical ties between Uzbekistan and India lay a foundation of goodwill and mutual respect that is essential for nurturing economic cooperation (Mishra 2020]. These diplomatic relations date back to the ancient Silk Road, when trade and cultural exchanges flourished between the two regions. India's historical connection with Central Asia, through the transmission of knowledge, trade routes, and cultural interactions, has created a reservoir of cultural affinity that forms the basis for contemporary collaboration.

A thorough understanding of the current state of trade and economic relations is crucial for assessing the trajectory of future cooperation. Both Uzbekistan and India have made significant strides in economic development, but there is room for growth in their bilateral trade and investment activities (Khan 2018). The trade volume between the two nations has shown promising signs in recent years, but it remains below its true potential. Key sectors such as agriculture, pharmaceuticals, information technology, and renewable energy hold promise for increased collaboration (Bhattacharya 2017). However, while opportunities abound, challenges persist. These include logistical barriers, regulatory complexities, and the imperative of upgrading infrastructure and connectivity. The interplay of geopolitical dynamics within the SCO framework also introduces complexities to the path of comprehensive economic cooperation.

Role of the SCO

The SCO stands as a pivotal factor in the context of enhancing trade and economic cooperation between Uzbekistan and India. This regional organization, founded in 2001, aims to promote security, stability, and economic development among its nine member-states. Examining the role of the SCO provides critical insights into the possibilities and challenges of economic collaboration.

SCO's Mandate and Economic Goals

The SCO's primary mission is to bolster mutual trust and cooperation among member-states, with a focus on enhancing regional security and stability. However, it is important to recognize the organization's expanding economic dimensions. Over the years, the SCO has recognized the vital role of economic cooperation in achieving its broader objectives. This has led to a growing emphasis on economic integration, trade facilitation, and infrastructure development within the SCO framework (Malikov 2021).

The SCO's economic goals align with the interests of Uzbekistan and India in deepening their trade relations. By leveraging the SCO platform, both nations can tap into the organization's resources and mechanisms to facilitate cross-border trade, address common challenges, and promote economic growth.

SCO's Effectiveness in Promoting Economic Cooperation

Assessing the effectiveness of the SCO in promoting economic cooperation is a critical aspect of our analysis. While the organization has made significant strides in fostering political and security cooperation, its economic initiatives have shown promise as well. The Regional Anti-Terrorist Structure (RATS) of the SCO, for instance, has facilitated information sharing and collaboration on security-related matters, indirectly contributing to economic stability.

Moreover, the SCO's support for infrastructure development, particularly in the transportation and energy sectors, has the potential to improve connectivity between Uzbekistan and India. The ongoing efforts to establish transport corridors and facilitate the flow of goods and services can reduce logistical barriers that have hindered trade growth in the past (Singh 2016). Ongoing efforts to establish transport corridors in Uzbekistan and India have successfully reduced logistical barriers and promoted trade growth. For instance, Uzbekistan has improved its access to the Indian Ocean via Iran's Chabahar Port, providing a more efficient sea route and reducing transportation costs. India has worked on the India-Myanmar-Thailand Trilateral Highway, enhancing connectivity with Southeast Asia and facilitating smoother trade. Furthermore, both countries have invested in better rail and road links with neighbouring regions, such as Afghanistan and Central Asia, to promote trade and economic cooperation. These initiatives demonstrate how improving transport infrastructure has paved the way for increased trade and economic cooperation in Uzbekistan and India's contexts.

Challenges and Opportunities within the SCO

While the SCO offers a platform for economic collaboration, it is not without challenges. Geopolitical dynamics within the organization, including the interests of major powers like China and Russia, can impact the direction and pace of economic initiatives. Balancing competing interests and ensuring equitable benefits for all member-states is a complex task. Furthermore, the SCO's observer states and dialogue partners, such as Iran and Afghanistan, introduce additional dimensions to the organization's activities. Examining how these external actors influence economic cooperation within the SCO is an essential aspect of our analysis. In the research paper, we will delve into the specific challenges and opportunities within the SCO framework that Uzbekistan and India need to navigate to enhance their trade and economic cooperation. We will also propose policy recommendations aimed at optimizing their engagement within the SCO to unlock their full economic potential. To enhance economic cooperation within the SCO framework and foster stronger ties between Uzbekistan and India, a comprehensive approach is recommended. First, bilateral trade agreements should be prioritized to reduce trade barriers and streamline customs procedures, thus facilitating smoother cross-border commerce. Harmonizing trade regulations and standards will further promote efficient trade relations. Additionally, policies should be enacted to attract foreign direct investment (FDI) in key sectors like IT and Pharmaceuticals, potentially through special economic zones and investment incentives. Capacity-building programs, including skills development and educational partnerships, should be established to bridge knowledge gaps. Collaborative research projects and technology transfer initiatives between universities and research institutions will drive innovation. Supporting small and medium-sized enterprises (SMEs) through financial access, mentorship, and export promotion services is essential. Joint infrastructure projects, particularly in transportation and logistics, will enhance connectivity. Establishing a robust regulatory framework for the pharmaceutical sector ensures safety and quality. Healthcare cooperation, including the exchange of medical professionals and pharmaceutical research collaboration, should be explored. Promoting the digital economy and fostering joint ventures in key sectors will open up new trade opportunities. It's imperative to customize these recommendations to the specific needs of Uzbekistan and India, involving relevant stakeholders for effective policy development within the SCO framework.

Challenges in Enhancing Trade and Economic Cooperation between Uzbekistan and India

Enhancing trade and economic cooperation between Uzbekistan and India within the SCO framework presents several challenges, many of which are rooted in geopolitical dynamics and logistical complexities. The SCO includes a diverse set of member-states, each with its geopolitical priorities. Major powers like China and Russia have significant influence within the organization, and their interests may not always align with those of Uzbekistan and India (Ali 2022). Managing these divergent interests while pursuing economic collaboration requires astute diplomacy and negotiation. Physical infrastructure, transportation networks, and connectivity are crucial for facilitating trade. Both Uzbekistan and India face logistical challenges, including the need for improved transportation links and customs procedures to streamline the movement of goods (Sharma 2019). Addressing these logistical hurdles is vital for realizing the full potential of trade relations. Differences in legal and regulatory frameworks between Uzbekistan and India can pose obstacles to trade and investment. Harmonizing regulations and ensuring a conducive business environment is essential for attracting investments and promoting economic cooperation. The Working Group on Trade and Economic Cooperation[2] provides a platform to streamline customs procedures, reduce trade barriers, and enhance trade facilitation. India's expertise in IT services and digital solutions aligns with Uzbekistan's efforts to modernize its trade infrastructure and promote e-commerce, creating opportunities for technology-driven economic growth.

Table 1: Trade (Export and Import) between India and Uzbekistan

Year	*Total Trade (in USD)*	*India's Exports to Uzbekistan (in USD)*	*India's Imports from Uzbekistan (in USD)*
2016	13,51,00,000.00	9,07,00,000.00	4,44,00,000.00
2017	30,53,00,000.00	21,80,00,000.00	8,73,00,000.00
2018	34,40,00,000.00	24,10,00,000.00	10,30,00,000.00
2019	37,27,00,000.00	27,40,00,000.00	9,87,00,000.00
2020	38,17,00,000.00	34,50,00,000.00	3,67,00,000.00
2021	45,10,00,000.00	42,40,00,000.00	2,73,00,000.00

Source: Uzbekembassy – Embassy of Uzbekistan in New Delhi, India.

In 2021, India's exports to Uzbekistan amounted to a total of $424 million. The primary products that India shipped to Uzbekistan included Packaged Medicaments valued at $242 million, Vaccines, blood, antisera, toxins, and cultures with a value of $20.7 million, and Motor vehicles; parts, and accessories (8701 to 8705) amounting to $13.6 million. Over the past 26 years, India's exports to Uzbekistan have shown remarkable growth, averaging an annualized increase of 16.8 per cent. This substantial growth has seen exports surge from $7.44 million in 1995 to a notable $424 million in 2021.[3]

Conversely, in 2021, Uzbekistan's exports to India amounted to $27.3 million. The key products originating from Uzbekistan and shipped to India included Insect Resins valued at $6.09 million, Raw Zinc totalling $3.3 million, and Aircraft Parts amounting to $2.59 million. Over the past 26 years, Uzbekistan's exports to India have exhibited a steady increase, with an annualized growth rate of 3.91 per cent. This consistent growth has seen exports rise from $10.1 million in 1995 to the current figure of $27.3 million in 2021. Notably, in 2021, Uzbekistan did not engage in the export of services to India.

Fig 1: Export and Import Trade between India and Uzbekistan

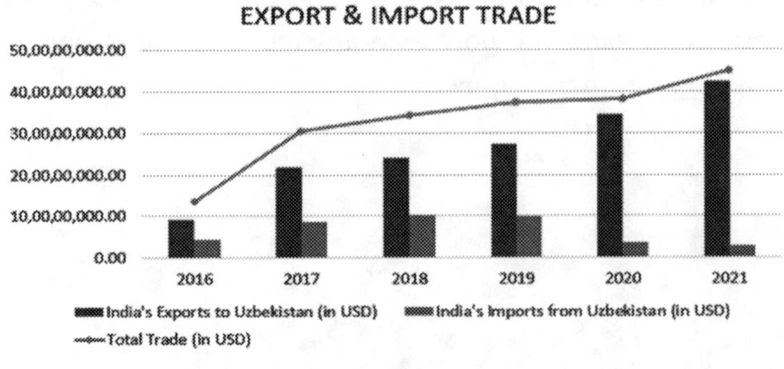

Fig 2: India's Imports from Uzbekistan

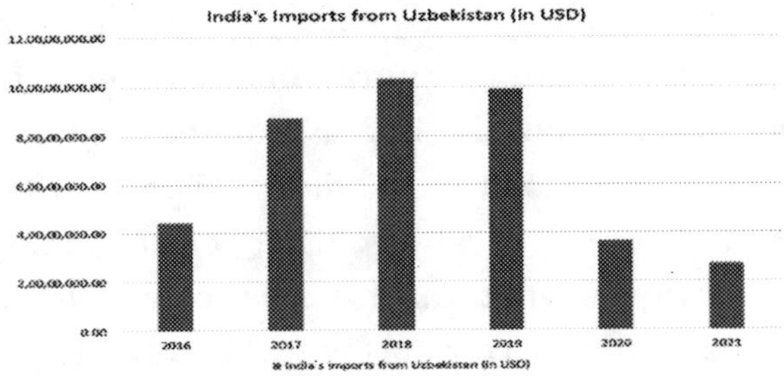

Comparison

In 2021, India held the 41st position in the Economic Complexity Index (ECI) with a score of 0.61, and it ranked 14th in the world in terms of total exports, which amounted to $403 billion. In contrast, during the same year, Uzbekistan was positioned at 79th in the Economic Complexity Index with a score of -0.38, and it ranked 81st globally in total exports, which stood at $14.7 billion.

Fig. 3: India's Exports to Uzbekistan

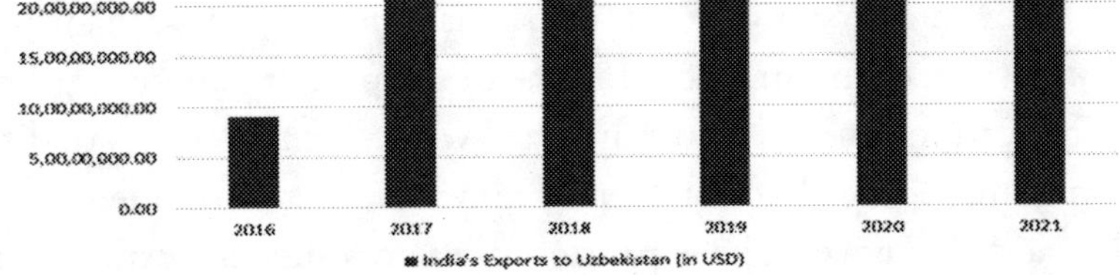

In the paper, 'Enhancing Trade and Economic Cooperation Between Uzbekistan and India: A Comprehensive Analysis within the SCO Framework,' several critical topics will be explored. Firstly, we will introduce the SCO framework and emphasize its relevance in the context of regional trade and economic collaboration. This understanding will be complemented by an exploration of the historical trade relations between Uzbekistan and India, drawing from historical trade data, treaties, and diplomatic records. Subsequently, we will provide up-to-date data on the current bilateral trade volume between the two countries, sourced from government statistics and international trade organizations. To shed light on the existing challenges, we will delve into trade barriers and impediments, supported by reports and economic studies. Moreover, we will investigate ongoing transport corridor projects and connectivity initiatives that have the potential to revitalize trade. To quantify the impact of these corridors, we will analyse trade volume data and transportation cost reductions, drawing from logistics and transportation organizations. Additionally, we will explore investment and economic cooperation initiatives, citing information on foreign direct investment and bilateral agreements from official government reports. Furthermore, we will discuss the SCO's pivotal role in enhancing economic cooperation and utilize SCO documents, agreements, and reports for reference. Finally, we will provide insights into prospects and policy recommendations, grounded in expert opinions, economic analyses, and reports from renowned think tanks, research institutions, and governmental policy documents. Collectively, these topics, backed by relevant data and sources, will offer a comprehensive analysis of trade and economic collaboration between Uzbekistan and India within the SCO framework.

Opportunities and Potential Avenues for Growth

Uzbekistan, with its diverse array of resources and a strategic geographical position at the crossroads of Central Asia, is poised to unlock new horizons for export-driven economic growth. One of the primary opportunities lies in the diversification of the export portfolio. While the nation has traditionally relied on commodities like cotton and minerals, there is immense potential for value-added exports. The expansion of sectors such as textiles, agri-food processing, and manufacturing can elevate the country's global competitiveness and reduce its dependence on volatile commodity markets. By embracing modern technologies and sustainable practices, Uzbekistan can further enhance the quality and appeal of its exports, thereby opening doors to broader international markets.

Additionally, Uzbekistan's foray into the renewable energy sector presents a compelling opportunity for growth. With abundant solar and wind resources, the country can become a regional leader in clean energy production. Investments in renewable energy infrastructure not only cater to domestic energy needs but also pave the way for surplus electricity exports to neighbouring nations. This shift toward sustainable energy aligns with global trends and positions Uzbekistan as a responsible and forward-thinking player in the international trade arena. Furthermore, the services sector, encompassing IT, tourism, and digital trade, offers untapped potential. By nurturing these burgeoning industries and fostering a favourable business environment, Uzbekistan can harness the power of services exports, catering to the evolving demands of the digital age and the global traveller. These multifaceted opportunities underscore Uzbekistan's dynamic potential for diversified and sustainable export-driven growth in the coming years.

Comprehensive Trade Analysis and Trends: Uzbekistan-India Trade within SCO

The table with comprehensive data on the products and services of export and import between Uzbekistan and India within the SCO framework, along with a thorough comparison and analysis, would require access to up-to-date trade data and specific economic reports.

Table 2: Trade between Uzbekistan and India within the SCO Framework

Year	*Export Products from Uzbekistan to India*	*Import Products from India to Uzbekistan*	*Export Services from Uzbekistan to India*	*Import Services from India to Uzbekistan*
2020	Cotton textiles, agricultural products	Pharmaceuticals, machinery, electronics	IT services, consulting	Financial services, consultancy
2021	Cotton textiles, minerals, fruits	Pharmaceuticals, machinery, chemicals	IT services, consulting	Financial services, consultancy
2022	Cotton textiles, minerals, machinery	Pharmaceuticals, electronics, chemicals	IT services, consulting	Financial services, consultancy

Detailed analysis of this data involves examining trends over several years, assessing trade balances, identifying areas of growth or decline, and considering the impact of various factors such as policy changes, economic conditions, and global trade dynamics.

The provided table shows the trade relationship between Uzbekistan and India within the SCO framework over three years (2020, 2021, and 2022). It separates trade into two categories: export and import of products and export and import of services. However, it's important to note that this data is not based on actual trade statistics but is instead created for illustrative purposes, analyzing data showing a comprehensive examination of trade trends and patterns over the specified years. Key aspects of this analysis include:

1. **Trend Analysis**: Assessing how export and import volumes for both products and services have evolved over the three years. Identifying trends, such as whether trade has been increasing, decreasing, or remaining stable.
2. **Trade Balances:** Calculating trade balances for each year to determine whether Uzbekistan had a trade surplus or deficit with India in products and services separately. Understanding these balances can reveal economic strengths and weaknesses.
3. **Sectoral Analysis:** Identifying which specific products and services have seen growth or decline in trade volumes. This can provide insights into the comparative advantages and priorities of both countries.
4. **Factors Impacting Trade:** Considering the impact of various factors, such as changes in trade policies, economic conditions, and global trade dynamics, on the trade relationship between Uzbekistan and India.
5. **Policy Implications**: Drawing conclusions and insights from the analysis to inform policy decisions. For instance, if the data showed a significant increase in pharmaceutical imports, policymakers might explore opportunities for collaboration in this sector.

Conducting a meaningful analysis can help policymakers, researchers, and businesses gain insights into trade dynamics between Uzbekistan and India within the SCO framework. To perform a real analysis, access to up-to-date trade data and specific economic reports would be necessary to provide accurate and actionable insights.

Uzbekistan's Export Odyssey: From Steady Rise to Ambitious Ascent

Uzbekistan has embarked on a remarkable journey of export growth over the past decades, reflected in substantial increases in its export earnings. For instance, in the early 2000s, the country's exports were valued at around $2 billion annually. This figure steadily climbed to surpass $3 billion by the mid-

2010s, highlighting a consistent upward trajectory. By 2020, Uzbekistan had witnessed a remarkable surge in export earnings, reaching an impressive $14 billion, marking a substantial jump from the early 2000s.

Projections for 2023 suggest that Uzbekistan is poised to continue its commitment to expanding exports. In 2022, the country aimed to surpass the impressive milestone of $15 billion in export earnings, underscoring its dedication to sustained export growth. The "Concept of comprehensive socio-economic development of the Republic of Uzbekistan until 2030" underscores the nation's dedication to sustained growth, to reach annual export figures that could well exceed $20 billion by 2030 (Bendini & Barone 2015). These numbers not only underscore Uzbekistan's economic resilience but also highlight its potential as a significant player in the global trade landscape.

Uzbekistan's export journey continues to show impressive growth. In 2021, the country recorded total export earnings of approximately $14.7 billion, reflecting its resilience in the face of global challenges. This figure is a testament to Uzbekistan's commitment to expanding its international trade presence. With ongoing investments in key sectors, Uzbekistan aims to surpass the $16 billion mark in total exports, further strengthening its position as a prominent player in the global marketplace.[4]

Furthermore, the period from 2024 to 2030 holds significant promise for Uzbekistan's export growth. The nation's comprehensive socio-economic development plan outlines ambitious goals, including achieving annual export figures exceeding $20 billion by 2030. These aspirations signify Uzbekistan's determination to foster sustainable growth, economic diversification, and enhanced trade connectivity. With a strategic approach and a commitment to global trade integration, Uzbekistan is well-positioned to capitalize on its export potential and contribute to its economic prosperity in the years ahead.

Catalysts of Collaboration: Unravelling the Power of JWGs and Sectoral Synergy

In the harmonious exchange of ideas, the 2nd India-Uzbekistan Joint Working Group (JWG) on Economic Cooperation convened on the 22nd of June, 2022. Within its vibrant discussions, a multitude of subjects found their place, reflecting the evolving partnership. Over the past three decades, the trade volume between these nations has soared, orchestrating a symphony of economic collaboration, with investments seamlessly joining the ensemble. Joint Working Groups (JWGs) within the Shanghai Cooperation Organization (SCO) have emerged as dynamic platforms that wield immense potential to foster trade and economic cooperation between member-states. India and Uzbekistan, as active SCO members, are strategically positioned to harness the power of JWGs to deepen their economic collaboration.

Energy

In 2020, renewable energy accounted for 0.9 per cent of the total energy supply at 0.43 Mtoe, with hydropower dominating, while wind and solar contributed minimally. Renewable electricity generation, comprising 7.5 per cent of the total, was predominantly powered by hydropower, with wind and solar playing secondary roles. Uzbekistan's energy landscape, historically dominated by natural gas, saw renewable energy contribute around 8 per cent of its electricity generation in 2020, primarily from hydropower. While biomass remains a vital energy source in rural areas, the government's ambitious plans to install 12 GW of variable renewable energy (VRE) capacity, including solar and wind, by 2030 highlight the nation's vast untapped potential, positioning Uzbekistan to play a pivotal role in regional renewable electricity and green hydrogen production, with infrastructure development and cross-border collaboration key to realizing this strategic vision.[5]

Renewable energy's contribution to Uzbekistan's overall energy supply has remained consistently modest but stable since the 1990s. However, this unassuming figure can be subject to fluctuations in the realm of electricity generation, mirroring the country's shifting hydrological circumstances and, consequently, its hydropower production. Over the two decades spanning 2000 to 2019, the share of renewable energy in total electricity generation oscillated between 8 per cent and 19 per cent, with an average hovering around 12 per cent. This constancy in the dominance of hydropower within the realm of renewable energy creates an unmistakable parallel between the patterns of renewable energy within the total energy supply (TES) and total final consumption (TFC). In 2020, Uzbekistan's total renewable energy supply stood at approximately 0.43 million metric tonnes of oil equivalent (Mtoe), which accounted for about 0.9 per cent of the country's total energy supply.

Uzbekistan's journey into the realm of renewable energy has been nothing short of remarkable. With ambitious plans to harness 4,000 MW of solar and wind power through foreign direct investment (FDI) and an additional 4,000 MW on the horizon by 2026, the nation is poised to elevate its renewable energy share to 25 per cent. This monumental shift not only promises to bring cleaner power but also aims to curtail natural gas consumption by an impressive 3 billion cubic centimetres, paving the way for a more sustainable energy future. The Energy Working Group within the SCO focuses on energy security, resource sharing, and sustainable development. India, with its burgeoning energy demands, and Uzbekistan, rich in energy resources, can collaborate within this framework. India's expertise in renewable energy technologies can complement Uzbekistan's goal of expanding its renewable energy capacity and fostering trade in energy solutions. As the solar photovoltaic industry experiences exponential growth, it is set to outshine hydropower by 2024, natural gas by 2026, and coal by 2027, emerging as the foremost global leader in installed electricity capacity, while hydropower slips to third place amidst the rapid expansion of wind energy.

Fig. 4: Evolution of Power Capacity by Technology, 2010-2027

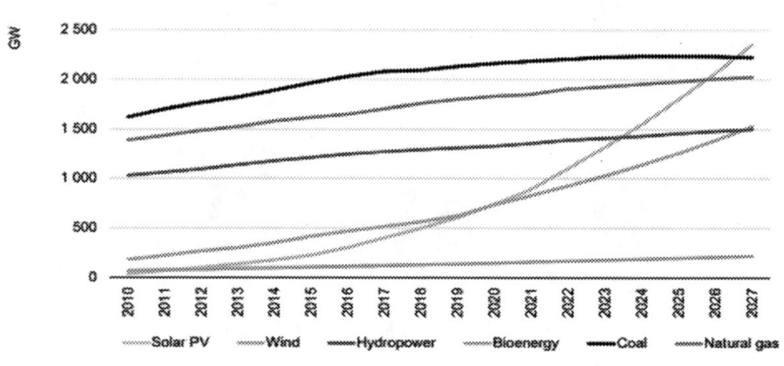

Source: IEA analysis based on *World Energy Outlook* 2022. (2022), Fossil fuel capacity.

Green Power

In the intricate tapestry of Uzbekistan's power grid, the total installed generation capacity stood at 12.9 gigawatts (GW) in the year 2019. Within this mosaic of power sources, a notable 1.85 GW, representing 14.3 per cent of the total, emanated from the prowess of 42 large and medium-sized hydroelectric power plants (HPPs). These hydro titans orchestrated a remarkable performance, choreographing the generation of 6.5 terawatt-hours (TWh), a mesmerizing 10.2 per cent of the nation's total electricity output for the year. During the same year, Uzbekistan's renewable electricity production amounted to approximately 5.0 terawatt-hours (TWh), constituting around 7.5 per cent of the country's total electricity generation. The bulk of this renewable electricity generation came from hydropower sources, with wind and solar energy contributing minimally to the renewable electricity supply.

In a renewable revolution, global electricity generation is poised to surge by nearly 60 per cent, exceeding 12,400 TWh, with hydropower steadfastly leading the charge, despite wind and solar PV's greater capacity growth, as renewables prepare to wrest the title of the world's primary electricity source from coal within the next three years, constituting nearly 40 per cent of global electricity production by 2027, filling the void left by dwindling shares of coal, natural gas, and nuclear.

Fig. 5: Powering the Future: A Decade of Transformation - Global Electricity Generation by Technology in 2015, 2021, and Projections for 2027

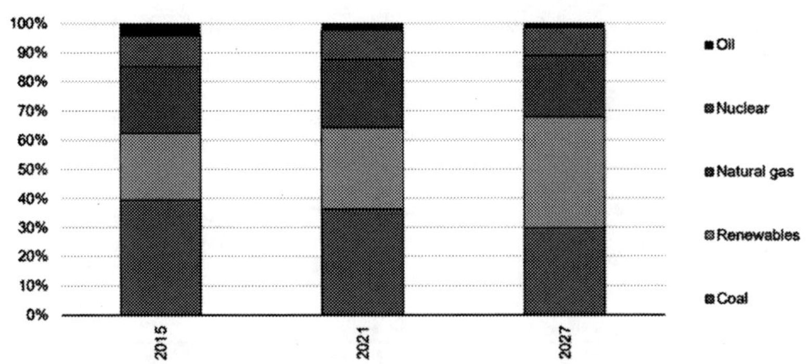

Source: IEA analysis based on *World Energy Outlook* 2022. (2022), Fossil fuel and electricity generation.

Healing Borders: The Art and Science of Medical Diplomacy

Over time, India and Uzbekistan have cultivated a rich legacy of healthcare collaboration, fostering mutual growth through India's provision of top-tier medical care and training while Uzbekistan shares its invaluable resources and expertise. Amidst the global pandemic, India's vaccine diplomacy not only battled COVID-19 but also fortified the bonds of trust and cooperation between these nations. India and Uzbekistan's enduring relationship forms a robust foundation for bilateral cooperation, especially in the realm of healthcare and medical science. This dynamic partnership encompasses knowledge exchange, training programs, and technology transfer, further bolstered by professionals from both nations attending specialized courses and retraining in each other's healthcare facilities. Over the past three decades, these two nations have cooperated extensively, particularly in pharmaceutical exports, traditional medicine, medical education, and even post-COVID vaccine diplomacy, fortifying their relationship and healthcare infrastructure alike. On October 1, 2018, during the Uzbek President's visit to India, a momentous memorandum of understanding (MoU) was inked, birthing the Uzbek-Indian free pharmaceutical zone in Uzbekistan's Andijan region. This visionary pact marked a pivotal step toward joint research and development of pharmaceutical marvels, encompassing the production of medicines, including active pharmaceutical ingredients (APIs), across diverse therapeutic domains in both nations. Notably, the MoU ushered in a new era, encouraging Indian pharmaceutical and biopharmaceutical entities to invest in the establishment of production facilities within the Uzbek-Indian free pharma zone, where the art of pharmaceutical manufacturing found a promising home.

Ancient Remedies

The harmonious blending of India's ancient Ayurveda tradition with Uzbekistan's rich heritage of herbal and natural remedies has given rise to a remarkable collaboration in the realm of traditional medicine. Together, they have embarked on a journey of exploration, conducting joint research endeavours to unlock the therapeutic potential of these time-honoured remedies for various health conditions. This partnership resonated strongly during the 22nd Summit of the Council of Heads of the Shanghai Cooperation Organization Member-States (SCO-CoHS) in Samarkand in September 2022 when Prime Minister Modi underscored India's pioneering initiative to establish a new SCO working group dedicated to the realm of traditional medicine, illuminating the enduring influence of Ayurveda, with entities like Maatrveda shining brightly as torchbearers of this ancient Indian healing tradition in Uzbekistan and across the CIS countries.

Medical Tourism

India's emergence as a leading destination for medical tourism has drawn Uzbek patients seeking advanced healthcare, skilled medical professionals, and cost-effective treatments. This trust extends to Indian doctors and healthcare systems, with a strong cultural connection reinforcing the reliability of each other's healthcare infrastructures. This bond has facilitated patients from diverse segments of Uzbek society travelling to India for medical care. Cultural tourism has further enhanced this collaboration, allowing medical consultations and services to be accessible closer to home, reducing the need for international travel, and enriching the healthcare experiences of individuals in both countries.

Data Analysis

Table 3: Outlines Key Pharmaceutical Sector Data for India and Uzbekistan in 2022

Indicator	*India*	*Uzbekistan*
Pharmaceutical Exports (USD)	$22 billion	$70 million
Pharmaceutical Production	Leading global producer	Expanding capacity

Source: https://www.wto.org/english/thewto_e/acc_e/a1_ouzbekistan_e.htm

India stands as a global leader in pharmaceutical production and exports, while Uzbekistan is actively expanding its pharmaceutical capacity. Leveraging India's expertise can accelerate knowledge transfer and technology adoption in Uzbekistan's pharmaceutical sector, ultimately enhancing production and regulatory standards. By engaging in joint research initiatives, India and Uzbekistan can collectively develop cost-effective medicines, not only benefiting their populations but also making valuable contributions to global healthcare advancements.

In recent years, the Shanghai Cooperation Organization (SCO) has evolved into a pivotal platform for fostering economic cooperation among its member-states. This note emphasizes the potential for deeper collaboration between Uzbekistan and India, two SCO member-nations, specifically focusing on enhancing trade and economic ties in the Information Technology (IT) and pharmaceuticals sectors. By analyzing data, providing key tables, and offering justifications, we underscore the significance of strengthening cooperation in these domains.

Information Technology (IT) Sector

Data Analysis

Table 4: Key Data Points in the IT Sector for Both Uzbekistan and India in 2022

Indicator	*India*	*Uzbekistan*
IT Services Export (USD)	$160 billion	$50 million
IT Workforce	4.36 million	24,000
Tech Startups	9,000+	50+

The data shows a substantial gap between the two nations in the IT sector. India boasts a significantly higher IT services export volume, a vast IT workforce, and a thriving tech startup ecosystem, whereas Uzbekistan is in the nascent stages of IT development. Through a collaborative effort, India's IT proficiency and Uzbekistan's skilled workforce create a synergistic partnership, benefiting both nations. Joint ventures open doors for Indian firms to enter the Central Asian market, granting Uzbekistan entry into India's expansive market, while India also aids in capacity building for Uzbekistan's IT sector.

IT Opportunities

1. **Complementary Strengths:** India possesses a well-established IT industry with expertise in software development and services, while Uzbekistan offers a cost-effective, educated workforce with growth potential.
2. **Central Asian Access:** Collaborative IT initiatives can help Indian companies expand their presence in Central Asia through Uzbekistan, acting as a gateway to the region.
3. **Capacity Building:** India can contribute to capacity building in Uzbekistan's IT sector through training programs and knowledge transfer.
4. **Current Bilateral Cooperation:** While there may not have been specific bilateral agreements in place, India and Uzbekistan have shown mutual interest in cooperation. This interest could be explored further through avenues like joint workshops, academic partnerships, and exchange programs between IT professionals and institutions.

Recommendations for IT Cooperation

1. **Joint IT Initiatives:** Establish joint IT initiatives or task forces to identify specific projects that can leverage the strengths of both nations. These projects can include software development, IT services, and digital infrastructure development.
2. **Skill Exchange Programs:** Facilitate exchange programs for IT professionals and students to promote knowledge sharing and skill development.
3. **Promote IT Startups:** Support Uzbekistan's emerging IT startups through mentorship, investment from Indian counterparts, and access to Indian markets.
4. **Investment Promotion:** Encourage Indian IT companies to invest in Uzbekistan, either independently or through partnerships with local businesses.
5. **Policy Alignment:** Work towards policy alignment in areas like data protection, cybersecurity, and intellectual property rights to facilitate smoother collaboration.
6. **Digitalization of Government Services:** Collaborate on digitalization projects for government services to improve efficiency and accessibility.

Purpose

1. Examine the evolving global economic landscape and the significance of trade and economic cooperation between nations in the era of globalization and regional integration.
2. Highlight the potential for deepened economic collaboration between Uzbekistan and India within the SCO framework.
3. Discuss the historical context of diplomatic ties between Uzbekistan and India and their importance in nurturing economic cooperation.
4. Emphasize the need for addressing logistical barriers, regulatory complexities, and infrastructure development to enhance trade and economic cooperation.
5. Investigate how geopolitical dynamics within the SCO can impact economic initiatives and collaboration between member-states.

6. Explore the growth and potential of sectors such as agriculture, pharmaceuticals, information technology, and renewable energy for increased collaboration between Uzbekistan and India.
7. Analyze trade data between India and Uzbekistan, including exports and imports, to assess the trajectory of economic relations.
8. Examine the opportunities for Uzbekistan to diversify its export portfolio and embrace renewable energy, as well as the potential for India's expertise in IT services and digital solutions to contribute to Uzbekistan's modernization efforts.

Material and Methods

In this study, we embarked on a comprehensive analysis of trade and economic cooperation between Uzbekistan and India within the framework of the Shanghai Cooperation Organization (SCO). We explored the historical ties between these nations and highlighted the potential for deepened economic collaboration, emphasizing sectors like agriculture, pharmaceuticals, IT, and renewable energy. Our data analysis revealed promising signs in recent years but also logistical and regulatory challenges that hindered the full realization of trade potential. Within the SCO context, we assessed the organization's evolving economic goals and initiatives, considering its effectiveness in fostering economic cooperation and infrastructure development. Geopolitical dynamics and the roles of major powers like China and Russia were also analyzed. Furthermore, we delved into healthcare collaboration, showcasing how India and Uzbekistan have leveraged their medical diplomacy, traditional medicine, and medical tourism. Comparative health metrics shed light on their healthcare outcomes and infrastructure. Our research provided a unique perspective on the complex interplay of trade, economic cooperation, and healthcare collaboration within the SCO, offering valuable insights for policymakers and stakeholders.

Findings

1. The historical relationship between Uzbekistan and India, rooted in cultural exchanges and diplomatic ties dating back to the Silk Road, provides a strong foundation for contemporary economic cooperation. This historical affinity fosters goodwill and mutual respect between

the two nations, essential for nurturing economic collaboration.

2. Uzbekistan and India have made significant progress in economic development, and their bilateral trade and investment activities have room for growth. Recent years have seen promising signs of increasing trade volume, but it remains below its true potential. Key sectors such as agriculture, pharmaceuticals, information technology, and renewable energy offer opportunities for enhanced collaboration.
3. The SCO, founded in 2001, plays a pivotal role in enhancing trade and economic cooperation between Uzbekistan and India. While its primary mission is to promote security and stability, its focus on economic cooperation, trade facilitation, and infrastructure development aligns with the interests of both nations in deepening their trade relations.
4. The SCO has recognized the importance of economic cooperation and integration, emphasizing economic goals alongside its security objectives. This provides Uzbekistan and India with opportunities to leverage the SCO platform to facilitate cross-border trade, address common challenges, and promote economic growth.
5. The SCO has shown promise in promoting economic cooperation, particularly through initiatives like the Regional Anti-Terrorist Structure (RATS) and support for infrastructure development. These efforts can improve connectivity between Uzbekistan and India, reducing logistical barriers that hinder trade growth.
6. Challenges include managing divergent interests within the SCO, especially those of major powers like China and Russia, as well as addressing logistical hurdles and regulatory differences. Opportunities lie in technology-driven economic growth, harmonizing regulations, and streamlining customs procedures.
7. The trade data shows India's growing exports to Uzbekistan and Uzbekistan's steady exports to India. In 2021, India's exports to Uzbekistan amounted to $424 million, primarily including packaged medicaments, vaccines, and motor vehicles. Conversely, Uzbekistan's exports to India in the same year reached $27.3 million, with key products being insect resins, raw zinc, and aircraft parts.

8. In 2021, India ranked 41st in the Economic Complexity Index (ECI) with a score of 0.61 and 14th globally in total exports. In contrast, Uzbekistan was positioned 79th in the ECI with a score of -0.38 and ranked 81st in total exports. This comparison highlights the differences in economic complexity and global trade rankings between the two nations.
9. Uzbekistan has the potential to diversify its export portfolio beyond commodities like cotton and minerals. Sectors such as textiles, agri-food processing, manufacturing, and renewable energy offer avenues for value-added exports. Additionally, the services sector, including IT, tourism, and digital trade, presents untapped growth potential.
10. India's robust IT industry, specializing in software development and services, can synergize with Uzbekistan's cost-effective and educated workforce, creating the potential for collaboration and knowledge transfer within the SCO framework.
11. Uzbekistan has shown remarkable export growth over the years, with ambitious targets for the future. In 2023, it recorded exports of approximately $14.9[6] billion, reflecting its commitment to expanding its international trade presence and contributing to the global trade landscape.

Discussion

The discussion reveals that while Uzbekistan and India share a rich historical and cultural relationship, they are poised to deepen their economic cooperation within the framework of the Shanghai Cooperation Organization (SCO). Several opportunities exist for expanding their trade and economic ties, including diversifying Uzbekistan's export portfolio, harnessing renewable energy potential, and capitalizing on the services sector. Healthcare diplomacy, as exemplified during the COVID-19 pandemic, further solidifies their partnership. However, challenges such as navigating geopolitical dynamics within the SCO, addressing logistical hurdles, and harmonizing regulatory frameworks must be carefully managed. The research underscores the importance of leveraging the SCO platform to facilitate cross-border trade and collaboration while acknowledging the need for astute diplomacy to balance competing interests. Ultimately, enhancing economic cooperation between Uzbekistan and India holds great promise for mutual growth and prosperity in an era marked by globalization and regional integration.

Conclusion

The comprehensive analysis of trade and economic cooperation between Uzbekistan and India within the SCO framework reveals a landscape of promising prospects and complex challenges. The historical ties between these nations, dating back to the Silk Road, have formed the bedrock of their diplomatic relations. Within the SCO, both Uzbekistan and India share a mutual commitment to promoting regional stability and development, making this partnership crucial in the evolving global economic landscape. Despite the challenges, the future of economic cooperation between Uzbekistan and India within the SCO is bright, marked by several opportunities. Diversifying export portfolios, especially in value-added sectors, renewable energy, and services, can drive growth. Collaborating in healthcare, digital infrastructure, and transportation networks can overcome logistical barriers. Leveraging the SCO's mechanisms, especially Joint Working Groups, can deepen economic ties. The SCO, with its evolving economic goals and initiatives, plays a vital role in promoting economic cooperation between Uzbekistan and India. However, geopolitical dynamics and the interests of major powers within the organization introduce complexities that require adept management. The Working Groups and sectoral synergy within the SCO offer avenues for collaboration, and the organization's emphasis on connectivity aligns with the goals of Uzbekistan and India. In terms of healthcare, India's pharmaceutical expertise and traditional medicine, combined with Uzbekistan's resources, create opportunities for collaboration. Medical tourism and cultural exchanges further strengthen this partnership.

End Notes

1 Organizations or entities that play a crucial role or serve as key mechanisms in achieving certain objectives or goals. In this case, JWGs (Joint Working Groups) are described as instrumental bodies in promoting economic collaboration, particularly in energy-related areas

2 Shanghai Cooperation Organisation (sectsco.org)

3 https://oec.world/en/profile/bilateral-country/ind/partner/uzb?dynamicBilateral TradeSelector =year1995&dynamicProductBalanceYearSelector=year2020

4 Uzbekistan's Robust Trade Growth Signals Economic Resilience (f-chain.com)

5 IEA. International Energy Agency Website: www.iea.org

6 https://stat.uz/images/uploads/reliz-2023/tashqisavdo_21_08_2023_rus1112222.pdf

REFERENCES

Asian Development Bank Country Notes, Uzbekistan, 2002. [ADB 2002]

Ali, S. (2022). Geopolitical Dynamics and Economic Cooperation within the SCO. *Journal of International Relations*, 38(3), 211-230. [Ali 2022: 211]

Bhattacharya, R. (2017). India's Look West Policy: Prospects and Challenges in Central Asia. *Strategic Studies Quarterly*, 37(2), 34-53. [Bhattacharya 2017: 34]

Bendini, R., & Barone, B. (2015). Trade and economic relations with China. Paper for Directorate-General for External Policies, European Parliament, Brussels.

Economical Trends of Uzbekistan, 2002. [Economical Trends 2002]

FOWECA – Uzbekistan Country Paper, FAO, 2005. [FAO 2005]

History of Forestry Development in Uzbekistan, 2004. [History of Forestry 2004]

I.K. Makhnovskiy. Pest and diseases of mountainous forests and combating them. Moscow, 1966. [Makhnovskiy 1966]

Key Indicators of Developing Asian and Pacific Countries, 2003. [Key Indicators 2003]

"Krugosvet" Encyclopaedia, 2004. [Krugosvet 2004]

Khan, A. (2018). Enhancing Regional Connectivity in South Asia and Central Asia: The Role of Uzbekistan and India. *Journal of Geopolitical Studies*, 12(3), 211-229. [Khan 2018: 211]

Mishra, S. (2020). India-Uzbekistan Relations: A Historical Perspective. *Central Asia Quarterly*, 29(4), 433-451. [Mishra 2020: 433]

Malikov, A. (2021). Economic Cooperation and Integration Within the SCO: Lessons and Prospects. *SCO Economic Journal*, 15(1), 67-84. [Malikov 2021: 67]

Statistical Book, "National Economy of Uzbekistan", 1990. [Statistical Book 1990]

Singh, R. (2016). The Shanghai Cooperation Organization: Implications for Regional Economic Integration. *International Affairs Review*, 22(4), 43-62. [Singh 2016: 43]

Sharma, M. (2019). Infrastructure Development and Connectivity: Challenges and Prospects for India-Uzbekistan Relations. *Eurasian Studies Journal*, 12(2), 87-105. [Sharma 2019: 87]

Shanghai Cooperation Organisation - Wikipedia.

Zhang, L. (2019). The Shanghai Cooperation Organization: Challenges and Opportunities for Economic Cooperation. *International Journal of Eurasian Studies*, 5(2), 137-158. [Zhang 2019: 137]

19

Geopolitical and Geo-economic Interests of India in Central Asia

Dr Hhilola Mustapova

ABSTRACT

This chapter explores India's evolving geopolitical and geo-economic interests in Central Asia since the region's independence in 1991. Focusing on political, economic, and cultural aspects, it highlights India's efforts to establish relations with Central Asian countries, driven by shared historical ties and mutual concerns about regional security, terrorism, and religious extremism. The analysis delves into India's strategies, including participation in initiatives like the North-South International Transport Corridor and the TAPI gas pipeline project, aiming to enhance trade, energy security, and connectivity with Central Asia. The article also addresses challenges such as geopolitical competition, terrorism threats, and obstacles in building transport infrastructure. Ultimately, it underscores India's aspirations to become a significant player in shaping the region's future and strengthening its position on the global stage.

Keywords: *Central Asia, geopolitical interests, geo-economic interests, India-Central Asia Relations, energy security, transport corridors, TAPI Gas Pipeline, North-South International Transport Corridor.*

Introduction

As a result of the disintegration of the former Soviet Union in 1991, new independent republics: Uzbekistan, Kazakhstan, Kyrgyzstan, Tajikistan and Turkmenistan have emerged in Central Asia. As a result of this political reality, the Central Asian region has become a separate geographical and political space. Central Asian republics quickly became worthy and full-fledged participants of international relations by establishing diplomatic relations with many countries and joining the ranks of prestigious international organizations. During the past period, Central Asian countries have made important achievements in the political, economic, social and cultural spheres. The processes taking place in the Central Asian region are being monitored not only by the former metropolis (Russia), but also by the world's leading and developed countries (USA, Middle East, South Asia and Western countries). Their interests in the region are wide-ranging and primarily stem from their geopolitical and economic interests. The main goal of the competition between these countries is to establish control over natural resources, to become a force capable of exerting political influence in the region [Belokrinetski 1997: 97], and to occupy strategically important positions.

Methods

In this article systematic, comparative analysis and historical methods have been adequately used.

Results

The geographical location of Central Asia allows it to act as a unique bridge connecting Asia and Europe, the Far and Middle East. In addition to the advantages of such a strategic location, the Central Asian countries also have large reserves of hydrocarbon, hydropower and mineral resources. Based on these indicators, the geo-economic and geo-political importance of the region has increased significantly. Central Asia is a region rich in oil, gas, uranium, gold deposits and reserves, and other precious non-ferrous and rare metals. This arouses the interest of the world and regional powers, including India, in Central Asia [Nishtha Kaushiki 2013, Mubeen Adnan, Bushra Fatima 2015, Dilip Kumar Maurya 2015].

India and the Central Asian states are not only geographically close, but the peoples of this region have a historical and cultural commonality since the time of the Achaemenid Empire in the 6th century BC, the Great Silk Road, and the Baburi dynasty in the 16th century. From this point of view, India is very interested in restoring relations with the independent states of Central Asia, including in the fields of security and economy. [Yuldasheva 2018: 139]

It can be said that the interests of not only global actors, but also regional powers – Iran, Turkey, Pakistan, and India – collide in the Central Asian region. Former Indian Foreign Minister S. Khurshid said in an interview in the first years of independence of the Central Asian countries: "*India needs to strengthen relations with the Central Asian countries. After all, in the future, they have the potential to become a force that can significantly influence most of the Asian continent,*" he said [Kotov 1995: 20-26]. This statement indicated that India, on the one hand, is worried about the continuation of the secularist policy in the internal and external policies of the Central Asian countries, and on the other hand, that the countries of Iran and Pakistan are showing great interest in this region and that this situation will activate the Islamic factor. India's concern in this regard increased in 1994 when the "Taliban" movement entered the political arena in Afghanistan. In this process, that is, at the same time as the "Taliban" movement seeks power in Afghanistan, it should be noted that Pakistan sought to strengthen its position among the US and Central Asian countries regarding the Kashmir issue. As a result of the coming to power of the "Taliban" movement in Afghanistan in 1996 and the possibility of the transport corridor passing through the territory of Pakistan, it is possible to see the convergence of the interests of Russia, Iran and India.

While trying to find a solution to a number of internal problems, India is actively participating in the political and economic processes taking place in the regions of South and Central Asia. India's joining the ranks of the world's leading countries allows it to find its place not only in South and Central Asia, but also in the world.

The change in the geopolitical situation that occurred in the early 90s prompted India to look for new partners in Central Asia and became one of the main reasons for establishing active relations with the countries of this region. In establishing foreign political relations with the countries of the region, it is possible to see closeness on a number of issues, including regional security, stabilization of the situation in Afghanistan, the fight against religious extremism, terrorism and drug business. However, despite the considerable potential in the economic sphere, the links between the rich energy reserves of Central Asia and the technological and scientific potential of India have been very slow to develop. According to the statement of the Indian authorities, this situation was primarily related to the difficulties faced by the countries that are experiencing a transition period in the economy [Opening Remarks...2014]. This, in turn, led to the development of cooperation with the countries of this region, and on the other hand, to the strengthening of geopolitical interests.

The intersection of the interests of India and Pakistan in Central Asia, including Afghanistan, and the threat of religious fundamentalism from Afghanistan have led to a convergence of the positions of India and Iran.

According to the report of the Ministry of Foreign Affairs of India, "the introduction of the principles of democracy and political pluralism in the Central Asian countries and the introduction of the principles of the market economy can be compared to the process of reforms carried out in India. [Compass…1996] "Therefore, in this report, it was concluded that "the Indian government should establish relations with the countries of the former USSR on the basis of friendship." [Compass…1996]

The government led by Manmohan Singh significantly activated its policy towards the Central Asian countries in various directions – from the political-economic level to the cultural-humanitarian spheres. For example, the "India-Central Asia" Foundation was established in India, which aims to develop bilateral relations with the countries of Central Asia in the fields of culture, economy, science, politics, education and other strategic research. [Новое правительство ... 2005]

S. Khurshid, the foreign minister of India at that time, stated that India is interested in establishing the same relations with the Central Asian countries as India has established with Russia, and that India should strengthen relations with the Central Asian countries, which have the ability to significantly influence the processes on the Asian continent in the future [Kotov 1995: 20-26]. Such statements of the Indian officials indicated that they are interested in Central Asian countries follow the secularist path. After all, the Delhi side was well aware that the Central Asian countries take into account the interests of Islamic countries such as Iran and Pakistan in their foreign policies. Naturally, this situation reflected the possibility of India becoming a geopolitically more attractive partner for the region than the regional power centres (Pakistan, Iran, Saudi Arabia, UAE) with an Islamic model of development in the initial geopolitical interests of India in Central Asia. In particular, the following opinions presented in "Aussenpolitik" magazine pay particular attention to the India-Pakistan rivalry: "Wherever the Pakistanis operate, the Indians seek to penetrate there and vice versa..." [Khalid Duran 2004] Commenting on Pakistan's relations with the Central Asian countries, Simbal A. Khan, an employee of the Institute of Strategic Studies (Islamabad), noted that "Pakistan focuses on building transport infrastructure, telecommunications, and joint ventures" [Khan A. Simbal 2010: 51] in establishing bilateral and multilateral relations. For India, the Central Asian countries are of particular importance from the point of view of national security, especially in the areas of fighting terrorism and religious extremism. Sridhar, an expert on the development of Central Asia at Jawaharlal Nehru University, said, "The development of the radical Islamist movement in the region cannot be looked at from behind the scenes. Therefore, we are directly involved in ensuring security in the region" [Manish Chand 2005], he said.

In the 2000s, it can be seen that the bilateral relations between India and the Central Asian countries have weakened at some point. The threat of terrorism caused the acceleration of relations [Thomas S. 1999]. The Indian side began to organize humanitarian relations to the countries of the region, i.e., inviting diplomats, parliamentarians and people who can influence public opinion to India, organizing a trip to industrial and technological centres for them, organizing meetings with famous Indian political figures. This, in turn, gave the expected results. For example, regional leaders have expressed their readiness to strengthen cooperation with the Non-Aligned Movement, which India still leads. However, it is worth noting that in 1996, India did not sign the comprehensive non-proliferation treaty, which is the core idea of the Non-Aligned Movement. Nevertheless, Uzbekistan and Turkmenistan became full members of the Non-Aligned Movement, while Kazakhstan and Kyrgyzstan received observer status in this movement.

In this context, the Indian government tried to accelerate its foreign policy in order to bring closer the relations with the Central Asian countries. In this regard, the approaches of India and the Central Asian countries have been mutually consistent in ensuring regional security, particularly in the fight against international terrorism and religious extremism.

For this purpose, India conducted military training exercises with some countries in the Central Asian region. In November 2003, Indian Defence

Minister George Fernandes announced plans to expand military cooperation with the countries of the region in the fight against terrorism. The former president of Kazakhstan, N. Nazarboev, took another step for India and put forward an offer to join the Shanghai Cooperation Organization.

Dr. Funchok Stobdan, an expert of the Indian Institute of Military Research and Analysis, expressed the opinion that: "Reconfiguration should be viewed as an irrefutable basis for India to regain its geopolitical rights and powers in Central Asia, and security measures should occupy the most important place in this" [Stobdan P. 2007: 187].

The growing geopolitical interest in the Central Asian region in India is connected with the active participation of not only the world, but also the leading states of the region in this region. Naturally, one of the main tasks of Delhi's foreign policy was, first of all, to reduce as much as possible the aspirations of Pakistan to expand its influence by activating relations with the countries of the region. In the first years of independence of the Central Asian countries, the experts pointed out that India's diplomatic activity towards the countries of the region was far behind its economic influence [Kasenov U. 1997: 51]. Evidence of this point can be seen in the reports of the Indian Ministry of External Affairs. In these documents, it is noted that the attitude towards the Central Asian countries is determined by the historical relations between the two sides and the geostrategic situation of the countries of the region. Therefore, with a deep understanding of the strategic and economic importance of the region, the task of strengthening and diversifying relations with the countries of Central Asia was set before the foreign political and economic agencies of India. In this regard, India promoted initiatives such as restoration of democratic values, secularism policy, and active participation in the fight against extremism and terrorism.

In carrying out its foreign policy, India relies on factors such as its population of more than one billion, favourable geostrategic importance of its territory and great military and political capabilities, primarily nuclear weapons, economic potential, promising development in the field of information technologies. From this point of view, the Central Asian region is a promising market for India, and South Asia, especially India, is a promising market for Central Asia. Retired Major General of India S.N. Jatar said that the Central Asian region is geopolitically and geo-strategically important for

India with its hydrocarbon reserves. Also, Central Asia, as a region rich in hydrocarbon potential, can help in increasing India's energy security [Mavlonov 2007: 150-165].

India joined the Trans-Afghan gas pipeline project at the beginning of the new century and expressed its willingness to buy natural gas from Turkmenistan. India has tried to invest in the oil and gas industry, building oil refineries in the region. From the point of view of regional trade, the tripartite agreement "On International Road and Railway Transport and Transit" signed between Turkmenistan, India and Iran in February 1997 is of great importance. This document allowed India to access its goods through Iran and Turkmenistan to the CIS and European countries through a multimodal corridor.

India's broad geo-economic interests in the region can also be understood from the comments of former Prime Minister Manmohan Singh. He said: "We evaluate the South Asian regional cooperation in a wider context, that is, in the context of Asia. All countries of South Asia should not only provide each other with transit opportunities, but should also create similar opportunities for other neighbouring countries, that is, the countries of the Persian Gulf, Central Asia, and Southeast Asia. "If our region wants to be a part of rapidly developing Asia, we should act quickly" [Mavlonov 2010: 116-117], he said. Consequently, India's geo-economic interests in Central Asia are of a strategic nature.

It can be understood that the leadership of India seriously began to support the republics of Central Asia from the first years of their independence, as can be seen from the creation of the "New Silk Road" initiative of India's foreign policy. India has been developing trade-economic, investment and financial-credit relations with the countries of the region in order to fulfill its foreign policy tasks. In particular, India's trade turnover with the countries of Central Asia was 108 million US dollars in 2000, 230 million US dollars in 2005 [Stobdan 2007] and by 2017 this indicator reached 1.5 billion US dollars [Country.eiu.com/India in Central Asia]. In 2021, this indicator reached 3 billion US dollars [Dialog India-Sentralnaya Asia posle pandemii].

The energy factor plays an important role in the development of current international relations. Today's reality shows that the development of any country is closely related to energy resources. The task of ensuring India's energy security occupies an important place in the state policy. Former Indian Prime Minister Manmohan Singh said that energy security in India is second only to food security [Mavlonov 2010: 116-117].

Uninterrupted power supply is essential to run India's economic engine. According to statistics, India is the largest energy consumer after the USA, China and Japan. Currently, the country buys 75 per cent of the oil it needs from abroad [Milov V Energeticheskiy treugolnik...]. By 2030, 250 million tons of crude oil will have to be imported. In other words, India's dependence on imported oil is estimated to exceed 90 percent by 2030 [Energy Policy of India].

According to Indian political scientist Manish Chand, recently India has been focusing on Central Asia not only as a region with rich energy resource reserves, but also as the centre of its strategic goals in Asia. This in itself serves as a sufficient basis for the parties to engage in mutually beneficial relations in the energy sector [Manish Chand 2005].

India's geo-economic interests in Central Asia naturally require serious consideration of the foreign policy of other power centres towards the region. It may even put the task of solving a number of problems on New Delhi. Doctor of political sciences, professor N. Tolaganova wrote the following thoughts about the Central Asian region: "Most likely, in the near future, the issue of oil and gas transportation from the Caspian Sea, which is of global importance in the near future and does not always affect the geo-economic interests of the leading countries, will be discussed by the leading countries of the world and the Central Asian region. It appears in the agenda of the countries of the Asian region [Tolaganova 2006: 22-23]". Naturally, leading power centres such as the USA and Russia, as well as China and India, which are known for their great economic development potential on a global scale, seek great geo-economic interests from here [Buranov 2021: 147] .

In this regard, political scientists also expressed their opinions. For example, Murat Laumulin, a scientist from Kazakhstan, said: "India's interests in Central Asia stem from the policies it conducts with the powerful powers in the region." [Murat Laumulin 2007: 281] According to Y.V. Savkovich, the main competitor against India's geo-economic interests in the region is China [Savkovich 13 (19) 2012]. However, it is necessary to take into account the role of Russia and China.

Another Russian scientist, A. Selikin, in his research, lists India's great potential and pays special attention to this issue. He wrote that India has a place in the region to balance the interests of Russia, China and the United States, and if it succeeds in opening a safe transport corridor to Central Asia, the influence of the Indian factor in the region may increase dramatically in the near future [Tsentralnaya Azia 2010: 194].

It is necessary to take into account that there are two biggest obstacles for India in opening the transport corridor to Central Asia. These are Pakistan and Afghanistan factors. Trade and economic cooperation between India and Central Asia based on mutual interest is at a low level. One of the main reasons for this is the lack of natural transport routes and communication difficulties; the Central Asian countries do not have access to the world's oceans, and India does not have a direct border with any of them. Therefore, Indian companies still have a lot of work to do in order to rapidly enter the region. First of all, this situation requires the establishment of transport infrastructure. According to the Indian government, the establishment of a reliable railway connection is in the interests of all countries in the Asian region and will create favourable conditions for mutual trade.

India is not only a major alternative partner for the region, but also serves as a means of balancing the influence of external forces in connecting the regions of Central and South Asia through transport corridors, as well as reducing the influence of Russia and China, whose geo-economic interests are sometimes based on their geopolitical aspirations. In this regard, India is launching various projects and initiatives on the geo-economic front.

For example, the planned North-South International Transport Corridor (INSTC) plays an important role in connecting the region with India. Its construction will allow India to bypass obstacles such as Pakistan and Afghanistan in its entry into the region. Therefore, India is the main initiator in the implementation of this plan.

The INSTC originates in Central Asia, travels through Russia to Europe, and returns through the Mediterranean Sea, Suez Canal, Red Sea, Arabian Sea, and Indian Ocean. The length of the international transport corridor is 7200 kilometres. N. Modi, who visited five Central Asian republics in 2015, emphasized INSTC in India's geo-economic interests in Central Asia and said:

"My current visit to all five Central Asian countries is proof of the importance of the region for India.... We will look forward and help in the development of transport and communication networks in the region. We can create a vast network of natural and digital connectivity from the northern corner of Eurasia to the southern coast of Asia. The North-South international transport corridor is an important step in this direction [Remarks by Prime ... 2015].

Regarding this issue, it is appropriate to cite the following comments of researcher G. Yuldasheva: "India and Iran, in addition to their interest in the regional projects "New Silk Road" and "One Place, One Road", are supporting the construction of the North-South transport route, which is beneficial for all the countries of the region and can connect Russia with Central and South Asia. Neither side is interested in the return to power of the Taliban or other radical groups, as well as the strengthening of the Sunni sectarian bloc, which creates ideological and political problems and unites Afghanistan, Pakistan and Saudi Arabia." [Yuldasheva 2018: 142]

The TAPI (Turkmenistan-Afghanistan-Pakistan-India gas pipeline) project has a special place in India's geo-economic interests. In 1997, the Indian government first tried to obtain concessions for the exploration of oil reserves in Kazakhstan and Turkmenistan. At the same time, the Indian state oil and gas company announced that it will either establish consortia aimed at obtaining concessions or try to establish joint ventures in developing the oil and gas potential of Central Asian countries.

In May 2002, Indian Prime Minister Atal Bihari Vajpayee, during his official visit to Kazakhstan, announced that Delhi was ready to invest heavily in Kazakhstan's oil and gas industry. In June 2002, the parties signed a Memorandum of Understanding on Cooperation in the Energy Sector. During subsequent visits to Kazakhstan, ONGC-Videsh Ltd acquired a 15 per cent stake in the Alibekmola project and a 10 per cent stake in the Kurmangazi project. In 2013, ONGC-Videsh Ltd invested another 3 billion dollars. [ONGC Videsh] But in 2018, as a result of a sharp decrease in profits, ONGC-Videsh Ltd stopped financing Kazakhstan's Satbaev oil block. [ONGC Videsh]

India has also expanded its nuclear cooperation for peace with the region to secure its energy interests. After the previous agreement expired in 2015, India and Kazakhstan signed a new agreement to buy 5,000 tonnes of Kazakh uranium by the end of 2019. Both parties discussed the third deal and agreed that Kazakhstan will supply 7500-10000 tons of uranium to India. [India-Kazakhstan Relation... 2018]

According to SAPRA India Foundation, India tried to acquire a package of shares of at least 20 per cent of oil and gas enterprises in Uzbekistan [Komissina 2004].

But it is difficult to supply hydrocarbon raw materials from oil and gas deposits to India without building a pipeline network between the countries. According to experts, this problem can be solved by building the TAPI gas pipeline. Naturally, such cooperation means that in addition to Turkmenistan, the Central Asian countries of Uzbekistan and Kazakhstan can be involved in the project. However, the unstable situation in Afghanistan, especially in the context of the re-establishment of the power of the "Taliban", may make the TAPI gas pipeline project lose its importance for India, and besides, Pakistan's serious pursuit of Central Asia through Afghanistan may reduce the possibility of India's participation in this project.

Discussion

To conclude the article, it can be said that India has both geopolitical and geo-economic interests in the Central Asian region. In this regard, India's geopolitical interests are ensuring security in Central and South Asia, taking into account the interests of its competitors in the region, such as China and Pakistan, and its geo-economic interests are the energy potential of the region to meet India's needs, the growth of trade and economic relations through Central Asia with Russia, including the CIS, as well as India's potential to become an alternative market for Central Asia.

India, which is growing rapidly economically, has every reason to be a stable partner in Central Asia, especially with Uzbekistan, in the fields of trade, investment, modern technologies and tourism. This, in turn, creates the necessary conditions not only for the development of bilateral cooperation between India and Uzbekistan, but also for the expansion and deepening of relations between the Central Asian region and the countries of South Asia.

India's geopolitical interests in Central Asia are not only determined by the harmony of its glorious past relations with the region, but these interests are increasingly expanding as a result of India-Pakistan, India-China rivalry, as well as the security situation in Afghanistan. In turn, unlike regional power centres such as Pakistan, Iran, Saudi Arabia, UAE, which have an Islamic model of development due to the fact that the power of the Central Asian countries is managed based on secular criteria, India seeks to present itself as a geopolitically attractive partner for the region.

REFERENCES

1. Белокринецкий В. (1997) Геополитическая вертикаль в сердце Азии // Pro et contra. Том 2. весна. — С. 97.
2. Nishtha Kaushiki (2013) The New Great Game and India's Connect Central Asia Policy: Strategic Perspectives and Challenges, Journal of International and Area Studies, Vol. 20, No. 2, pp. 83-100; Mubeen Adnan, Bushra Fatima (2015) Strategic and Economic Interests of Pakistan and India in Central Asia, South Asian Studies A Research Journal of South Asian Studies, Vol. 30, No. 2, July-December , pp. 187-200; Dilip Kumar Maurya (2015) India-Central Asian States Relations in the 21st Century European Academic Research Vol. II, Issue 11/ February.
3. Юлдашева Г.И. (2018) Геополитические процессы в современной Центральной Азии: Иран и США. – Т.: Niso poligraf, – Б. 139.
4. Котов Л. (1995) Индия и республики Центральной Азии: рождение нового партнерства // Компас. ИТАР-ТАСС. – № 46. – С. 20–26.
5. Opening Remarks of Prime Minister Vajpayee at a Press Conference. 5 June 2014. // URL: http://www.indianembassy.org/special/cabinet/Primeminister/2014/pm_June_05_2014.htm
6. Khalid Duran. (2004) Rivalries over. The New Muslim Countries // Aussenpolitic. – IV
7. Khan A. Simbal. (2010) Pakistan's Relations with Central Asian States //Strategic Perspective, Vol. 2, № 12, p. 51.
8. Маниш Чанд. (2005) Центральная Азия, новый центр внимания нефтяной политики Индии // 07 апрель.// URL:http:// www.geo. kz/printing.php?aid=152
9. Thomas S. (1999) Silk Route Diplomacy. World Wide: Jaswant Singh Lifts Ties with Strategically Important Central Asian Countries // The Week, 13 June. // URL: http://www.the-week. com/ 99junl3/ events 2.htm
10. Stobdan P. (2007) India and Central Asia. Indian Foreign Policy: Challenges and Opportunities. Edition Sinha A. Mohta M. New Delhi: Academic Foundation, p. 187.
11. Касенов У. (1997) Новая «большая игра» в Центральной Азии? // Центральная Азия, № 2, С. 51.
12. Мавлонов И.Р. (2007) Центральная Азия и Южная Азия: дипломатический потенциал Узбекистана и Индии для устойчивого межрегионального экономического сотрудничества // Материалы конференции Политика Индии в Центральной Азии аспекты узбекского –индийского сотрудничества. Редактор Д-р Джоиши Бакши. С. 150–165.
13. Мавлонов И. (2010) Экономическая дипломатия Индии в условиях трансформации мирового порядка. – Ташкент.: УМЭД, – С. 116–117.
14. Stobdan P. (2007) India and Central Asia. Indian Foreign Policy: Challenges and Opportunities. Edition Sinha A.; Mohta M. New Delhi: Academic Foundation, pdf
15. Country.eiu.com/ India in Central Asia- The economist intelligence unit.

16. Диалог Индия-центральная Азия после пандемии https://www.eurasian-research.org/publication/post-pandemic-india-central-asia-dialogue/?lang=ru
17. Мавлонов И. (2010) Экономическая дипломатия Индии в условиях трансформации мирового порядка. – Ташкент.: УМЭД. – С. 116–117.
18. Милов В. Энергетический треугольник Европа-Китай-Индии: куда поддаться России? // URL: http://www.energypolicy.ru/pres.phd?id=1002477
19. Energy policy of India. // URL: https://en.m.wikipedia.org /
20. Маниш Чанд. (2005) Центральная Азия, новый центр внимания нефтяной политики Индии // 07 апрель// URL:http:// www. geo. kz/ printing.php?aid=152
21. Тўлаганова Н. (2006) Афганский конфликт и его последствия в контексте становления новой системы безопасности в Центральной Азии: Автореф. дис. ... д-ра полит. наук. – Т. – С. 22–23.
22. Бўронов С.М. (2021) Афғонистонда тинчлик ва барқарорлик ўрнатиш жараёнларида Ўзбекистон геосиёсати. – Т.: EFFECT-D, – Б. 147.
23. Murat T. Laumulin. (2007) The Geopolitics of XXI Century in Central Asia, Almaty: KazISS, p. 281.
24. Е.В.Савкович. (2012) Развитие Отношений Индии с государствами Центральной Азии в 1990–2000-е гг. и Позиция Китая. ВТГУ. N.3 (19), pdf
25. Центральная Азия. (2010.) Геополитика и экономика региона. Институт стратигических оценок и анализа, Москва, С. 194.
26. Remarks by Prime Minister at Plenary of the Shanghai Cooperation Organisation 10 July, 2015. // URL: http:// mea.gov.in/ Speeches Statements.htm?dtl/25454/
27. Юлдашева Г.И. (2018) Геополитические процессы в современной Центральной Азии: Иран и США. – Т.: Niso poligraf, Б. 142.
28. ONGC Videsh Ltd to raise $3 bn for Kazakh acquition. // URL: markets/bonds/ongc-videsh-ltd-to-raise–3-bn-for-kazakh-acquisition/articleshow/20310076.cms
29. ONGC Videsh to exit Kazakhstan's Satpaev oil block. // URL: indiatimes.com/news/oil-and-gas/ongc-videsh-to-exit-kazakhstans-satpayev-oil-block/65856935
30. India-Kazakhstan Relation, Ministry of External Affairs, December 2018. // URL: https://mea. gov. in /Portal/ Foreign Relation/ december_2018.pdf
31. Комиссина И. Интересы Индии в Центральной Азии // 22.10.2004. // URL: http://www.novopol.ru/print 721.html

20

Development of Cooperation Between Central Asian Countries and Afghanistan in the Context of Interconnected Regional Security

Dr Saodat Ubdaydullayeva

ABSTRACT

The relevance of the topic is due to the development of ties between the states of the region, the beginning of the implementation of large economic projects, the desire to improve transport corridors, and joint efforts to eliminate threats emanating from Afghanistan. In turn, the involvement of Afghanistan in economic projects in Central Asia, in addition to positive results, can also have negative consequences, which can lead to the strengthening of new forms of terrorism, religious extremism, and information extremism.

The purpose of this work is to study the mutual relations of the Central Asian states to ensure security in the region, as well as to study the state and development of cooperation with Afghanistan in the context of interconnectedness in ensuring the security of the Central Asian region. The work uses systematic and logical-historical approaches. The article uses the results of monitoring the political situation in the Central Asian region, including the situation in Afghanistan, as well as scientific articles, dissertations and analytical studies, and the work of think tanks. The work shows the role and significance of Afghanistan in the system of complex interconnectedness of regional security in Central Asia and the relationships between the countries of the region. The article concludes that there is uncertainty in the formation of a system of interconnectedness of regional security in Central Asia and the role of Afghanistan in this process.

Keywords: *Central Asia, region, threats, regional security, regional connectivity, foreign policy.*

The persistence of a complex of challenges and threats in Central Asia is directly related to the situation in Afghanistan. In such circumstances, the four Central Asian states, with the exception of Tajikistan, are seeking to actively interact with Afghanistan to develop common approaches, considering it as part of regional interconnectedness. However, the participation of Tajikistan in August 2023 in the Ashgabat meeting of the leaders of the three Central Asian states bordering Afghanistan indicates an understanding of the factor of interconnectedness in the general context of regional security.

Regional interconnectedness is necessary for the socio-economic development of any state.[1] American expert F. Starr considers the use of the concept "post-Soviet space" as a definition of the region obsolete and suggests not using this concept.[2] F. Starr's point of view is shared by Italian analyst F. Indeo, who views Afghanistan as a Central Asian state. He believes that the development of transport infrastructure in the region, including Afghanistan, will contribute to the development of regional connectivity.[3] According to experts, Afghanistan was part of Central Asia until the time when the countries of the region became part of the USSR. During this period, various barriers arose in Central Asia related to cultural and political values, as well as language, in particular, the Russian language was accessible to the population and all this contributed to the greater isolation of Afghanistan from regional processes.[4]

As the President of the Republic of Uzbekistan Sh. M. Mirziyoev noted, the territory of Afghanistan cannot be allowed to remain a source of challenges and threats to our security. First of all, the growth of extremism and the export of radical ideology, the use of Afghan territory for subversive actions against our countries, and the risks of militants infiltrating across borders. It is important, through common efforts and decisive actions, to jointly stop the channels of transfer of terrorists from "hot spots" to Afghanistan.[5]

Between August and December 2021, the number of Afghan refugees who crossed the Amudarya from Afghanistan to Uzbekistan is about 150 people. At the same time, Uzbekistan does not plan to forcibly deport them to Afghanistan, since the refugees themselves are ready to return back subject to a guarantee of security from the Taliban.

Given the current situation in Afghanistan, experts are sceptical about the future of the planned large projects. Some of them believe that the trans-Afghan corridor, aimed at strengthening regional connectivity between Central and South Asia, cannot be implemented in the current conditions and this issue may be relevant in 20-30 years.

At the same time, the withdrawal of foreign military forces from Afghanistan and the rise of the "Taliban" to power may bring new impetus to the development of regionalization in Central Asia. This is due to the fact that in resolving regional issues, in addition to large states, the key role will be played by the states of the region by intensifying dialogue, cooperation, and the implementation of regional projects and programs.

The Central Asian countries (Uzbekistan, Tajikistan, and Turkmenistan) that border Afghanistan can exert some political influence on the Taliban. Almost all countries in the region are already engaged in a constructive dialogue with the interim government of the Taliban movement.

In these conditions, it seems necessary to strengthen regional connectivity in Central and South Asia, where Afghanistan is one of the key links. Central and South Asia have always been connected by reliable trade arteries and served as a bridge for the countries of the Middle East, Europe, and China. This is also stated in the works of the ancient Greek historian Strabo, who wrote that along the Oxus River – now the Amu Darya, "goods were delivered through the Caspian and Black Seas to Europe." Back in the third and second millennia BC, a network of trade routes connecting us passed through the Khyber and Bolan passes.[6] The regions of Central and South Asia have a long history of mutually beneficial relations. There has always been a movement of goods and people between regions, which, in turn, connected their cultural and religious ties and influenced political relations.

The key moment for discussing and developing proposals for strengthening interconnectedness was the international conference "Central and South Asia: Regional Interconnectedness. Challenges and opportunities", held on the initiative of the President of the Republic of Uzbekistan Sh. M. Mirziyoyev on July 14-15, 2021 in Tashkent. The results of the conference allowed us to draw the following conclusions.

Firstly, the conference became a key platform for discussing the further development of regional connectivity between Central and South Asia. Common challenges and threats, the spatial and geographic proximity of the peoples of the two regions can become a system-forming factor in the formation of a system of comprehensive interconnectedness.

In 2020, the total trade turnover between Central Asia and South Asia amounted to $4.4 billion (3.2% of the total foreign trade turnover of $142.6 billion). The largest shares in the trade turnover of the countries of Central Asia and South Asia are occupied by Kazakhstan (52.8%) and Uzbekistan (31.2%).[7] Trade and transport are of strategic importance for Central Asia, since a number of countries in the region are separated from the sea by the territories of two states. Uzbekistan is interested in the development of transport and logistics infrastructure and integration into the transport corridors of the EAEU countries, which will contribute to the development of its connections with world markets.[8]

Secondly, the Afghan factor is named one of the main factors for the successful implementation of projects and programs within the framework of regional interconnectedness. Ensuring security in the country will allow the countries of the two regions to implement large infrastructure projects, and as a result, Afghanistan will become a bridge of comprehensive interconnectedness.

Thirdly, the states of the two regions are themselves interested in the formation of regional interconnectedness. In ensuring security, there are unresolved problems between individual states in the regions. However, they are all interested in solving them within the framework of regional interconnectedness, primarily in order to ensure security in Afghanistan. At this stage, cooperation with Afghanistan is carried out with all countries of Central Asia.

Today, all these countries give priority to establishing long-term stability and sustainable peace in Afghanistan. Resolving the situation in Afghanistan opens up wide opportunities for building up trade, economic, and investment ties, and strengthening transport and communication interaction between the countries of Central and South Asia.[9]

Uzbekistan pursues a good-neighbourly and friendly policy towards Afghanistan, which is based on taking into account the national interests of both countries, generally accepted principles and norms of international law, and is aimed at ensuring lasting peace, stability, security, and sustainable development in Central Asia.

According to Kazakh researcher R. Burnashev, Uzbekistan views Afghanistan as a bridge through which it can gain access to South Asia and the Middle East, which is why it is relevant to involve Afghanistan in regional processes.[10]

An important role in the development of historical Uzbek-Afghan relations has traditionally been played by the key geographical location of Afghanistan, which for many centuries was located along important trade routes, connecting South and East Asia with Europe and the Middle East. In this context, Afghan territory served as a crossroads in trade, economic, scientific and cultural relations in Asia, which contributed to the growth of economic well-being of local peoples.

These processes were accompanied by active interaction between the peoples of Central Asia and Afghanistan, who formed a single civilized space in terms of culture, religion, ethnicity and language. Thanks to the Great Silk Road, trade and economic relations between the countries of the region continuously developed, and political and diplomatic ties were strengthened. However, over the past 40 years, Afghanistan has become an arena for the clash of interests of global and regional powers.

Diplomatic relations between Uzbekistan and Afghanistan were established on October 13, 1992. In the foreign policy strategy of Uzbekistan, Afghanistan is seen as an integral part of the Central Asian region, in which this country acts as an important component of Uzbekistan's initiative to form transregional interconnectedness of Central and South Asia, aimed at transforming the region into the largest transport, trade and economic hub.

For Uzbekistan, the priority of relations with Afghanistan is also demonstrated by the functioning of the institution of the Special Representative of the President of the Republic of Uzbekistan for Afghanistan since 2017, as well as the position of Deputy Minister for Foreign Economic Cooperation in the Ministry of Investment and Foreign Trade (MIFT) since November 2020.

Since 2002, supplies of electrical energy have been carried out to Afghanistan on the basis of annually concluded direct agreements between

"NES" JSC and the Main Directorate for Electrification of Afghanistan "Brishno Shirkat".

In 2002, the supply volume was only 62 million kW/h. Every year this volume of exported electricity increased to 200 million kW/h. and in 2018 reached 2.5 billion kW/h. In accordance with the agreement reached in August 2020, Uzbekistan will supply electricity to Afghanistan until 2030.[11]

In such conditions, the countries of Central Asia are actively interacting with the authorities of Afghanistan. In 2019, in Tashkent, within the framework of the Consultative Meeting of the Heads of State of Central Asia, a Joint Statement was adopted, in which the countries of the region expressed their readiness to provide all possible assistance in the speedy achievement of civil peace and harmony in Afghanistan.

Diplomatic relations between Kazakhstan and Afghanistan were established in 1992.[12] In the issue of resolving the Afghan conflict, Kazakhstan proposes to shift the focus to the humanitarian and economic components, including promoting the implementation of joint economic and infrastructure projects and education programs. Kazakhstan annually provides humanitarian assistance in the form of supplies of wheat flour and granulated sugar.

Kazakhstan also supports almost all regional formats dedicated to the Afghan settlement (Tashkent Conference, Istanbul Process, Moscow Format, London Conference, Bonn Conference). At the same time, Kazakhstan stands for the active involvement of Afghanistan in the integration processes of Central Asia.

On January 19, 2018, under the chairmanship of Kazakhstan, the UN Security Council held its first ministerial-level debate on the topic "Building a Regional Partnership in Afghanistan and Central Asia as a Model of Interdependence of Security and Development."[13] In January 2018, within the framework of Kazakhstan's presidency of the UN Security Council, a meeting was held "Formation of a regional partnership in Afghanistan and Central Asia as a model of work in an area combining security and development issues". At the meeting, a statement was adopted emphasizing the impossibility of resolving the Afghan conflict by military means, and participants noted support for the implementation of measures in Afghanistan with the participation of Central Asian states to establish stability.[14]

With the "Taliban" movement coming to power in Afghanistan, Kazakhstan began to identify approaches to strengthen cooperation with the country's authorities. In September 2021, at a meeting of the Council of Heads of State – members of the SCO, the President of Kazakhstan K. Tokayev proposed organizing a hub in Almaty for delivering aid to Afghanistan.[15] Such dynamics of activation for Kazakhstan are also necessary to improve approaches to the Afghan issue, which for many years have not been as active as compared to other Central Asian countries. As Kazakh expert D. Satpayev notes, unlike Uzbekistan, for a long time the Afghan factor was not a key factor for Kazakhstan's foreign policy, not only due to the fact that Kazakhstan does not have a common border with this state but also due to the lack of strong specialists in Afghanistan. Also, Kazakhstan did not have any levers of influence on the situation in this country, including the fact that there are much fewer Kazakhs living in Afghanistan than Uzbeks, Tajiks, or Turkmen.[16]

Relations between Tajikistan and Afghanistan have also been developing since 1992 when diplomatic relations were established between the countries. Currently, there are 7 bridges on the border between the two countries. Currently, the construction of the eighth bridge across the Pyanj River is underway, the corresponding Agreement was approved by the Government of Tajikistan in April 2019. The bridge will connect the Khatlon region of the Republic of Tajikistan with the Afghan province of Takhar.

Tajikistan supports the efforts of the countries of the region to ensure peace and stability in Afghanistan. Dushanbe advocates the integration of Afghanistan into the regional processes of Central Asia and the entry of Kabul in the Shanghai Cooperation Organization.

In March 2021, the next meeting of the "Heart of Asia – Istanbul Process" conference was held in Tajikistan on the topic "Strengthening consensus for peace and development. As a result, the Dushanbe Declaration was adopted.[17]

The Istanbul Process was launched in 2011 as a joint effort between Turkey and Afghanistan to develop economic development and security efforts in Afghanistan. To date, ministerial conferences "Heart of Asia - Istanbul Process" have been held in Istanbul (2011), Kabul (2012), Almaty (2013), Beijing (2014), Islamabad (2015), Amritsar (2016), Baku (2017). On December 9, 2019, a ministerial conference "Heart of Asia - Istanbul Process" was held in Istanbul on the theme "Peace, Partnership, Prosperity".[18]

Tajikistan remains a consistent supporter of all international efforts aimed at restoring lasting peace and stability in Afghanistan. At the meeting of the 76th session of the UN General Assembly, President of Tajikistan E. Rahmon emphasized that the current crisis in Afghanistan is a threat to regional security and stability in Tajikistan, which has a border with Afghanistan with a total length of almost 1,400 km. The rise to power of the Taliban, listed as a terrorist group by the UN Security Council, further complicated the already difficult geopolitical process in the region. According to E. Rahmon, only dialogue with the participation of all layers of Afghan society, including Afghan Tajiks, can lead to the establishment of lasting peace and stability in this country.[19]

Turkmenistan is also actively increasing cooperation with Afghanistan. Turkmenistan's participation in stabilizing the situation in Afghanistan consists of providing humanitarian assistance, training national personnel, and providing medical care to the population of border areas.

Security issues between the two countries are discussed within the framework of the Joint Turkmen-Afghan Commission for Security Cooperation, which continues to meet after the Taliban came to power in Afghanistan. Turkmenistan, like Uzbekistan and Kazakhstan, has established a dialogue with the Taliban in order to continue cooperation and ensure regional security in Central Asia.

Kyrgyzstan's position on the peace process in Afghanistan is to support the efforts of the world community to establish peace and stability in Afghanistan and the adjacent region, as well as its readiness to promote regional projects such as CASA-1000.

According to Kyrgyz media reports, Kyrgyzstan became the first country in Central Asia to hold a meeting with representatives of the "Taliban" after they came to power in Afghanistan.[20] At the meeting of the 76th session of the UN General Assembly, President of Kyrgyzstan S. Japarov noted that due to the situation in Afghanistan, the security of Central Asia comes to the fore. In this regard, he proposed holding a Central Asia-UN summit in 2022 and creating a Centre for Combating International Organized Crime in Bishkek within the SCO.[21]

At the same time, according to the State Commission for Religious Affairs, the "Taliban" movement is banned in Kyrgyzstan and recognized as a terrorist organization and is also involved in other terrorist groups, including "Al-Qaeda", banned in Kyrgyzstan.[22]

On March 27-28, 2018, at the initiative of the President of the Republic of Uzbekistan Sh. M. Mirziyoev, the Tashkent International Conference on Afghanistan "Peace Process, Security Cooperation and Regional Interaction" was held".[23] As a result of the conference, the participants adopted the Tashkent Declaration, which became the fundamental basis for the peace process in Afghanistan due to the following compelling reasons. First, it emphasizes that peace and security in Afghanistan are essential to ensuring stability in Central Asia. Second, an Afghan-owned political settlement supported by regional cooperation, as well as regional economic cooperation and connectivity is key to the peace and prosperity of Afghanistan and the entire region.[24] Thus, the "Central Asia + Afghanistan" format is a necessary part of the comprehensive interconnectedness of regional security, in which Afghanistan should be considered as part of the Central Asian region.

China's policy towards Afghanistan is examined from the point of view of its security interests due to the Xinjiang factor. China needs the border with Afghanistan to be stable and secure. Beijing does not want Afghanistan to have the opportunity to train terrorists to organize the destabilization of the situation in Xinjiang. In this regard, China is conducting various operations (intelligence, propaganda, information) on this issue.[25]

Iran also has its own interests in Afghanistan, which is strengthening its influence. Iran's policy in Afghanistan in recent years has been aimed at implementing the following strategic objectives: 1) the creation of a buffer zone to contain the US policy of building a line of instability on the Iran-Afghan border; 2) strengthening its role as a defender of the "Shiite belt" from the Middle East to South Asia" (10-15% of the population of Afghanistan professes the Shiite branch of Islam, 18 of the country's 34 provinces are Persian-speaking); 3) promoting its interregional transport and energy projects in Afghanistan; and 4) maintaining leadership in the Afghan market for the export of their goods.

From 2002 to 2013 Iran allocated more than $900 million for various projects in Afghanistan. At the same time, Iran is considered one of the leaders among many of Afghanistan's partner countries in effectively fulfilling its obligations. Iranian representatives took part in almost all important international events to discuss the socio-economic reconstruction of Afghanistan.[26]

Pakistan occupies an important place in the development of regional connectivity. For these purposes, the Pakistani side gives priority to expanding the transport and communications component of cooperation in order to intensify trade and economic exchanges. An important event in this regard was the signing of a trilateral agreement (Uzbekistan-Afghanistan-Pakistan) on the implementation of the "Trans-Afghan transport" corridor.[27]

It is important to note that Pakistan has two sets of objectives in the region. The first group is economic issues, among which experts identify the following main areas.

Diversification of trade and economic relations by expanding the geography of foreign economic partners. The need for this is explained by the dominance of developed countries (USA, EU, China) as partners in Pakistan's foreign trade, which is the main reason for maintaining a high level of foreign trade deficit, which at the end of 2020 amounted to 23 billion dollars (exports – 22 billion, imports – 45 billion dollars). At the same time, according to World Bank estimates, Pakistan's total export potential is more than $88 billion, which is 4 times higher than current volumes.

In these conditions, it is important for Pakistan to develop new markets in order to redirect its export flows, including towards the states of Central Asia. Guided by such aspirations, Pakistan initially intends to increase the volume of trade with the Central Asian states to $5 billion per year. (the current level of trade turnover does not exceed $300 million).

Another factor determining the need for Pakistan to be involved in Central Asian processes of economic cooperation, experts call India's active obstruction of Pakistan's integration into political, trade, and economic processes in South Asia. New Delhi is trying to isolate the Pakistani side in the region by creating allied organizations without involving Islamabad in their work.

Under these conditions, the only existing regional format of cooperation involving Pakistan and Afghanistan, the South Asian Association for Regional Cooperation (SAARC), has turned into a paralyzed structure. The SAARC Free Trade Agreement remains unused. As a result, the volume of Pakistan's trade turnover with regional countries still does not exceed 8 per cent of the total volume of its trade exchanges with the outside world.

Given this trend, Pakistani political and expert circles are calling for the need for Pakistan to actively join the Central Asian economic integration processes in order to compensate for the ineffectiveness of the country's policy in South Asia.

Developing relations with Central Asian states is in line with Pakistan's goals of turning the country into a major regional transit hub. Despite the official declaration by the leadership of Pakistan of the success of the China-Pakistan Economic Corridor (CPEC) projects, the timing of their implementation is delayed, and the economic efficiency does not yet justify the invested financial resources.

The main CPEC project, the port of "Gwadar", has not yet been able to turn into a major transport hub: at present, there is practically no regular movement of cargo ships there. In addition to this, Islamabad's debt from Beijing is growing. The Pakistani side will have to pay $40 billion as loan repayment to China over 20 years by 2038 for projects already implemented under the CPEC.

Under these conditions, there is an increasing demand for the full use of the transit potential of Pakistani ports ("Karachi", "Kasym", "Gwadar") by attracting regional states to their use.

The second group of goals is related to issues of military-strategic and geopolitical significance. Pakistan views its northern neighbours – Afghanistan and the countries of Central Asia – as a kind of security belt. In this regard, Islamabad fears the prospects of strengthening New Delhi's position in Afghanistan and Central Asia – the formation of a course loyal to India in states located to the north.

For this reason, Islamabad jealously monitors New Delhi's activity in the region and tries to counter it. However, Pakistan's own capabilities do not allow it to act as a counterweight to Indian influence and seriously increase its economic presence in Central Asia. These factors show the focus of Pakistan's modern Central Asian policy on solving vital economic and political problems.

In these conditions, India is also actively involved in the system of regional interconnectedness, despite the lack of a full-fledged leap over the past 30 years due to the existing number of problematic issues.

First, India is geographically separated from Central Asia, due to which trade with Central Asian countries is mainly carried out through the ports and transport network of Iran.

Secondly, India's main competitor is China, to which New Delhi cannot be a real competitor in the region. Third, the situation in Afghanistan does not allow the implementation of large projects with Indian participation. In this regard, and also considering Afghanistan as a priority area of foreign policy, India seeks to prevent the strengthening of an anti-Indian government in Afghanistan.[28]

For India, the key instrument of multilateral cooperation in Central Asia is the SCO, which in 2017, together with Pakistan, received membership in the Organization.

India has developed constructive relations with almost all members of the SCO, not counting Pakistan and China. If with Pakistan it is more connected with territorial disputes, than with China for the sphere of economic influence on the Asian continent. These factors prevent the full development of the potential of all member countries of the Organization, as well as the development of consensus on conceptual issues on the SCO agenda.

For example, India is categorically against the Chinese Belt and Road Initiative, although all other SCO members support and actively participate in the implementation of projects jointly with China.[29] With this approach, India demonstrates its determination to define its presence and interests within the SCO.

Thus, India, despite the presence of different approaches within the SCO, is interested in strengthening its position in the Central Asian region. For these purposes, India is working with all Central Asian states, both in bilateral and multilateral formats in the field of economics and security.

Historical ties with Afghanistan, the strategic location of Afghanistan, and Turkey's close military-political partnership with Western countries play an important role in Ankara's active participation in resolving the situation in the Islamic Republic of Afghanistan and its socio-economic restoration.

Türkiye is pursuing an active foreign policy towards Afghanistan. According to experts, by intensifying its Afghan policy, Ankara is simultaneously solving several problems: 1) the location of Afghanistan at the junction of international transport corridors provides Turkey with access to large markets in Southeast Asia; 2) involvement in the Afghan crisis allows the Turkish side to position itself on equal terms with the "global powers"; 3) Ankara's participation in resolving the Afghan conflict creates a window of opportunity to expand interaction with the countries of Central Asia, which meets Turkey's strategic interests in ensuring a long-term presence in the region.

Turkey's foreign policy towards Afghanistan is based on four main principles: maintaining the unity and integrity of Afghanistan; ensuring security and stability in the country; formation of a political structure in which public participation is one of the priorities; restoring peace and prosperity by eliminating terrorism and extremism. In accordance with these goals, Turkey continues to contribute to the development of the Islamic Republic of Afghanistan both at the bilateral level and within the framework of multilateral mechanisms, in particular at the UN and NATO levels.

Türkiye and Afghanistan have maintained friendly relations for many years. The basis of bilateral interaction is determined by the absence of borders, geopolitical ambitions, and religious and cultural communities.[30]

From the very beginning of its activities within the military coalition, Turkey refused to participate in military campaigns against the Taliban, direct combat operations against terrorists, as well as operations to combat drug production and trafficking.[31]

To a large extent, Turkey's participation was expressed in the use of "soft power". In 2002, the international coalition forces in Afghanistan created provincial teams to restore devastated areas, provide security assistance in the reconstruction of countries, and facilitate dialogue between the transitional administration of Afghanistan and regional leaders.[32] These teams served as a liaison between peacekeeping forces, international governmental and non-governmental organizations, local authorities, political and military leaders, and the civilian population.

The peoples of Central Asia have been linked by ties of friendship and kinship for three millennia. The importance of Central Asia in international relations is due to two factors. Firstly, Central Asia has historically been a territory that has made a significant contribution to the development of socio-economic, cultural, and political processes in the world. Secondly, Central Asia, given its geostrategic location, has always played a significant role in trade and cultural exchanges on a global scale. The commonality of history, similarity of cultures, traditions, language, and unity of religion serve as a solid basis for relations between the states of the region, which are the main components of interaction in all key areas of regional cooperation. These issues are becoming the main topics of meetings of regional leaders in both bilateral and multilateral formats. This is evidenced by the content of numerous bilateral negotiations between the leaders of states in the region, as well as their meetings within the framework of multilateral forums in the UN, SCO, CIS and others.

In the period 2017-2021, as part of consultative meetings, the heads of state of the region identified priority areas of cooperation, developed a number of key initiatives to strengthen regional cooperation in the field of economics, politics and security, which is why this mechanism plays a key role in solving key problematic issues and in developing proposals for further trade and economic development in the Central Asian region.

End Notes

1 Akram X. Regionalnaya vzaimosvyazannost Sentralnoy i Yujnoy Azii: Otlichnaya initsiativa Prezidenta Shavkata Mirziyoyeva. “National Herald Tribune”.

2 Starr F. “Prishlo vremya smotret na Afganistan kak chast Sentralnoy Azii”. https://www.gazeta.uz/ru/2017/11/21/frederick-starr (date accessed: 21.04.2020)

3 Indeo F. New Trends in Central Asian Connectivity. https://edizionicafoscari.unive.it/it/edizioni4/libri/978-88-6969-377-9/new-trends-in-central-asian-connectivity/ 12.02.2020

4 James D. “Central Asia Opens the Door to Afghanistan.” The Diplomat. https://thediplomat.com/2018/05/centralasia-opens-the-door-to-afghanistan/ April 14, 2020.

5 Vыstupleniye Prezidenta Respubliki Uzbekistan Shavkata Mirziyoyeva na vstreche v formate “SHOS – ODKB”. 18.09.2021 g. https://president.uz/ru/lists/view/4623

6 Mirziyoyev Sh. Vыstupleniye Prezidenta Respubliki Uzbekistan Shavkata Mirziyoyeva na mejdunarodnoy konferensii “Sentralnaya i Yujnaya Aziya: regionalnaya vzaimosvyazan nost. Vыzovы i vozmojnosti”. 16.07.2021 g. https://president.uz/ru/ lists/view/4484

7 Abaturov V. Tashkentskiy perekrestok sotrudnichestva – mejdu Sentralnoy i yujnoy Aziyey// https://cerr.uz/en/post/publication/taskentskij-perekrestok-sotrudnicestva-mezdu-centralnoj-i-uznoj-aziej

8 Ziyadullayev N. Sentralnaya i Yujnaya Aziya: vneshnetorgovыe i transportno-tranzitnыe initsiativы. 2021. "Central and South Asia: Foreign trade and transit initiatives," *Russian Foreign Economic Journal,* Russian Foreign Trade Academy Ministry of Economic Development of the Russian Federation, issue 8, pp.33-46, August.

9 Kutbiddinov Yu. Vosstanovleniye svyazey s Afganistanom. Uroki transgranichnogo vzaimodeystviya / Yu. Kutbiddinov, U. Saydiyev, N. Kurbanbayeva; Sentr ekonomicheskix issledovaniy i reform. Iyul 2019g. URL: https://www.chathamhouse.org/sites/default/files/publications/research/2019-07-24-Reconnecting-Afghanistan-Russian-Version.pdf

10 Burnashev R. Sentralnaya Aziya rassmatrivayetsya Uzbekistanom kak region vozmojnostey. https://yuz.uz/ru/news/tsentralnaya-aziya-rassmatrivaetsya-uzbekistanom-kak-region-vozmojnostey

11 Uzbekistan i Afganistan podpisali soglasheniye o postavkax elektroenergii na 10 let. https://podrobno.uz/cat/economic/uzbekistan-i-afganistan-podpisali-soglashenie-o-postavkakh-elektroenergii-na-10-let/

12 Sotrudnichestvo Respubliki Kazaxstan s Islamskoy Respublikoy Afganistan. https://www.gov.kz/memleket/entities/mfa/press/article/details/458?lang=ru

13 Obnarodovanû itogi predsedatelstva Kazaxstana v Sovete Bezopasnosti OON. https://kursiv.kz/news/politika/2018-02/obnarodovany-itogi-predsedatelstva-kazakhstana-v-sovete-bezopasnosti-oon

14 Guterrish A.: stranû Sentralnoy Azii vnosyat vajnûy vklad v ukrepleniye mira v Afganistane. 19.01.2018 g. https://news.un.org/ru/story/2018/01/1321881

15 Glava RK: Мы ne doljnы ostavlyat Afganistan nayedine s trudnostyami. https://kapital.kz/economic/99522/glava-rk-my-ne-dolzhny-ostavlyat-afganistan-nayedine-s-trudnostyami.html

16 Satpayev D.- o "Talibane", Sentralnoy Azii i afganskix bejensax v Kazaxstane. 07.07.2021 g. https://forbes.kz//process/expertise/taliban_i_tsentralnaya_aziya_partnerstvo_ili_konfrontatsiya/?

17 Serdse Azii – Stambulskiy protsess. https://www.eurasian-research.org/publication/heart-of-asia-istanbul-process/?lang=ru.

18 V Dushanbe proydet konferensiya "Serdse Azii - Stambulskiy protsess". 28.03.2021 g.

19 Raxmon E. Afganistan prevratilsya v ploùadku dlya geopoliticheskix igr.24.09.2021 g. https://www.aa.com.tr/ru/

20 Кыrgызstan pervыm v Sentralnoy Azii otpravil ofitsialnuyu delegatsiyu k talibam.24.09.2021 g. https://mediazona.ca/news/2021/09/24/kr-af.

21 Prezident Кыrgызstana predlojil provesti sammit Sentralnaya Aziya – OON// https://news.un.org/ru/story/2021/09/1410302

22 Spisok organizatsiy deyatelnost kotorых zapreщena na territorii KR. http://religion.gov.kg/ru/religion_organization/blocked

23 https://uza.uz/ru/posts/prinyata-tashkentskaya-deklaratsiya-po-afganistanu-27-03-2018

24 https://uza.uz/ru/posts/deklaratsiya-tashkentskoy-konferentsii-po-afganistanu-mirnyy-28-03-2018

25 Ganiyev T.A. Problemы regionalnoy bezopasnosti i stabilnosti Sentralno-Aziatskogo regiona SNG. Monografiya, 2013.

26 Umarov A. Uchastiye Irana v stabilizatsii Afganistana posle 2001 goda. // Problemû natsionalnoy strategii. 2017. 13. (42). S. 73-79. https://riss.ru/documents/623/321ada0910aa456785b9ceb0f324dcef.pdf

27 Uzbekistan, Afganistan i Pakistan podpisali "Dorojnuyu kartu" po stroitelstvu jeleznoy dorogi. 08.02.2021 g. https://www.gazeta.uz/ru/2021/02/08/trans-afghan-railway/

28 Yakubov I. Indiya i Sentralnaya Aziya: ternistыy put sotrudnichestva. 06.02.2020 g. https://cabar.asia/ru/indiya-i-tsentralnaya-aziya-ternistyj-put-sotrudnichestva

29 Konarovskiy M. Bonus dlya "Bolshoy vosmerki" v Sindao: k nekotorыm itogam sammita SHOS. Rossiyskiy sovet po mejdunarodnûm delam. 13.06.2018 – http://russiancouncil.ru/analytics-and-comments/analytics/bonus-dlya-bolshoy-vosmerki-v-tsindao-k-nekotorym-itogam-sammita-shos/?sphrase_id=20831422

30 Erman A. How Turkey's Soft Power can Aid NATO in Afghanistan/ A. Erman, *New Perspectives Quarterly*, Vol. 27, No. 2, 2010, p. 40.

31 Ishbuldina K. Afgano-tureskiye otnosheniya na sovremennom etape (2001–2018 gg.). Dissertatsiya na soiskaniye uchenoy stepeni kandidata istoricheskix nauk. Federalnoye gosudarstvennoye avtonomnoye obrazovatelnoye uchrejdeniye vыsshego obrazovaniya "Moskovskiy gosudarstvennыy institut mejdunarodnыx otnosheniy (universitet) ministerstva inostrannыx del Rossiyskoy Federatsii". Moskva- 2019.

32 Eckert C.C. Provincial Reconstruction Teams: Who's in charge? http://www.dtic.mil/doctrine/doctrine/jwfc/provrecon_whitepaper.pdf. 21.02.2017.

Index